LOGISTICS IN MANUFACTURING

The BUSINESS ONE IRWIN/APICS Series
in Production Management

Supported by the American Production
and Inventory Control Society

OTHER BOOKS PUBLISHED IN THE BUSINESS ONE IRWIN/APICS
SERIES IN PRODUCTION MANAGEMENT

Attaining Manufacturing Excellence   *Robert W. Hall*

Bills of Materials   *Hal Mather*

Common Sense Manufacturing   *James A. Gardner*

Forecasting Systems for Operations Management   *Stephen A. Delurgio,*
Carl D. Bhame

Manufacturing Planning and Control Systems, Second Edition
Thomas E. Vollmann, William Lee Berry, D. Clay Whybark

Microcomputers in Production and Inventory Management
Thomas H. Fuller, Jr.

The New Performance Challenge: Measuring Operations for World-
Class Competition   *J. Robb Dixon, Alfred J. Nanni, Thomas E. Vollmann*

Production Activity Control   *Steven A. Melnyk and Phillip L. Carter*

Purchasing Strategies for Total Quality   *Greg Hutchins*

Shop Floor Control   *Steven A. Melnyk and Phillip L. Carter*

The Spirit of Manufacturing Excellence   *Ernest Huge*

Strategic Manufacturing: Dynamic New Directions for the 1990s
Patricia Moody

Time-Based Competition: The Next Battle Ground in American
Manufacturing   *Joseph Blackburn*

Total Quality: An Executive's Guide for the 1990s   *The Ernst & Young*
Quality Improvement Consulting Group

BUSINESS ONE IRWIN/APICS Series in
Production Management

APICS ADVISORY BOARD
L. James Burlingame
Eliyahu M. Goldratt
Robert W. Hall
Ed Heard
Ernest C. Huge
Henry H. Jordan
George W. Plossl
Richard Schonberger
Thomas E. Vollmann
D. Clay Whybark

LOGISTICS IN MANUFACTURING

Christopher Gopal
Gerard Cahill

BUSINESS ONE IRWIN
Homewood, Illinois 60430

© RICHARD D. IRWIN, INC., 1992

Executive editor: Jeffrey A. Krames
Project editor: Rebecca Dodson
Production manager: Mary Jo Parke
Art manager: Kim Meriwether
Compositor: Eastern Graphics
Typeface: 11/13 Times Roman
Printer: Arcata Graphics/Kingsport

Library of Congress Cataloging-in-Publication Data

Gopal, Christopher.
   Logistics in manufacturing / Christopher Gopal, Gerry Cahill.
      p.   cm.—(The Business One Irwin/APICS series in production management)
   Includes index.
   ISBN 1-55623-389-2
   1. Business logistics—United States.   2. Competition—United States.   I. Cahill, Gerry.   II. Title.   III. Series.
HD38.5.G67   1992
658.5—dc20   91-25189
                                                        CIP

Printed in the United States of America

1 2 3 4 5 6 7 8 9 0 AGK 8 7 6 5 4 3 2 1

PREFACE

U.S. manufacturers are operating today in a business environment characterized by unprecedented global, competitive, and technological change. While several leading edge and excellent manufacturers are adapting successfully, or even leading and defining the change, the majority are in a highly reactive mode. They are responding to single points of a shifting environment by applying single point solutions. They are striving to maintain a static operational framework in a dynamic environment.

Our combined experiences in industry, academia, and management consulting have accorded us the privilege of working with, and observing, a large number of manufacturing firms in a wide variety of industries. Excellent companies (where "excellence" translates into market success) approach their competitive environment through truly enterprise-wide and integrated business processes. Other firms use functional-based approaches such as across-the-board cost reduction efforts, or adopt the trappings of enterprise management without the commitment or infrastructure required to support it. For instance, many firms implement total quality control by providing education only, without the organizational structure, rigorous measurement and reward systems, true empowerment of the work force, or the focus on the underlying business processes that drive company performance. Among these key cross-functional processes is the management of material and information flow from supplier to customer and vice versa—the logistics process. Logistics joins sales and sales generation, design, and transformation as the four fundamental processes of a business. Traditionally, the focus of management and management education has been on sales/sales generation and, more recently, on transformation. It is the other two processes, however, that now define the basis of business competition: design in time to market and logistics in customer service and response.

Widespread corporate activities such as total quality control and the publicity accorded the Baldrige Award have succeeded in establishing the concepts and orientation of customer service in U.S. industry—at least as far as the business press is concerned. Achieving competitive, cost-effective customer service requires a new definition of the enterprise—one that includes suppliers, customers, and third-party vendors of goods and services. Tom Gunn addressed the issues and approach necessary for enterprise-wide design and transformation through his world class manufacturing framework and planning process. Others, such as George Stalk, addressed the time to market issues.

This book is less ambitious—it deals with the strategy development and management of integrated materials management through the supply chain. It emphasizes excellence in meeting customer service needs at a competitive total cost. It attempts to span the gap between the corporate strategy formulation texts—which work at an industry and market level—and those that focus on the detailed operations of various components of logistics management—for example, warehouse management, traffic, inventory control, operations research, demand management, and customer service. It does, however, include elements of all of them. Current management literature does address these issues, albeit in a fragmented fashion. This book seeks to tie it all together in a comprehensive methodology for developing and assessing logistics strategies. We have outlined the steps involved and discussed those major issues that must be addressed in each step. The book, essentially, focuses on the Corporate Profit Equation:

$$\text{Profit} = \frac{\text{Quality} + \text{Customer Service}}{\text{Cost} + \text{Cycle Time}}$$

Managing this profit equation requires that strategies be developed and implemented across the supply chain for all stages of the product life cycle to increase customer service and response and reduce costs and cycle times. As such, the book has two main objectives:

- To provide logistics executives with a methodological approach and guide to developing, assessing the effectiveness of, and managing the implementation of integrated materials management strategies
- To provide all executives in the manufacturing organization with an understanding of logistics, its issues and strategic importance, and a vision of the competitive logistics organization of the future

The concepts, approach, and applications outlined in the following pages owe a great deal to leading edge management in the many excellent companies that we have worked with, as well as to such visionary management thinkers as Stanley Davis, Gene Tyndall, Tom Gunn, Robert Hayes, Steven Wheelwright, Michael Porter, Scott Flaig, Keki Bhote, Donald Bowersox, Warren Bennis, Tom Davenport, and Phil Pyburn—all of whose concepts and ideas form the framework of this book.

The authors would especially like to thank Diane Rosenberg, Tom Gunn of Gunn & Associates, Gene Tyndall and Terry Ozan of Ernst & Young's Management Consulting Group, Scott Flaig and Bud Mathaisel of Ernst & Young's Center for Information Technology & Strategy, Pat Guerra, Frank Frederick of the Emerson Electric Co., and Jim Codner for their time, encouragement, and insightful comments.

Christopher Gopal
Gerry Cahill

CONTENTS

CHAPTER 1

LOGISTICS AND COMPETITION—
THE FUTURE

COMPETITIVE FOCUS

The focus of business thought vis-à-vis success and competition has changed dramatically since the strategic planning/generalist era of the 1960s and 70s. This evolution has progressed from **the traditional top-down strategy** of:

- Plan the exclusive purview of the strategy department
- Decide first on strategy and direction, then go to operations and try to execute (tactics)
- Make long-term plans based on predicting future competitive moves

The evolution has progressed to **the response-based strategy** of today, where:

- Bottom-up strategy takes hold as the issues of ownership and accountability prevail
- Joint management-employee teams focus on the critical issues of competitiveness
- Consultants become "expert" facilitators of the process versus MBA-trained architects of the strategy
- Time and response-based strategies focus on speed becoming the difference between winners and losers in the marketplace—the "playing field"—where quality is a given

This evolution translates into a continuous improvement process where:

- Speed and response are major differentiators
- Focus is on the customer-oriented value-chain to provide excellent customer service
- Change and flexibility are vital given the competitive environment and rapidly changing market dynamics

This evolution in management thought has progressed from an emphasis on efficiency to effectiveness and, further, to flexibility and quick response. It has been driven by several market factors that have changed the face of competition, and by advanced management thinkers in academia and industry. The latter includes Hayes and Abernathy (the orientation of senior management), Gunn (world class manufacturing), Hayes and Wheelwright (process-product relationships), Skinner and Schonberger (managing manufacturing and manufacturing strategy), Ishikawa (total quality control), and Deming and Juran, among others.

The key characteristics of this evolution have revolved around products, technology, operations, and the voice of the customer.

Briefly, the industrial battlefields of the 1970s were characterized by product portfolio management and market positioning, with power residing at corporate staff and higher-level product management functions. These analytically-driven concepts paid little attention to the customer or customer service, product quality, or the timely development and introduction of new products to satisfy an increasingly demanding market.

The 1980s exposed the inherent operational weaknesses in this approach to competitive management, as an increasing number of firms and industries succumbed to foreign and domestic competitors who manufactured with higher quality and provided improved customer value. Driven by necessity and the success of foreign (principally Japanese) manufacturers, focus shifted to world class manufacturing and the empowerment of line employees. Ishikawa's thoughts on total quality control were enthusiastically adopted by firms such as Hewlett-Packard. Like H-P, a large number of U.S. manufacturers used total quality control and just-in-time techniques, along with improved information technology (IT), to improve their competitive ability and achieve manufacturing excellence. As a result, they emerged stronger than ever. Unfortunately, many other firms, still driven by the excessively financial-legal bent of their senior management and traditional hierarchical management principles, and unaware of the changing basis of competition, started the long slide toward bankruptcy or acquisition.

The 1980s further demonstrated that good product quality and short production cycle times—a focus within a company's plants and those of its suppliers—would not alone guarantee success in a competitive environment characterized by increasingly short product life cycles, rapidly changing customer demands and expectations, and the globalization of markets and firms. Too many companies have succeeded in divorcing those functions which interface with and serve the customer from those responsible for sourcing the material and manufacturing the product. As if such horizontal fragmentation weren't bad enough, even more of these firms have isolated their functions vertically—research from engineering from manufacturing from procurement from packaging from distribution. The "virtual factory" had to encompass the entire business of serving customers and responding rapidly to their needs.

Tom Gunn identified these trends and developed a global world class manufacturing framework (Figure 1–1), where an operating philosophy consisting of a commitment to quality, planning, technology, and people drives a vertically and horizontally integrated firm to serve customer needs. Integration includes the supplier base, and execution is based on three operational "pillars"—total quality control (TQC), just-in-time (JIT), and computer-integrated manufacturing (CIM). Several leading companies have used this framework as a basis for operation and have moved to leadership positions within their industries.

The 1990s and beyond: Today's competitive environment and industry dynamics have resulted in two strategic imperatives for success:

Integrated materials management or logistics—The management of material from supplier to the customer

Competitive product response or time to market—The management of the process and cycle time from product concept to availability to the customer

The enterprise operating structure of the 90s is described in Flaig's "virtual factory" (Figure 1–2), a time-based, information integrated extension of Gunn's work. It highlights the use of information technology in extending the scope of management to the supplier and customer chains to ensure integrated supply chain management and rapid response to customer and market needs in terms of time to market and product delivery. This is where the competitive future of manufacturing companies lies.

FIGURE 1–1
Tom Gunn's World Class Manufacturing Framework

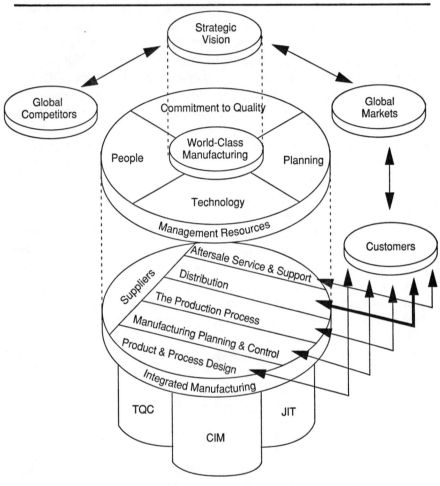

Source: Thomas G. Gunn, *Manufacturing for Competitive Advantage* (Cambridge, Mass.: Ballinger Publishing Company, 1987).

These evolutionary (and, occasionally, revolutionary) changes in management focus are illustrated in Figure 1–3, for a wide range of important competitive characteristics.

While most successful manufacturing companies converge in their achievement of manufacturing excellence, success or failure in the competitive battlefield of the 90s and beyond will be determined by successful management of the logistics value chain and time-to-market. This book

FIGURE 1–2 The "Virtual Factory" Framework

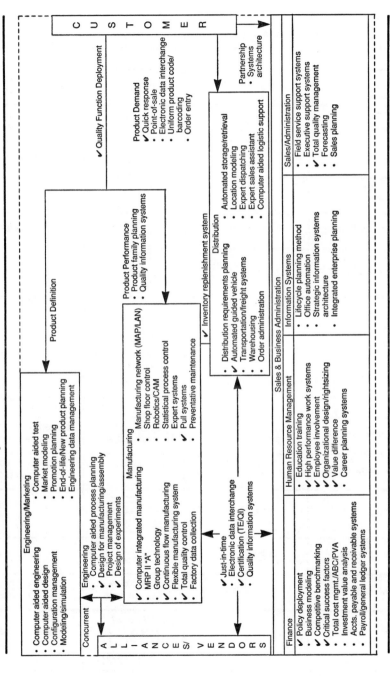

CUSTOMER

Engineering/Marketing
- Computer aided engineering
- Computer aided design
- Configuration management
- Modeling/simulation
- Computer aided test
- Market modeling
- Promotion planning
- End-of-life/New product planning
- Engineering data management

✓ Quality Function Deployment

Product Definition

Product Demand
- ✓ Quick response
- Point-of-sale
- Electronic data interchange
- Uniform product code/barcoding
- Order entry

ALLIANCE VENDORS

Concurrent

Engineering
- Computer aided process planning
- ✓ Design for manufacturing/assembly
- ✓ Project management
- ✓ Design of experiments

Manufacturing
- ✓ Computer integrated manufacturing
- ✓ MRP II "A"
- Group technology
- ✓ Continuous flow manufacturing
- ✓ Flexible manufacturing system
- ✓ Total quality control
- ✓ Factory data collection
- Manufacturing network (MAP/LAN)
- Shop floor control
- Robotics/CAM
- Statistical process control
- ✓ Expert systems
- ✓ Pull systems
- ✓ Preventative maintenance

- ✓ Just-in-time
- Electronic data interchange
- ✓ Certification (TE/QI)
- ✓ Quality information systems

Product Performance
- Product family planning
- ✓ Quality information systems

✓ Inventory replenishment system

Distribution
- Distribution requirements planning
- ✓ Automated guided vehicle
- Transportation/freight systems
- Warehousing
- Order administration
- Automated storage/retrieval
- Location modeling
- Expert dispatching
- Expert sales assistant
- Computer aided logistic support

- Partnership
- Systems architecture

Sales & Business Administration

Finance
- ✓ Policy deployment
- ✓ Business modeling
- ✓ Competitive benchmarking
- ✓ Critical success factors
- Total cost mgmt./ABC/PVA
- Investment value analysis
- Accts. payable and receivable systems
- Payroll/general ledger systems

Human Resource Management
- ✓ Education training
- ✓ High performance work systems
- ✓ Employee involvement
- ✓ Organizational design/rightsizing
- ✓ Value difference
- Career planning systems

Information Systems
- Lifecycle planning method
- ✓ Office automation
- Strategic information systems architecture
- Integrated enterprise planning

Sales/Administration
- Field service support systems
- Executive support systems
- ✓ Total quality management
- Forecasting
- Sales planning

Source: Scott Flaig, Ernst & Young Center for Information Technology & Strategy.^{SM} All rights reserved.

5

FIGURE 1–3
Changes in Competitive Management Focus

	← 70s	80s	90s →
Manufacturing Focus	Efficiency	Effectiveness	Flexibility/quick response
Product Features/ Demand	Discrete	Options/features	Customer-demanded variety
Product Life Cycle	Managing for cash flow	New product introduction	Time to market BET
Technology Rate of Change	Stable	High	Very high
Technology Focus	Automation	Information and interface	Integration
Information Focus	MRP II Management information systems	CIM	Integrated logistics systems/executive information systems
Information Management	Centralized MIS dept.-driven information disconnect	Centralized/ distributed MIS-supported/user-driven information interface	Distributed user-driven and supported information integration
Management Type	Generalist/functional specialists	Cross-functional	Multi-functional
Management Focus	Strategic planning/ portfolio-driven	Manufacturing excellence	Logistics excellence/ enterprise excellence
Supply Management	Suppliers as resources/adversarial	Supplier excellence	Strategic alliances/ the "virtual factory"
Customer Orientation	Product-focused	Customer service—quality, cost, delivery	Total customer satisfaction
Cost-Emphasis	Direct labor	"Within plant" cost	Total cost
People-Emphasis	Viewed as resource	Employee involvement	Employee empowerment
New Product Introduction	"Over the wall"	"Voice of customer"/ design for manufacturability	Competitive product response

addresses the development and implementation of logistics strategies— the integrated movement of material through the value chain from supplier to customer. It is intended to serve as a conceptual guide and thought-generator for senior executives in directing and overseeing integrated materials management, as well as a useful middle management guide—a "management consultant on paper"—for effectively managing the logistics function.

THE ROLE OF LOGISTICS IN TODAY'S BUSINESS ENVIRONMENT

Logistics, as defined by the Council for Logistics Management, is:

> The process of planning, implementing, and controlling the efficient cost-effective flow and storage of raw materials, in-process inventory, finished goods, and related information from point of origin to point of consumption for the purpose of conforming to customer requirements.

Today's competitive trends require a modification:

> for the purpose of meeting felt and unfelt customer requirements and achieving a competitive advantage.

This definition has been further augmented to include:

> the potential contribution of logistics to achieving the goals of commercial enterprise is based upon (1) the integrated management of all activities related to inventory to achieve operating objectives at lowest possible costs; and (2) the proactive use of logistics to help achieve customer satisfaction.

Driving Forces

Today's business environment is characterized by several dynamic factors that have been noted, in one form or another, by several journal articles and books. These driving forces have severely strained the operations of the "traditional" functional organization. All indications point toward the acceleration of these forces in the future, not their abatement. Companies that cannot, or will not, adapt to and lead these trends are not likely to survive in their current form over the coming decade. These driving forces are familiar to most executives, but they bear repeating as they form the basis for the new competitive framework of U.S. industry, and have major logistics implications for manufacturing companies. These implications are, however, seldom discussed in the same context. The driving forces include:

Shorter product life cycles. The life cycles of personal computers are measured in months, while those of many consumer foods products barely exceed a year.

Increased product/feature/option proliferation. Consumers demand personal computers for a variety of uses and applications with a wide variety of peripherals and features (speed, capacity, memory, footprint, enhancements, and functionality).

Consumer electronics, such as TVs and VCRs, are now differentiated based on their breadth of features and complexity of functions.

Several new hit movie/TV characters generate new cereal SKUs (stock keeping units) with different packaging (often with remarkably similar content).

Increasing customer service level and product expectations. A larger number of companies are selecting suppliers based on delivery, quality, reliability, response to ad-hoc demands, and other service considerations, rather than pure price. Increasingly, non-availability on the shelf results in lost, rather than deferred, sales for many consumer products.

Advances in process, product, and information technologies. Advances in semiconductor manufacturing equipment often drive chip development and manufacture.

Advances in integrated circuit, display screen, and process miniaturization technologies have resulted in smaller, more powerful computers—moving from desktop to portable to laptop to notebook.

Developments in computing, networking, and database technologies have given rise to integrated systems, distributed applications and processing, and on-line access to worldwide information. These advances have changed the ways we operate and compete, and created new businesses.

Globalization of the marketplace. Companies are sourcing, manufacturing, and selling internationally. Many computer companies source in the Far East, Europe, and the U.S., manufacture in the Far East and the U.S., and distribute worldwide. The logistics supply chain now spans several countries, encouraged by the evolution of multi-nationals into global companies. This assumes even greater importance when one considers that logistics costs are greater as a percentage of revenue for international companies than purely domestic firms.

The changes occurring in the European Economic Community and Eastern Europe will also pose great challenges and impose severe strains on many organizations. The opportunities are tremendous—so are the pitfalls, not the least being the logistics network configuration vis-à-vis IRS tax regulations.

Just-in-time manufacturing and management. Companies are improving operations flows and, in the process, minimizing inventory levels. The new delivery requirements (smaller lots, frequent deliveries, little safety stock to hedge against quality rejects and process breakdowns) are being forced upstream in the supply chain.

Balance of power shifting from the manufacturer to the distributor. The increase in system-wide capacity in many industries, coupled with the shortage of available shelf space and distribution channel outlets, has tilted the balance of power toward the distributors.

Furthermore, the reduction in size of many firms through restructuring has reduced their bargaining power over major, concentrated distributors.

Wide capacity swings. Changes in market demand for volume, technology, and product mix have led many companies to encounter frequent over- and under-capacity conditions. Often, these conditions are exacerbated by over-optimistic market projections and the tendency to build large automated plants.

Increased competition across all dimensions and pressure on margins. Virtually every industry is experiencing an increased intensity of competition. For some, the basis of competition has changed—witness the successes of Lexus and Acura against the German automobile manufacturers, and the loss of the U.S. semiconductor memory business to the Japanese.

In most industries, the increased intensity of competition has put severe pressure on margins, forcing less-than-efficient manufacturers (particularly those that have a productivity focus instead of a customer service and quality focus) out of business or into acquisition.

Impact on Logistics—Using Logistics As A Competitive Weapon

The impact of these driving forces on the logistics function is significant, and has forced a number of competitive imperatives on U.S. manufacturers, including:

Increase and maintain customer service levels across all dimensions and channels, from delivery performance to ad-hoc customer response and last minute order changes

Reduce overall cycle time—from order placement/demand projection to customer delivery and availability to a matter of hours and days

Improve the total quality of the delivered product and service, including the quality and convenience of packaging, product reliability, and after-sales service

Plan for, and manage, the value-added flow and movement of material from the supplier to the customer to match market demand—including supply-demand planning, demand management and forecasting, and distribution planning—and to enhance flexibility of response

Reduce total costs—inventory levels across the value chain, transportation, warehousing, packaging, costs of lost sales, non-quality, etc.

Plan and structure for increased product modularity, serviceability, customization, options, and configuration (one unique product for one customer)

Integrate information technology into process flows to obtain quantum leap improvements in performance (specifically, to acquire, develop, and implement information technologies and systems to increase market response and system-wide visibility, and enhance decision support)

Optimize and balance worldwide resources and maximize flexibility of assets and response

Figure 1–4 summarizes these factors and the strategic logistics imperatives they have forced on manufacturers across virtually all industrial segments. The importance of logistics and integration of management functions are all the more important when one considers that:

- Logistics is an integral part of the customer service/marketing mix.
- Service now plays a major role in customers' buying decisions—whether consumer or industrial—and logistics is targeted at customer service.

FIGURE 1–4
Industry Dynamics and Strategic Imperatives

Changing Industry Dynamics		Strategic Logistics Imperatives
• Shorter product life cycles • Increased product/feature/option/ configuration/proliferation • Increased customer service level and product expectations • Advances in process, product, and information technologies • Globalization of the marketplace • Just-in-time manufacturing and management • Balance of power shifting from the manufacturer to the distributor • Wide capacity swings • Increased competition across all dimensions and pressure on margins	**Results In** IIII➡	• Increase and maintain customer service levels—availability, delivery, response • Reduce overall cycle time-order placement to delivery and availability • Plan for and structure for increased customization, option, and configuration management • Strategy and implementation of information and automation technologies to manage, plan, and control worldwide supply- demand, resource, and inventory deployment • Strategic alliances with customers, carriers, and suppliers with better information and communications technologies and management methods • Improve total quality of delivered product, support, and service • Supply-demand planning for delivery, availability, flexibility, and response • Reduce total costs

Source: Ernst & Young Center for Information Technology & Strategy.^{SM} All rights reserved.

Excellence in logistics can result in strong customer relationships, and improve the firm's value to the customer. Increasingly, customers are moving toward single sourcing, and are examining total procurement costs and total costs of ownership, not merely purchase price. Additionally, with many firms adopting just-in-time/synchronous manufacturing, suppliers are being evaluated and selected based on their ability to deliver product in small lots, frequently, to point of use, and in a consistent, reliable manner. Customers now demand packaging for use on their lines (for example, semiconductors packaged in cartridges, and components packaged in kits). For such JIT-driven customers, service includes all activities on the suppliers' part to deliver the right amount of product to the point of use at precisely the right time, along with the attendant planning and status information (for instance, shipment schedules and notice of late deliveries to enable them to plan ahead).

• Logistics accounts for a major portion of a company's value chain costs (some studies estimate it to range from 5 to 25 percent of sales), and savings through improved logistics strategies and improved or redesigned processes go straight to the bottom line.

Logistics can serve to increase customer switching costs and build barriers to entry in the industry, thereby providing a true sustainable competitive advantage. An increasing number of companies have recognized this relationship and have used it to their competitive advantage. A recent study has shown that the key rationale behind many of the major mergers has been the "desire to combine distribution and achieve synergy and the desire to increase market penetration" (James E. Morehouse and Richard J. Rice, "Combined Distribution: Strategic Advantage or Strategist's Folly?" *Council of Logistics Management Annual Meeting Proceedings*, vol. 1, 1987, pp. 101–118).

Further, the study stated that "the specific rationale for combining distribution in merged companies included, first, increased marketing clout with the trade . . . , second, increasing the number of products offered to the customer usually increases throughput to that customer, resulting in better inventory turnover. Third, combined distribution represents the easiest way to expand geographical scope of regional brands."

We are familiar with the success stories of McKesson and General Electric. There are, however, numerous instances of companies that are using logistics as a competitive weapon.

• A major electronics firm located a manufacturing plant near a significant potential market in order to respond quickly to anticipated market needs. This went against prevailing wisdom (and narrowly-defined cost analysis) that the plant location should be decided to take advantage of lower direct labor and manufacturing engineering labor costs. A total cost analysis, however, revealed that increased labor, duplication, and inventory stocking costs would be more than offset by reduced transportation, warehousing, and value-added costs, as well as increased market share (due to rapid response to customer requirements for short-notice and just-in-time deliveries) and competitive position against larger overseas manufacturers.

• A major consumer products firm, providing a full line of products, developed a logistics information system to tie in its distributors and retailers to its inventory system. By providing its customers features that gave product stock visibility while enabling them to manage their own inventory levels, it effectively closed out its lower-priced competition. Additionally, it provided its retailers a powerful value-added service.

• Some forward-thinking semiconductor manufacturers have adopted similar strategies, tying in their inventory systems to those of their distributors, moving toward the "virtual factory." When end-users require chips, the distributors have a built-in bias to satisfy their orders with product from these suppliers.

• Other semiconductor firms have formed backward and forward strategic alliances with their customers. Engineering departments are linked with customers' design facilities to speed up the development process to match customer needs, while electronic data interchange (EDI) links distribution inventory to customers' procurement and ordering processes and systems. This provides an invaluable time and response-based competitive advantage for both firms.

On the other hand, the opposite is also true. One electronics firm decided to locate overseas because of lower labor and engineering personnel costs. Its product lines were design-intensive, while direct labor accounted for less than five percent of total costs. The enormous distance between product design (in the U.S.) and manufacturing (Far East) led to significant quality and manufacturability problems. Additionally, it was found that shipping components from the Far East was less expensive than shipping the final product. This company collapsed, while a major competitor, who located *its* new plant in the U.S. near a large customer and close to its design center, has achieved excellent market position.

A common thread runs through these situations, where decisions along the logistics chain have resulted in a decided competitive advantage. These companies considered the management of materials in an integrated fashion, rather than from a functional "silo" perspective. Decisions were made, based not on functional performance or the cost/profit center concept, but on the logistics perspective of an integrated approach to satisfying the customer. One study concluded that:

[such integrated] companies show an increased operating profit contribution of 1.9–2.4 percent higher than for less integrated companies.

While integration does not necessarily imply placing all functions under a single organizational umbrella (although several leading edge firms have done just that), it does require multi-functional decision-making and an enterprise-wide awareness that decisions in one area have major impacts on others and on the company as a whole. It also requires a management philosophy and measurement structure that prevents "optimizing the parts, while sub-optimizing the whole."

The Logistics Supply Chain

The value chain, described by Michael Porter, provides the framework for analyzing and managing the integrated flow of material and information from the supplier to the customer and back. Figure 1–5 illustrates the materials flow across the logistics supply chain. Effectively managing the flow of material and information through this chain, and its assets, requires focusing on the highest *competitive* customer service levels at the least possible total cost. To do so, a manufacturing firm must:

- Develop a robust logistics strategy, driven by the corporate strategy and integrated with the marketing and manufacturing strategies.
- Set up and manage the supply chain in terms of the physical structure, resource allocation, the driving policies and decisions, and the cost drivers/performance indicators in order to decide on policy and monitor its success.
- Integrate IT into the process, and then evaluate, plan for, acquire, and implement key enabling information and automation technologies. The key factors in setting up and managing the logistics supply chain along these dimensions are shown in Figures 1–6—1–11.

The structural factors of the logistics network (Figure 1–7) include the physical configuration of the components of the value chain. The components include the number and location of vendors (components, raw material, value-added, subassembly, etc.); manufacturing facilities stage, scope, location, mix, and size; and the type, scope, and location of distribution centers or, alternatively, public or contract warehousing. The

FIGURE 1–5
Logistics Supply Chain

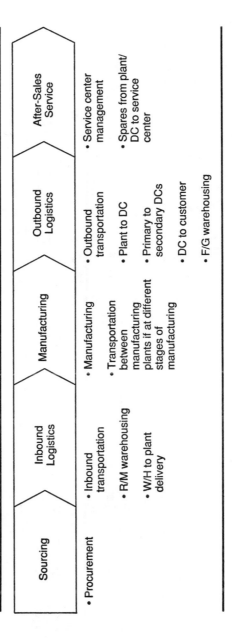

Sourcing	Inbound Logistics	Manufacturing	Outbound Logistics	After-Sales Service
• Procurement	• Inbound transportation • R/M warehousing • W/H to plant delivery	• Manufacturing • Transportation between manufacturing plants if at different stages of manufacturing	• Outbound transportation • Plant to DC • Primary to secondary DCs • DC to customer • F/G warehousing	• Service center management • Spares from plant/DC to service center

FIGURE 1–6
The Logistics Supply Chain Key Factors

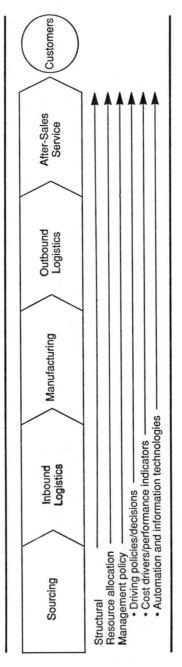

FIGURE 1-7
Key Factors in the Logistics Supply Chain Configuration (Network) Structural

Sourcing	Inbound Logistics	Manufacturing	Outbound Logistics	After-Sales Service
• Number of vendors per product • Vendor location(s) • Capacity allocated • Local regulations and tax implications • Local market implications • Local labor and material costs • Local technologies • Local economy • Political	• W/H location(s) (plant adjacent or remote) • Number of W/Hs • W/H size, capacity, and function • In-house fleet vs. contract carriers • Modes of transportation • Number of carriers • Local regulations and tax implications	• Plant location(s) • Concentrated vs. dispersed manufacture (plans per product line) • Single plant or plants at different stages of manufacture • Level of technologies • Capacities • Manufacturing flexibility (dedicated vs. flexible) • Local regulations and tax implications • Local market implications • Local labor and material costs • Local economy • Political	• DC location(s) and functions • Number of DCs • DC size and capacity • In-house fleet vs. contract carriers • Number of carriers • Modes of transportation • Local regulations and tax implications • Political	• Number of service centers and functions • Service centers location(s) • Size and autonomy of service centers • Local demand and market implications

decisions are typically major and long-term in scope and involve large capital and working capital investment and commitment.

The resource allocation factors (Figure 1–8) involve decisions to allocate and control costs for the ongoing operations of the value chain. They reflect management priorities regarding costs and development. An important aspect here is education and learning costs—exposing management and employees to the best practices in industry (particularly, other industries) and new, improved ways of conducting business.

Management policies involve policies, methods, management parameters, and technology options required to analyze, conduct, and effectively manage the business. They can be classified into three major areas:

1. Driving policies and decisions, (Figure 1–9) involve the key decisions and policies for managing the business—including supply management, justification and acquisition of technologies, organizational structure, roles and responsibilities, and customer service levels.

2. Cost drivers and performance indicators, (Figure 1–10) illustrate the major cost drivers and market-based performance measures in the logistics value chain. The basis for effective management is a knowledge of the total cost structure, its drivers, and the development of performance indicators. These provide the total cost picture as well as form the basis for attributing costs by product-service-segment in order to:

- Monitor and control costs
- Make informed decisions based on the true cost picture
- Analyze the process and improve or redesign it to meet competitive market and cost objectives
- Identify performance indicators to monitor the business, its success and investment requirements

3. Information and automation technologies, (Figure 1–11) provide the key technologies and technology planning requirements that must be considered if the firm is to:

- Redesign its business processes to match its "vision"
- Possess effective decision support to management
- Support the management and execution of ongoing operations
- Manage the supply-demand planning/forecasting/delivery processes

FIGURE 1–8
Key Resource Allocation Factors in the Logistics Supply Chain Resource Allocation

Sourcing	Inbound Logistics	Manufacturing	Outbound Logistics	After-Sales Service
Education/ Learning	Education/ Learning	Education/ Learning	Education/ Learning	Education/ Learning
• Supplier development • Supplier learning costs • Overlap costs • Systems • Component engineering and on-site quality control	• R/M inventory • Systems and automation • Fleet maintenance/ replacement • Packaging engineering • Transportation costs • Space • Flexibility costs • Direct labor • Indirect labor	• Plant • Equipment • Preventative maintenance • Systems automation • WIP inventory • Direct labor • Indirect labor	• F/G inventory • Systems and automation • Fleet maintenance/ replacement • DC space and equipment • Flexibility costs • Transportation costs • Packaging engineering	• Service center costs • Service spares inventory

FIGURE 1–9
Key Management Policies/Decisions in the Logistics Supply Chain Management Policy

Sourcing	Inbound Logistics	Manufacturing	Outbound Logistics	After-Sales Service
• Logistics network configuration • Technology justification • Carrier modes in-house vs. contract/backhauls • Performance measures and objectives • Supply management • Delivery patterns	• R/M inventory levels and safety stock • Technologies	• Staffing levels (direct/indirect) • Coordination of activities • Policies and procedures • WIP inventory levels • Delivery performance • Capabilities • Technologies • Product lines per plant • Manufacturing mission • Quality	• Planning/forecasting methodologies and policies • Organizational roles and responsibilities • Customer service levels • F/G inventory levels and safety stock • Technologies • Delivery patterns • Quality	• Service offered

FIGURE 1–10
Key Cost Drivers/Performance Indicators in Logistics Supply Chain Management Policy

Sourcing	Inbound Logistics	Manufacturing	Outbound Logistics	After-Sales Service
• R/M cost • R/M quality and reliability • R/M delivery • R/M flexibility and lead times	• R/M inventory levels • Freight costs • W/H storage space and facings • W/H indirect labor and overhead • Order-pick-delivery response time (turnaround time) • Spoilage/damage/breakage	• Quality • Process variability • Yield • Scrap • Rework • Process cycle time • Direct labor cost • Indirect labor and overhead support staff • Delivery performance • WIP inventory levels	• Freight costs • F/G inventory levels • Customer service leads • Costs of expediting stockouts • Turnaround time • W/H storage space and facings • W/H indirect labor and overhead • Spoilage/damage/breakage	• MTBF • Service response time • Cost of servicing product(s) • Spare inventory levels

FIGURE 1–11
Key Automation and Information Technology Considerations in the Logistics Supply Chain
Management Policy

Sourcing	Inbound Logistics	Manufacturing	Outbound Logistics	After-Sales Service

• EDI supplier links
• Supplier evaluation
• P.O. information tracking
• R/M cost, quality, delivery
• Integration of business systems
	• Carrier tracking
	• AS/RS
	• Loading/unloading technologies
	• Material handling technologies
	• R/M visibility
	  • In-transit
	  • Receipts and scheduled receipts
	  • Inventory levels and movement
	  • Spoilage/aging
	• Freight monitoring
	• LCL/LTL
	• Integration of business systems
	• W/H management systems
		• CAD/CAM/CAE
		• FMS/FM cells
		• Robotics
		• Group technology
		• Integration of business systems
		• Manufacturing, planning, and control systems
		• Plans/schedules
		• Process control
		• Process cycle times
		• WIP tracking
		• Quality information
			• DRP
			• AS/RS
			• Loading/unloading technologies
			• Carrier tracking
			• Optimization models
			• Order entry and taking technologies
			• EDI customer links
			• W/H management systems
			• Freight monitoring
			• LCL/LTL
			• F/G visibility
			• Integration of business systems
				• Service/spares management systems
				• Integration with DC and plants
				• Returns and analysis

22

- Have true multi-functional, enterprise-wide integration
- Make the quantum leap to outdistance its competition

The range and scope of available technologies are enormous. A key factor in making IT decisions is the company's technology justification process (discussed in a later chapter). It is vital that the company move away from the traditional solely-financial based techniques, and adopt rigorous methods that reflect the integrative nature of the technology, its strategic impacts, and its value to the firm and process.

A key word here is *rigorous*. A large company is in its second major in-house development effort for a forecasting and demand management information system. Previous efforts have failed and have been enormously expensive. Yet the same in-house MIS team is at it again, driven by corporate needs—and is being greeted with a great deal of skepticism by the users. It would be safe to predict that another multi-year, multi-million dollar effort is already dead in the water.

The New Paradigm of Logistics Management

Traditionally, companies have organized, operated, and measured themselves along functional lines—even the Council for Logistics Management was formerly called the National Association for Physical Distribution. Within this business framework, distribution operated to reduce transportation costs and provide safe storage and quick order turnaround. Procurement, inbound traffic, manufacturing and distribution planning, customer service, and materials/inventory management typically operated in isolation from each other—functional "silos" that sought to optimize their own operations, sometimes at the expense of the enterprise. Functional performance measures (often in conflict with each other) encourage this situation. Warren Bennis placed the new role of logistics in its proper perspective when he said:

> while marketing is a demand-creating activity, [logistics] is a demand-satisfying activity.

Bowersox and Murray state:

> Management focus is moving beyond the walls of the existing business structure to encompass suppliers and customers. Inter-organizational partnerships that share information and coordinate functional preference are evolving (Donald J. Bowersox and Robert W. Murray, "Logistics Strategic Planning for the 1990s," *Council of Logistics Management, Annual Meeting Proceedings*, vol. 1, 1987, pp. 231–244).

Among the characteristics of the new, emerging logistics enterprise are:

1. Consistent customer service across all dimensions and channels—delivery, response, quality, convenience of use and packaging, and reliability. This will include a new role for distributors—that of component integrators and single point-of-contact vendors. These are value-added services that some distributors are promoting and some customers are demanding (for example, total procurement cost management—which results in reducing customer purchasing, incoming inspection, and inventory management costs), and include:

- Consolidation of procured parts from multiple sources, kitting and consolidated shipments in a just-in-time mode
- Value-added work (non-critical assembly, cable harness, etc.)
- Management of the customer's floor stock inventory
- Single billing
- Incoming inspection and testing

2. Strategic alliances and partnerships with key stakeholders—customers, suppliers, carriers, warehousers, information technology developers, and integrators. This will further emphasize the interdependence of the key stakeholders.

3. Outsourcing of traditional functions and value-added activities across the value chain. Outsourcing is particularly useful if:

- Specialized skills are required
- The organization is to focus on its core competencies and stay lean and mean
- The outside resource is able to deliver product and service quicker and more reliably, at less cost, or at consistently better quality

Many companies currently outsource for new products outside their current lines and channels when greater flexibility is required, and to cope with major changes in the business environment. Outsourcing has touched virtually every aspect of the manufacturing business including supply (less vertical integration, OEMs), manufacturing (contract manufacturing, assembly, co-packing), warehousing and distribution (contract warehousing, full-service logistics carriers, and freight forwarders), information systems (particularly new systems or re-engineering of existing systems), product engineering, process design, and after-sales service.

Contract warehousing, for instance, provides shared risks of delivery, higher control and flexibility, responsiveness, an often lower overall cost structure and, very importantly, a business partnership versus an arm's-length relationship.

Outsourcing is giving rise to the "new hollow corporation," where the hollowness results from focusing on core competencies, flexibility, and risk minimization (for example, during production ramp-up for a new product) and assuring best customer service and cost structures.

4. Direct customer involvement in the definition of the product and its packaging ("voice of the customer"), specification of service requirements, and the pull-through/call-out of inventory.

5. Information technology and communications—linking key members of the supply chain, as well as providing worldwide visibility, control, intelligence, and decision support. The key issues here involve IT strategic alignment, integration with business processes, and information integration and sharing for the "virtual factory". Information integration enables the company to anticipate the customer's needs and respond more quickly, rather than react to the competition.

The changing industry dynamics and resulting management roles and imperatives necessitate an enhanced framework for viewing and managing the business. This is presented in Figure 1–12, and encompasses these elements:

- Methods of management and improvement
- Business focus
- Product-market strategies and focus
- Organization
- Scope of the organization
- Operations focus
- Operating/multi-functional focus
- Information technology parameters
- Problem-solving/employee operating focus

The paradigm transcends the functional and enterprise-wide perspectives to "virtual supply chain integration". It involves a vision of the logistics company of the near future with "breaking glass" rethinking on the roles of suppliers, customers, delivery response, and total cost. Figure 1–13 illustrates some of the issues that surfaced during an executive session held by one company to define its vision.

FIGURE 1–12
Framework for Business Enterprise Viewpoint

	Local		Industry	Global
Enterprise — Impact on corporate competitiveness — Product line/ Business Unit	• Functional "silo" optimization • Operations improvements (SPC, JIT, etc.) Operational/ Functional Focus		Value Chain Focus • Global supply/ demand planning • Integrated materials management	Virtual Supply Chain Focus • Outsourcing • Strategic alliances with stakeholders • System-wide planning
	Short-Medium Term		Strategic Time Horizon	Visionary
Methods of management	Budgets	Product cost	Cost management	Total cost management
Business focus	Product	Process	Customer	Time/customer/process
Methods of improvement	Statistical process control		Continuous process improvement	Business process redesign
Organizational operations	Functional		Multi-functioning teams	Multi-functional international teams
IT Parameters	Functional applications		Vertical/value chain integration	Stakeholder/global access and networks
Motivation	Functional targets/ team incentives		"System" performance incentives	Ownership/business success rewards

Management viewpoint: Strategic — Management viewpoint — Operational

Source: Ernst & Young Center for Information Technology & Strategy.

FIGURE 1–13
Developing a New Paradigm for Logistics: Key Issues Surfaced

- Total configuration at point-of-sale
- Customer as an operational part of supply-demand planning
- Product design specified by customer as part of new product design and manufacture
- Individual customers managed as accounts
- Customers initiate planning, shipment, production
- The "transparent" corporation
- The "hollow" outsourced corporation
- Tight linkage between customer and supplier—zero inventory, make and deliver at customer initiation and to customer specification
- Information technology integration with all customers (global IT)

CONCLUSION

In order to survive and compete effectively today, manufacturers must abandon the functional model of management and operation, and move toward an enterprise and "virtual supply chain" view. An increasing number of corporations in various industries are, indeed, adopting such a paradigm of management, moving toward managing material and value-added through the logistics supply chain in an integrated fashion.

This text discusses the enterprise-wide paradigm of logistics management for competitive advantage. It provides frameworks and methods for planning, analysis, and assessment of competitive logistics, as well as the information technology aspects of integrated materials management. Additionally, it describes the characteristics the new logistics manager needs in today's business environment, and shows how managers can plan and control the logistics function to support the company's corporate and marketing strategies.

CHAPTER 2

LOGISTICS STRATEGY PLANNING FRAMEWORK

The previous chapter established the strategic importance to, and role of, logistics in the firm's competitive success and survival, through the achievement of the strategic imperatives imposed by the marketplace. The first step in the process is the development of a coherent logistics strategy, and the adoption of a simple (though not simplistic), yet comprehensive framework within which to view, plan, execute, and monitor competitive logistics strategies.

There are several good and useful frameworks within which a company can work effectively to guide the development and implementation of a logistics strategy. Figure 2–1 presents one such logistics strategy planning framework that will also be used as the framework of the book. This framework has the virtues of being easy-to-comprehend and feedback-oriented. In other words, it emphasizes the continuous nature of the process. This approach is by no means unique. It draws upon earlier approaches, such as the one developed and implemented by Ernst & Whinney in the CLM-sponsored book on the effective management of logistics—*Corporate Profitability & Logistics: Innovative Guidelines for Executives*. While frameworks may differ to some extent, most experience-based approaches to logistics strategy will prove useful, provided they incorporate the essential steps in some sort of rational sequence.

Logistics strategies must be consistent with the corporate goals and strategies of the organization, and should be the third line management leg (generating sales, transformation, movement) developed in conjunction with the firm's marketing and manufacturing strategies. The marketing strategy (generated sales) is typically oriented toward the firm's external environment, and includes:

FIGURE 2–1
Logistics Strategy Planning Framework

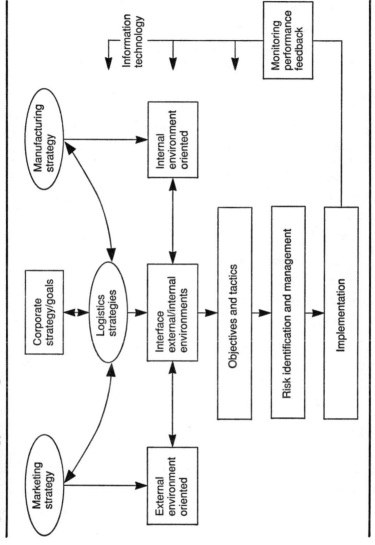

29

Product-market strategies

New product introduction, phase-in/phase-outs

Promotion at the national and regional level

Trade/channel management, etc.

while the manufacturing strategy (transformation) is internally-focused, and deals with product technologies, manufacturing processes, automation—"hard" and "soft," plant focus, cost reduction, etc. Table 2–1 presents the major components of a manufacturing strategy and their logistics impacts.

Logistics strategies (material movement) provide the interface between the external and internal environments, and consist of five interrelated components:

- Configuration/facilities network strategy
- Coordination/organization strategy
- Customer service strategy
- Integrated inventory strategy
- Information technology strategy

Supporting these is transportation, the link between supply and delivery points that binds the supply chain together. (Each of these components is discussed in subsequent chapters.)

DEVELOPING LOGISTICS STRATEGIES

The charter of logistics is as follows: Within corporate strategic, marketing, and manufacturing guidelines:

Establishing, planning for, and controlling facilities, material, and information flow

to

Create and sustain a competitive advantage at the *least total cost*

While exceeding *competitive customer expectations of service*, and maintaining flexibility, and building/maintaining barriers to competitive entry.

It is important to recognize that competitors are actively pursuing similar charters, and that logistics can be used as a competitive weapon by the enterprise—or against it! The previous chapter discussed the con-

TABLE 2–1
Major Components of Manufacturing Strategy and Their Logistics Impacts

Major Components of Manufacturing Strategy	Logistics Impact
Capacity	• Product mix to service regions • Volume by product mix • Maximum capacity
Facilities	• Location and proximity to supplier/customer/co-location • Multi-plant/multi-stage • Product prices/type • Expandability
Equipment and process technologies	• Flexibility to customer demands • Returns/repair facilities • Product mix flexibility • Product phase-in/phase-out
Vertical integration	• Transportation between stages • Consolidated shipments
Vendors	• Number and volume • Distances/frequency of delivery/size of delivery/JIT • Alliances
New products	• Phase-in/phase-outs and volume • Packaging • Supply/demand planning • Volume ramp up
Systems	• Integration • EDI/stakeholder links • Worldwide inventory visibility • Decision support tools • Costing systems • Supply/demand planning systems • Order management

Source: Hayes and Wheelright, "Competing Through Manufacturing," *Harvard Business Review*, Jan./Feb. 1985.

cepts of the logistics supply chain and its key structural, resource allocation, management decision, and cost driver aspects. Logistics management involves planning and executing along this value-added chain to
match supply and demand. The goal of this supply-demand management
process is to support marketing in helping the company create and sustain
a competitive advantage in the marketplace. The objectives are to exceed
competitive customer expectations of service (note: they do not include
providing an *absolute* level of service—this can prove very expensive),

FIGURE 2–2
Meeting/Exceeding Customer Expectations of Service
Wasted Effort/Lost Opportunities

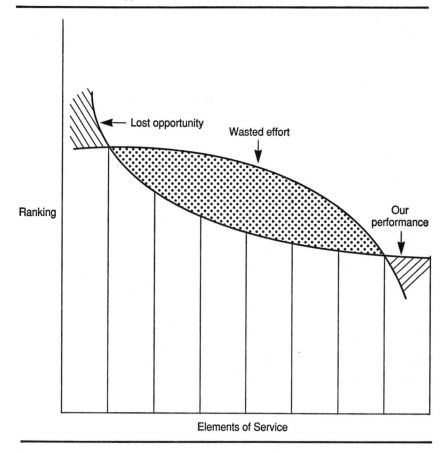

while attaining the *least total cost* along the supply chain (see Figures 2–2 and 2–3).

If the firm provides service at a much higher level than that expected by the customer, much of the effort may be misdirected or wasted. If, additionally, the firm's performance is greater than that of the competition as well, it is probably spending money on *unnecessary excellence*. However, if, as shown, performance in some service dimensions falls below customer expectations, there exist areas of *lost opportunity*. If, on

FIGURE 2–3
Meeting/Exceeding Customer Expectations of Service
Vulnerabilities/Unnecessary Excellence

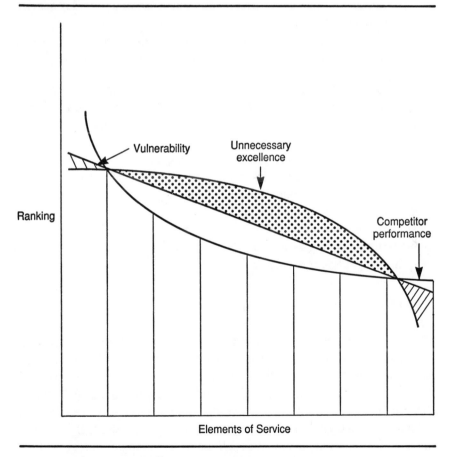

the other hand (as in Figure 2–3), performance falls below that of the competition *and* customer service expectations, there probably exist serious areas of vulnerability and potential lost sales, which must be acted upon.

Implicit here is the requirement that the enterprise know its competitive targets along all dimensions of customer service. Methods to obtain such information include the various benchmarking tools to arrive at "Best of Industry" or "Best in Class" measures:

1. Ask customers (channels/end customers) about their current expectations regarding company performance vis-à-vis the competition, their needs, and expectations.

- Define their needs specifically and quantitatively (one-day service means the next day!).
- Determine the consequences in terms of stockouts. Are they prepared to wait for a day, or two days, or will they go elsewhere?

2. Survey line management within the firm. Front-line managers often have good ideas about customer needs and competitor performance.

3. Analyze past performance along all dimensions of customer service. Does the firm measure up?

4. Conduct secondary research in trade and business journals.

This information provides a baseline for customer needs, firm performance, and improvement targets. It provides a basis to develop and implement logistics strategies to gain a competitive advantage. By redesigning the processes and integrating information technology (IT) to achieve these strategies and objectives, the firm can obtain a quantum leap in competitiveness (Figure 2–4).

The First Step: Develop the Mission and Criteria

The mission statement sets the overall tone for the logistics function and forms the basis for its key success criteria. It must reflect the corporate strategic objectives of the firm. Without it, the company is reduced to using logistics in a purely reactive mode, and will obtain little benefit from its potential to influence its competitive ability. At worst, this lack of general direction can adversely affect the company's market performance. The mission statement should be short (a single, non-convoluted sentence, ideally) and derived from the overall corporate mission state-

FIGURE 2–4
Innovative Logistics Strategies Can Provide a Quantum Leap in Competitiveness

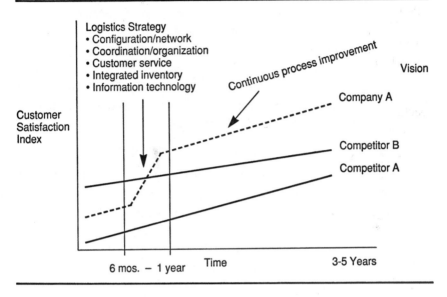

ment (sometimes it *is* the corporate mission statement). Examples from some companies include:

> We will be our customers' preferred vendor of choice.

> We are responsible for the high quality, cost effective gathering and distribution of our product and delivery to our customers on time.

These two mission statements have different implications and key success criteria for the logistics functions. The criteria for the first include:

- Incorporating the firm's delivery and inventory planning mechanisms into the customer's procurement and manufacturing functions to provide just-in-time and quick response delivery
- Designing packaging for customer convenience in receiving, stocking, inventory management, and production use

- Providing the customer visibility into the finished goods and available to promise or allocated semi-finished inventory
- Labeling the product and packaging for customer convenience
- Using part numbers compatible with those of customers' systems (even using the customer's part numbers)
- Using continuous improvement techniques and sharing the data with customers
- Establishing communications, via EDI (electronic data interchange) and frequent customer satisfaction meetings, to exchange information and obtain feedback regarding problems and needs

The criteria for the second mission statement could include:

- System-wide inventory and availability system to monitor customer orders and status
- Comprehensive order processing/management system
- Centralized logistics planning and control for all components needed for complete order fill delivery
- Consolidated shipments (for cost control) within stated delivery windows by region
- Excellent forecasting/demand management processes and systems
- Inventory deployment geared toward high delivery performance at least total cost
- Uses of models for least total cost network (configuration) planning and deciding on/monitoring cost trade-offs

In general, the criteria should encompass control over customer service; product and service time and quality; inventory deployment; supply-demand planning, lack of "nervousness," and ability to react; and total cost management.

The mission statement should, therefore, be not merely a collection of "motherhood" and "nice to have" sentiments, but should, rather, represent the firm's strategic direction and must be thought out carefully—it must become the firm's operating credo and its strategic posture with respect to the market. Too many firms arrive at their logistics mission statement without thinking through the potential implications—worse, they often base them on popular business literature (for instance, some firms use the charter cited here—or words to that effect—as their mission statement—a case of wanting everything but having no coherent direction). Furthermore, the logistics mission statement can, and should, change with changes in market dynamics, the firm's competitive positioning, and overall corporate strategy.

Rao, Stenger, and Young have identified three types of generic logistics strategies, based on Porter's generic strategies of overall cost leadership, differentiation, and focus. They provide a useful framework within which to define the mission of the logistics environment. They include:

Cost minimization—based on service, customer requirements, and coverage trade-offs. This would be consistent if the corporate strategy were based on cost leadership.

Value-added maximization—"ways of expanding value-added contributions of the firm through its logistics activities."

A major office products firm provided a single supply point-of-contact for its customers, and undertook to stock and deliver products complementary to its own lines—in effect, becoming a distributor.

Control/flexibility enhancement—"ability to change even at the expense of some obvious costs or value-added benefits."

Certainly, key characteristics include outsourcing and fast response types of strategies.

In short, the mission statement must present a vision of excellence and competitiveness, align the logistics and business strategies, and encompass the integration of the logistics supply chain.

The Second Step: Define the Current Logistics Environment— "Know Thyself"

This step consists of defining the firm's logistics environment in terms of hard data, and includes the following five categories:

1. Product groupings and volumes
   - Product lines/SKUs
   - Major raw material, components, sub-assemblies
   - OEM material
   - Peripherals and software
   - Spares, etc.
2. Logistics network source-destination links/flows
   - Market and geographical segments
   - Countries
   - Plants, distribution centers

- Public, contract warehouses
- Dealers, value-added dealers, major accounts
- Sources of supply
- Field service centers and returns/repairs

3. Customer service levels
   - Service levels (delivery performance, backorders, lead time response, order cycle and accuracy, return and repair cycle, etc.)
   - Inventory management (inventory levels, safety stocks, aged inventories, obsolescence, stockouts)
   - Demand variations by country, region

4. Total cost
   - Manufacturing
   - Warehousing and packaging
   - Inventory carrying costs
   - Transportation
   - Order processing and filling
   - Subcontracting
   - Field service
   - Indirect and support costs

5. Asset utilization
   - Plants, distribution centers
   - In-house fleets
   - Warehousing
   - Field service centers

These five categories provide a complete picture of the logistics environment and form the baseline for determining and evaluating logistics options and strategies. A method for defining the "as-is" is outlined in chapter 9, which discusses logistics assessment.

The Third Step: Know the Industry

This includes the trends in the industry and competitors' actions and structures. It is important that the firm does not expose itself to areas of vulnerability or lost sales or, on the other hand, spend money and effort unnecessarily (see Figure 2–3). This step involves determining two facets of the industry:

• Trends: what changes are likely to occur in each major market/geographical segment? How will these changes affect the company?
• Competitors' actions, including product lines and market coverage/location, distribution network, value-added services, and customer service levels.

Answering these questions typically involves interviews with field sales personnel and customers, and analysis of secondary data. Additionally, they may necessitate benchmarking, defined by Robert Camp as "the search for industry best practices that lead to superior performance" (Robert C. Camp, *Benchmarking: The Search for Industry Best Practices that Lead to Superior Performance* [Milwaukee, Wis.: ASQC Quality Press, 1989]).

The Fourth Step: Develop Objectives for Each of the Five Major Areas of Logistics Strategy

Using this logistics mission statement/operating credo as a framework, and based on the firm's marketing and manufacturing strategies, the next step is to develop objectives for the logistics function, set within the guidelines of the marketing and manufacturing strategies. Corporate objectives often take the form of standard operating objectives—enterprise-wide and quantifiable. Most of the logistics strategy objectives are more developmental in nature, providing direction. The process of setting objectives is an iterative one, and must involve front-line managers. Key logistics standard operating objectives include:

• Return on operating logistics assets
• System-wide inventory investment levels
• High-level customer service policies
• Costs

As indicated earlier, there are five major interrelated areas of logistics strategy. These are listed here, along with their key components.

1. Configuration/facilities network strategy
   • Regional location of distribution centers
   • Policies governing facilities location

- Centralized or dispersion (satellite) strategies for distribution centers
- Aggregate size, function, and capacity for distribution centers
- Proximity/time issues, addressing the geographical dependencies of the critical internal and external functions and stakeholders

2. Coordination/organization strategy

   To support the logistics strategy:
   - Supply-demand planning policies through the supply chain
   - Key decisions that have to be made
   - Organization linkage to support strategy
   - Centralization and control policies of necessary functions

3. Customer service strategy
   - Alliances with customers/channels

     By major product line, spares/service, and broad regional/customer segment:
   - Policies governing customer service
   - Order cycle time
   - Order cycle time reliability
   - Order completeness and accuracy
   - On-time delivery
   - Order fill rate
   - Proximity/presence (distance to customer)
   - Customer access to order/inventory information

4. Integrated inventory strategy
   - Alliances with OEMs, suppliers, third-party service agents by major product line, spares/service, and broad regional/customer segment to satisfy customer service objectives:
   - Inventory deployment and management policies
   - Stocking locations and levels
   - Safety stocks

5. Information technology strategy
   - IT strategic alignment

     Along the supply chain:
   - Business process redesign using IT enablers

- IT planning
- Information integration/sharing
- Applications
- Architecture
- Worldwide/system-wide visibility
- Connectivity
    Supporting the logistics strategy transportation:
- Alliances with carriers
- Third party contracting
- Shipment (bulk, master packaging, unitization)
- Frequency/consolidation policies
- Modes of transportation
- Transportation management policies (contract carriers, freight forwarders, third party billing, etc.)

Some representative objectives (used by various companies) for each of these areas are presented in Table 2–2. As operational objectives ought to be, they are direct (not vague), concise, and measurable, and represent a combination of standard operating objectives and developmental objectives.

The Fifth Step: Develop Logistics Strategies

The development of configuration/network, coordination/organization, customer service, integrated inventory, and information technology strategies is discussed in the following chapters.

Logistics strategies, by virtue of being geared toward quick customer response and changing market conditions, must be:

Flexible

Robust (able to achieve key objectives satisfactorily under a variety of conditions)

Committed to the minimum possible capital expenditure—if possible, in a phased manner

Justified using both economic and strategic analysis

Integrated with risk identification and risk management programs (contingency planning)

TABLE 2–2
Representative Objectives

Logistics	Return on operating assets: 15%
System-wide	System-wide inventory turns: 10
Network/ configuration	To locate our inventory as close to our customers' point of use as is cost effective
	To maintain full service distribution centers (DCs) to best serve our customers' delivery needs
	To maintain satellite DCs only when it is necessary to maintain the business of a major customer
Coordination/ organization	To maintain quick, concerted response to customer demands by centrally planning and controlling worldwide finished goods inventory
	To staff the logistics function with those best suited through experience, training, and capabilities
	To maintain worldwide inventory status for effective planning
	To integrate the supply chain in terms of management and operations for the most competitive customer service
Customer service	To deliver 95% of orders 100% complete within 1 day of customer request date
	To offer our customers delivery of complete orders within a 1 week cycle time from receipt of order
	To offer our major customers 48 hour response with complete orders to their emergency requests
	To ensure, through our packaging efforts, that our customers receive undamaged products 100% of the time
Integrated inventory	To minimize our system-wide dollar investment in inventory while providing customer service levels to our stated objectives
	To continuously advance our order processing points through the integrated efforts of design engineering, manufacturing, and order management so that we can achieve our stated customer service level goals
	To manage our inventory investment to fully support our competitive customer service objectives
	To provide the best possible decision support tools to assist in managing our inventory to our stated objectives
Information technology	To provide the IT, consistent with our IT thrust, to ensure worldwide visibility of all material, provide on-line analytical tools, and integrate all functions along the supply chain
	To enable the linking with suppliers and customers for improved service
	To enable a single point of customer and supplier contact
	To ensure up-to-the-hour, accurate information for executive monitoring and decision-making
Transportation	To leverage our corporation-wide and system-wide traffic activities to obtain the lowest possible transportation costs and obtain the best possible service from our contractors
	To manage traffic such that it supports our stated customer service level objectives

A Point to Note: The structural and automation aspects of configuration and coordination strategies necessitate a long-term perspective—they are expensive to implement and equally expensive (if not more so) to change. One large electronics components manufacturer, in the heat of the "automation era" (when automation was viewed as the solution to most problems, and justified on the basis of direct labor cost savings), built an expensive automated storage/retrieval system facility to act as a major distribution center—and justified it on the basis of projected direct warehousing labor savings and quick order turnaround. A few years later, it was found that the facility required several high-paid engineers, technicians, and programmers to maintain it (the system kept breaking down), which more than offset the initially-projected direct labor savings. In addition, the very real cash outflow based on interest payments, combined with the fact that inventory reduction programs had rendered the facility grossly underutilized (undermining the volume projections on which most of the anticipated savings were based), made the facility very uneconomical. Further, its location—far from any major customer base—rendered the premise of quick order turnaround from the customer's perspective void. The company is now seriously reevaluating the entire decision—at a considerable projected expense.

Table 2–3 shows the typical components of a logistics strategy. It can be seen that these areas are similar to those for which objectives were developed—the objectives are built into the strategy. A strategy, after all, is a plan for achieving objectives. Similarly, the implementation plan will also be built into the strategy. The discussions in this book focus on the configuration/network, coordination/organization, customer service, integrated inventory, and information technology strategies. The development of transportation policy, though often called strategic, is really tactical. Its components provide a means to achieve an end. It is certainly part of the total cost solution, and a key part in attaining customer service strategies, but transportation policies for reducing costs and increasing customer service are typically decided at a tactical level, driven by the logistics strategies of network configuration, coordination and organization, customer service, and inventory through the pipeline.

Our discussions will not focus on transportation. However, there are several texts that more than satisfactorily address the issues of transportation policy-setting, management, and control.

Strategies must be developed using an industry-wide perspective. In other words, they must answer the questions:

TABLE 2–3
Components of Logistics Strategy

Logistics Strategy	Components
Configuration/Facilities	• Stage • Time/proximity • Location • Facility mission and type (e.g., public/contract warehouse) • Capacity and throughput • Links (source, destination, product, mode, lane)
Coordination/ Organization	• Multi-functional integration • Structure • Responsibilities • Planning, control, reporting • Human resources/skill required
Customer Service	• Customer Service • Alliances/linkage • Customer service levers • Packaging • Assuming customer functions • Convenience • Delivery preferences
Transportation	• Third party alliances • Modes • Contracts • Shipment frequency/consolidation • Routing/delivery patterns
Integrated Inventory	• Inventory deployment • Supply/demand management • Alliances
Information Technology Support	• EDI/internal-external links • Global material planning supplies (worldwide visibility/order tracking) • Satellite communication • Warehouse management • Order management/support • Management reporting • Decision support • Demand management/forecasting • Models/optimization/routing/scheduling

FIGURE 2-5
Major Logistics Stakeholders

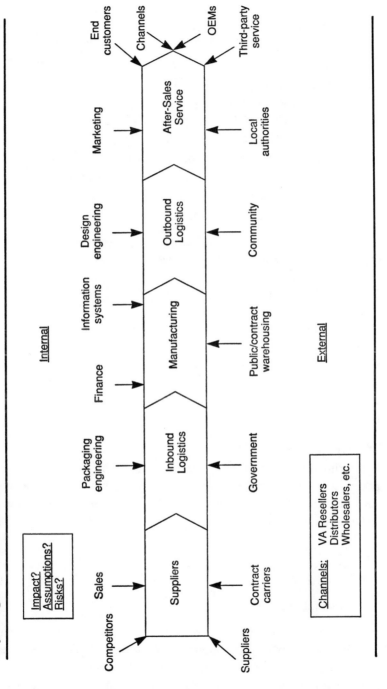

- What stakeholders are impacted by, and what stakeholders impact, this strategy? (Figure 2–5 shows the major logistics stakeholders.)
- What are the assumptions the firm is making about them?
- Are these assumptions valid?
- If not, what must the firm learn about these stakeholders to better understand their drivers and trends so as to satisfy them/co-opt them into the strategy (the "virtual factory")?
- What impact will it have on the strategy?
- What are the risks involved? (The major types of risk are discussed later in this chapter.)
- How can these risks be managed?

If the answers to these questions are not satisfactory, it means that the strategy is probably flawed and needs rethinking.

The Sixth Step: Develop Key Indicators and Performance Metrics

The key indicators and performance metrics must be derived directly from the objectives developed in the preceding step. Every major objective must have a series of cascading metrics that measures each function and level in the organization. They must be compatible with each other, measurable and quantifiable, attainable, and within the function's control.

Measure the Process
Every function and process in the organization has a customer and a supplier—whether internal or external. The process's measures should measure the effectiveness of the process and be based on the input of the function's internal customer. They should measure:

Cost

Process quality

Cycle time

Customer response

The logistics organization must be customer-oriented. If a particular function (whether direct, support, or corporate staff) cannot satisfy the internal customer, the corporation as a whole will never be able to satisfy the final arbiter of excellence—the external customer. Given these guidelines, these metrics must measure the *processes* along the value chain—inputs, activities, and outputs.

They must be compatible at, and cascade to, all levels in the organization. For instance, one major technology-driven electronics equipment manufacturer realized that its investment in inventory cost it a great deal of money, and developed the cascading metrics shown in Figure 2–6.

The performance measures selected must be tracked through an information system and monitored on an executive information system—to be as near real-time as possible. In this way, it will provide criteria for ongoing improvement and provide warning indicators of trouble areas that may impact key process outputs (customer service/response, quality, cost, cycle time). Setting up measurement tracking, aggregating, and reporting must be an integral part of the firm's information technology strategy.

Rationality Check

Most important, the firm must ask itself five key questions while setting performance measures in the organization:

1. Is this measure a key indicator of overall business performance?
2. Will this measure help in increasing customer satisfaction?
3. Will this measure help in terms of cost, customer response, quality, and cycle time?
4. Is this measure required by *line* management?
5. Is this measure appropriate for measuring and tracking at this particular level in the organization?

The first three issues—relevance—are self-explanatory. If, however, the answers to the last two are negative, the company is probably micro-managing, and probably with unfortunate results in terms of competitiveness, cost, and manager morale.

FIGURE 2–6
Cascading Metrics

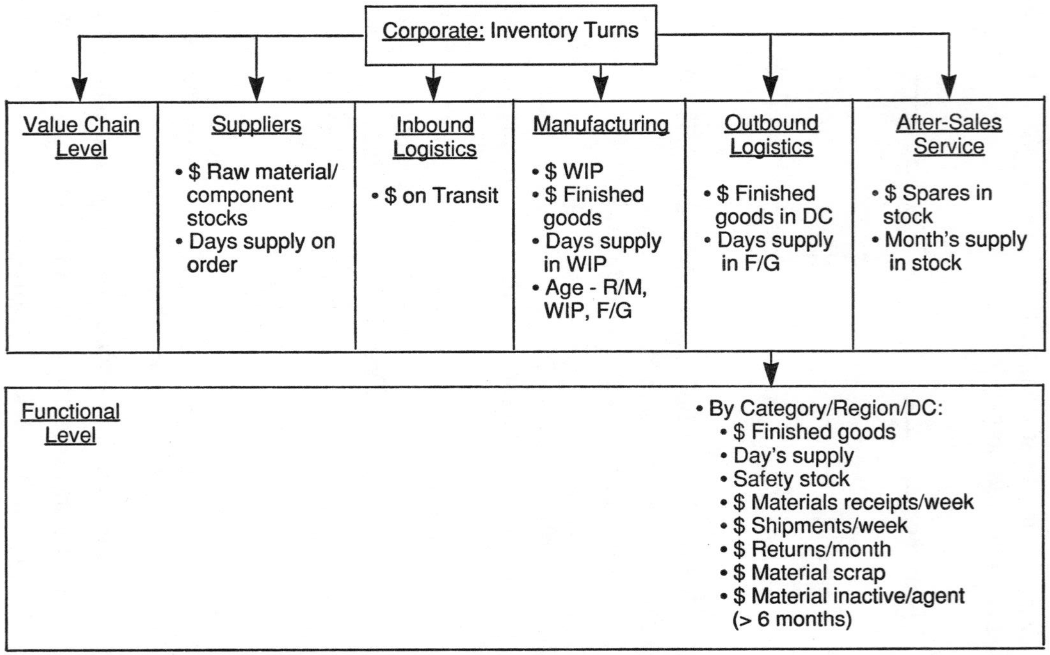

Corporate: Inventory Turns

Value Chain Level	Suppliers	Inbound Logistics	Manufacturing	Outbound Logistics	After-Sales Service
	• $ Raw material/ component stocks • Days supply on order	• $ on Transit	• $ WIP • $ Finished goods • Days supply in WIP • Age - R/M, WIP, F/G	• $ Finished goods in DC • Days supply in F/G	• $ Spares in stock • Month's supply in stock

Functional Level

• By Category/Region/DC:
  • $ Finished goods
  • Day's supply
  • Safety stock
  • $ Materials receipts/week
  • $ Shipments/week
  • $ Returns/month
  • $ Material scrap
  • $ Material inactive/agent (> 6 months)

One particular *Fortune 100* electronics company required that detailed metrics and information be collected, submitted, and explained by senior plant management to corporate staff on a weekly basis. In effect, senior corporate management undertook to manage, monitor, and improve the plant processes. Two years later, few significant cost reductions had been achieved, plant management morale was low, and turnover high. Plant management spent one full day every week accumulating and explaining the information to corporate staff—translating to 20 percent less time being spent on managing the plant and its processes! If the measure is one required by corporate staff, it probably is not worth too much to the company's competitiveness (as corporate staff often do not understand the processes involved, and can neither improve them nor comprehend the implications of operational decisions made at a remote location).

The Seventh Step: Identify the Risks Underlying the Strategies and Develop Risk Management ("Contingency") Programs

Every strategy entails five types of inherent risk which must be identified and for which contingency plans must be considered before implementation. (The process should be formal—it helps if it is incorporated formally into the planning process.) The implications of each strategy must be considered in terms of these five risks, vis-à-vis the major stakeholders. The major logistics stakeholders, some potential risks, and risk management programs are shown in Figure 2–7. The five risk categories are:

1. Business risk (or "bet your company/division").

If this strategy were to fail, the competitiveness of the company would be seriously and adversely affected.

A major consumer foods company with four plants and contiguous distribution centers covering various regions in the U.S. evaluated a series of plant rationalization scenarios with the objective of reducing system costs. A major option under consideration was the closure of the old, supposedly inefficient (higher labor costs per unit, older equipment) southern region plant, with the anticipation that a new, highly automated plant in the midwest would assume the capacity. A risk analysis showed that the midwest plant was militantly unionized, and had an ongoing dispute with local environmental authorities. Furthermore, the selection of automation rendered it quite inflexible in a period when new products

FIGURE 2–7
Stakeholders, Risks, Risk Management Programs

Stakeholders	Some Risks	Sample Risk Management Programs
Customers: • End • Channels • OEMs	• Mismatch of performance expectations • Stockouts/lost sales • Late deliveries • Slow service response	• Frequent customer interaction/linkage • Inventory management/ buffers • Satellite DCs/coverage • Use customer–requested due date not quote date • Field service locations/ third party service • Spare stocks • Migrated customer service partnerships
Third Party Service	• Slow response for spares/lack of factory support	• Organize to service third parties • Periodic upgrade/ technical updates • Training programs
Government	• Profit sharing/transfer pricing • Local tax/content regulations change	• Analyze process staging prior to foreign location • Consult tax experts prior to location/ transfer pricing policies • Document rationale
Local Authorities/ Community	• Regulations of tonnage	• Select infrastructure for transportation for contingencies
Suppliers	• Quality, delivery issues • Poor/expense response to engineering changes	• Supplier development/ evaluation programs • Supplier certification • Alternate sources of supply • Concurrent engineering to minimize engineering change costs

FIGURE 2–7 *(concluded)*

Stakeholders	*Some Risks*	*Sample Risk Management Programs*
Competitors	• Exceed our service levels • Alliance with our customers	• Monitor competitors through benchmarking, customer satisfaction/ requirements surveys, secondary research • Pro-active in innovative alliances for mutual benefit
Marketing	• Regional promotions • Leading to demand surge • Variable, nervous forecast	• Multi-functional interaction to obtain promotion plans in advance • Forecasting based on history with tracking mechanisms—multi-functional product planning
Design Engineering	• Frequent engineering changes • New product introduction/phase-out	• Concurrent engineering • Co-location • NPI/phase-out plans in advance
Information Systems	• New systems selection and installation leading to disruption • Slow response from central IS for modifications/changes	• Users involved in selection • Education and training programs • Phased implementation/parallel • Distributed systems • New IS organization—strategy at corporate/ modification at function

Source: Ernst & Young Center for Information Technology & Strategy.

were being tested at a rapid rate. The other plants in the system were at capacity. The study recommended that the company retain its southern region plant as a hedge against trouble in the midwest. Additionally, a total cost analysis revealed that the southern region plant's total cost of manufacturing and delivering the product to its regional market was as competitive as doing it from the Midwest plant. The company decided to keep the plant open. Less than a year later, production came to a halt in the Midwest plant. Had the company proceeded with its initial strategy, it would have been disastrous for its future. The loss of capacity at one plant—instead of two—was covered through arrangements with co-packers (though at slightly higher costs).

2. Competitive risk (if you don't, the competition will).

If the firm decided not to go ahead with this strategy, the competition might do so and gain a significant advantage.

A major health care firm decided to develop a major logistics customer service information system that would link their delivery systems with those of their customers and end users. This was a very expensive proposition, but one that was deemed necessary to gain a competitive advantage in a highly competitive industry with several major players. The company went ahead and, in a relatively short period of time following implementation, its major competitors emerged with similar systems. The time frame was much too short for the competition to have developed such logistics systems from ground zero to counter the health care company. Hence, a logical deduction was that all the major players were working on the concept simultaneously. Only by assuming the risk and proceeding with all speed was the company able to beat its competition to the market and gain a significant advantage. Had it not done so, it could have been shut out of the market.

3. Market risk (no impact on operations/competitiveness).

This strategy would cost a great deal in terms of time elapsed and money, and would make no appreciable difference to competitive position. In a worst case scenario, it would divert resources, capital, and management attention from other areas and business opportunities.

4. Implementation risk (implementation delayed beyond target date and/or significantly greater cost than anticipated).

Typically, poor upfront and contingency planning and inability to consider all relevant costs amplifies this risk, and the result can jeopardize competitive ability.

5. Operational risk (implementation of the strategy does not meet company goals).

This involves culture conflicts and non-resolution, lack of training, and inappropriate/incomplete skill-sets. Even excellent strategies, if coupled with poor execution, are a waste of time.

The Eighth Step: Implementation Planning

Implementation planning is a phase of the planning process that is often given scant attention by senior management. Every strategy implementation effort must include the following to minimize risk:

A detailed implementation plan with schedules, milestones, roles, and responsibilities

Communications forums to explain the strategies, their implementation and success requirements, and the roles and responsibilities of the organization members

Performance measuring and tracking systems

Identification of training needs and the necessary programs.

Typical logistics training needs include information systems use, data manipulation, total quality management concepts and continuous improvement processes, materials planning and scheduling concepts, and, in certain instances, modeling and simulation. One of the most powerful training methods is job rotation—moving personnel laterally to other functions. These prerequisites to implementation are essential to success.

To be successful in execution, every organization and every strategy must possess:

- Top management support for the effort and its consequences
- Line management involvement in policy making and execution
- A culture of continuous improvement
- A philosophy which views situations from a non-traditional and multi-functional perspective (including multi-functional planning, policy-making, and improvement teams)
- Stated policies and practices, supported by senior management, to eliminate functional "silos" and the resulting attitudes
- Rewards for policies that encourage customer satisfaction
- Performance measures, roles, and responsibilities, and monitoring mechanisms
- Information technology enablement and integration

It is in the organization that the major obstacles to successful logistics strategy formulation and execution lie. They include:

- Intra-organizational/functional conflicts brought on by "turf-doms," a functional "silo" attitude, and functionally-based (rather than enterprise-based) performance measures
- No translation of the strategy into a measurable, defined action plan
- The pressure to respond to changing customer needs, competitive actions, and poor supply-demand planning ("get it out of the door at the end of the month to book the sales" syndrome), and the lack of processes to manage the business for smooth scheduling and quick response
- Constraints of capital and cash due to competing entities within the organization—often through a lack of prioritization of enterprise-based critical success factors.

Structuring the organization for these attributes will be discussed in a later chapter.

It is worthwhile to conclude the discussion of implementation by highlighting the findings of *Corporate Profitability & Logistics* by Ernst & Whinney for the Council for Logistics Management. The ten findings address the principles for successful logistics management and operations:

1. Link logistics to corporate strategy.
2. Organize comprehensively.
3. Use the power of information.
4. Emphasize human resources.
5. Form strategic alliances.
6. Focus on financial performance.
7. Target optimum service levels.
8. Manage the details.
9. Leverage logistics volumes.
10. Measure and react to performance.

It can be seen that the planning framework addresses these issues from a strategic perspective. It is useful to mention a point that has been emphasized over and over, but appears to get lost somewhere in the translation:

FIGURE 2–8
Approach to Logistics Strategy Planning

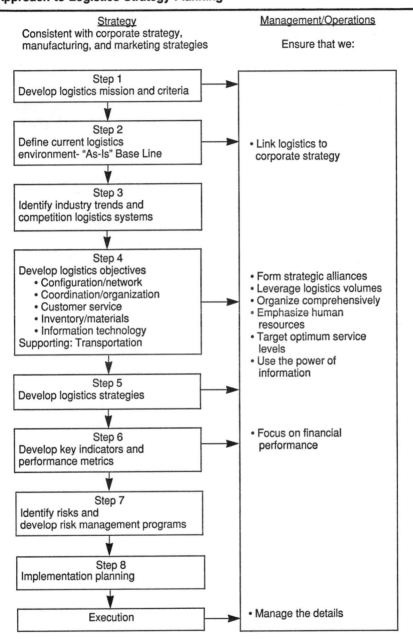

while logistics strategy formulation is the front end of gaining competitive advantage through the use of logistics, it is quite useless without implementation and management of the operations.

Figure 2–8 outlines the eight steps of the approach to logistics strategy planning, along with the logistics management principles for successful operation.

As indicated in the title, this book takes a methodological approach to logistics strategy planning. The overall approach outlined in Figure 2–8 is expanded upon and discussed in detail in the following chapters.

CHAPTER 3

CONFIGURATION/NETWORK STRATEGY

Following the development of the global logistics mission and key objectives (there might be several of these, depending on the company's worldwide thrust—truly global, international, or multi-national), the first important stage in logistics strategy formulation is the development of the firm's logistics network (configuration) strategy.

CONFIGURATION AND COORDINATION

There are two major structural aspects of logistics strategy. Michael Porter defines them as follows:

Configuration: "Location in the world where each activity in the logistics value chain is performed, and in how many places"

Coordination: "How like or linked activities performed at different locations are coordinated with each other" (Michael Porter, ed., *Competition in Global Industries* [Boston: Harvard Business School Press, 1986]).

Coordination, which includes management organization and structure; process and performance measurement; planning, control and reporting, is discussed in the next chapter.

Configuration and coordination are interdependent and reflect the firm's overall global posture. Michael Porter effectively illustrates the types of strategy (global posture) in the international arena, as shown in his coordination–configuration matrix (Figure 3–1). The logistics supply chain can be thought of as a pipeline conveying inventory (and adding value to it) from the supplier to the customer and demand information and

FIGURE 3–1
Types of International Strategy

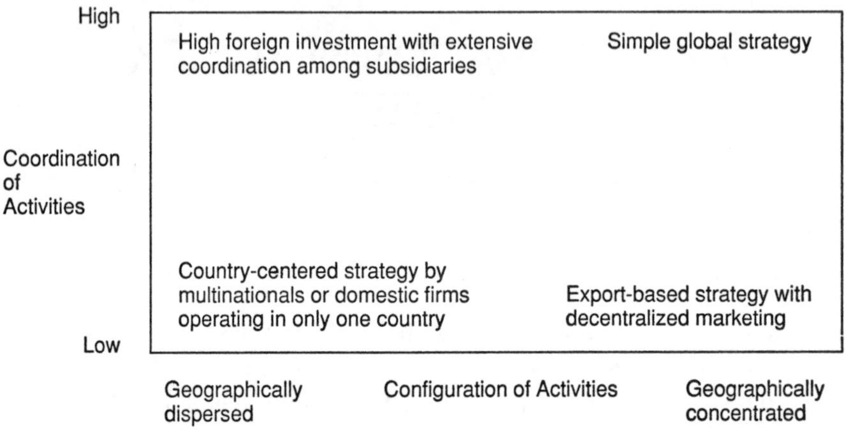

High	High foreign investment with extensive coordination among subsidiaries	Simple global strategy
Coordination of Activities		
Low	Country-centered strategy by multinationals or domestic firms operating in only one country	Export-based strategy with decentralized marketing
	Geographically dispersed	Configuration of Activities Geographically concentrated

Source: Michael Porter, ed., *Competition in Global Industries* (Boston: Harvard Business School Press, 1986), p. 28.

requirements from customer to supplier. The movement of inventory is triggered by various demand patterns downstream—starting with the customer. The value-added portions of the pipeline are the plants, distribution centers, and field service centers. Planning for this two-way flow is critical—field service and the management of returns are dimensions of customer service as important as on-time delivery and reliability, quality, convenience, packaging, and order response.

A key to managing this pipeline effectively is the location and mission of these value-added centers. The decisions must be driven by the overall corporate strategy, logistics system mission and objectives, and must reflect the company's customer service and investment goals. Customer service is an increasingly important part of the buyer's purchasing decision.

These are the customer service trends which, coupled with the increased competitive necessity for globalization, must drive the configuration strategy:

Cost—least *total network* cost

Market preferences—local market preferences and regional/major account customer service objectives

Time—proximity to suppliers (internal/external), customers (internal/external/channels), cross-functional proximity (product engineering—process engineering—manufacturing—procurement—packaging, etc.)

Local costs of business—local investment, joint-venture, and content laws

Process staging—ability to couple/decouple the manufacturing process

Tax—domestic and local tax regulations

Locating Offshore—Some Issues

Prior to discussing these major configuration strategy drivers and their roles in developing a network strategy, a few words should be said on an issue that has attracted and, ultimately, bedeviled several companies—that of offshore location.

Benefits
There are several good reasons for locating a facility offshore. They include:

1. Local technologies and proximity to key suppliers. For instance, many computer companies locate assembly plants offshore because major suppliers of terminals, printed circuit boards, and keyboards are in the Far East.

2. Proximity to market. Manufacturing companies frequently locate plants in Ireland and distribution centers in Germany, Belgium, and the Netherlands because of their proximity to key European customers.

3. Costs of supply. It is often cheaper to ship components and semi-finished products over longer distances than it is to ship finished or assembled products.

4. Local presence requirements and regulations. With the coming of EC92 (the regulations that accompany European Community '92), as well as the local regulations of many countries (e.g. Brazil and India), building plants abroad can be a necessary cost of doing business in those countries.

5. Local taxes. Taxes in many countries are much lower than U.S. taxes. This decision, however, must be made carefully—taxes may have a hidden "bite," courtesy of the IRS's Section 486 regulations which deal with inter-company transfer pricing.

Dangers

In today's global marketplace, however, the benefits of locating offshore rarely include cheaper labor, particularly for the more engineering-intensive products. In the 1960s and 70s, several companies, including many high technology firms, located manufacturing assembly plants in the Far East because of cheap manufacturing labor (just as today there appears to be a rush to locate in Ireland for tax advantages). Conversations with several executives have shown that this was often just a "gut" reaction— to compete with inexpensive imports—and reflected an unwillingness or inability to confront manufacturing/operations issues and problems at home.

Unfortunately, as many of these companies have discovered, there are several hidden and competitive costs associated with these decisions. These costs include:

Separation of design and procurement from manufacturing. This adversely impacts concurrent engineering and time to market and increases, by orders of magnitude, the costs of engineering and process changes.

Distances from major customers and market bases. This leads to decreased customer service levels, reduced customer response, and the necessity of carrying significantly higher levels of value-added inventory, which tends to become obsolete given market and life cycle changes, engineering and product changes/enhancements, supply changes, and new competitive products.

Increased complexity of supply-demand planning. The increased number of manufacturing stages, facilities, suppliers, and shipment points, and the proliferation of local part numbers all add to the already major challenges in multi-national supply-demand planning.

Local political uncertainties. Witness the status of facilities in the Philippines and Korea, and the enthusiasm (or lack of it) of engineers and managers to travel back and forth.

Technology transfer. Many local governments, on perceiving that the foreign-owned manufacturing facility produces old generation technology products, and that the process consists mainly of assembling products from imported components and sub-assemblies, may insist that the company transfer more advanced technologies and value-added processes to these facilities. U.S. companies have lost a great deal by transferring technology to foreign countries, only to see it absorbed and improved upon, generating increased competition.

Differences in culture. Many enlightened companies are implementing total quality management worldwide. This involves changing and redesigning processes, work patterns and flow, and the roles of employees. Such changes are met with different degrees of enthusiasm (occasionally hostility) in different areas, (including domestically) across different geographic regions.

Structural changes in the company's total cost. In many companies today, labor is only a small fraction of total product cost. Major costs lie in materials, overhead, indirect and support costs (engineering, procurement, design, management, etc.), and in the cost of capital involved in building or updating facilities. An offshore location decision that considers only a few of these cost elements can result in unpleasant cash flow and margin surprises.

Costs of quality. These include costs of uncertainty, including inventory buffers against uncertain and long delivery lead times, costs of rework and the length of time for execution, and process control at large distances.

An example: A major peripherals company located an assembly plant in the Far East, thereby virtually mothballing an expensive automated facility in the U.S. In an industry well known for tight margins and the need to reinvest in new products, this was probably not the most efficient use of capital. The industry, furthermore, is characterized by the engineering complexity and tight manufacturability constraints of its products, and by short product life cycles driven, in part, by the rapid new product introduction that characterizes its major customer base—the computer industry.

The company's stated rationale for this decision was the desire to cut costs (manufacturing costs actually comprised a little over 5 percent of total product cost) and take advantage of cheap manufacturing and manufacturing engineering labor. Its engineering group was, however, located in the U.S.

The result. Huge engineering change, logistics and quality costs, coupled with a decrease in customer service levels, severely impacted the company's ability to compete effectively.

A lesson. Locating offshore can be dangerous if done for reasons selected in a operational vacuum. It can be an excellent business decision, provided that it is done for sound business reasons—considering the major drivers, making the necessary trade-offs, and functioning as part of the overall logistics strategy.

DRIVERS OF CONFIGURATION STRATEGY

There are six major drivers of a configuration strategy, as mentioned earlier—process staging, time/proximity, market preferences, total cost, local costs of doing business, and tax regulations. The last two are not within the scope of this book nor the expertise of the authors, and require special real estate and tax expertise. The discussion which follows focuses on the first four, and ties them together at the end of the chapter (see Figure 3–14) in a framework for determining a configuration strategy.

Process Staging

Process staging involves the coupling or decoupling of a firm's core transformation activities—the manufacturing process. It involves making the trade-offs between large manufacturing plants and smaller plants/ stages located close to suppliers, customers, and distance-critical functions such as engineering. It is typical to think of facility location and network in terms of discrete, managed units—international procurement offices (IPOs), distribution centers, manufacturing plants, and sales offices. Yet today's manufacturing environment provides the product, process, and, particularly, the information technology to decouple or couple these units as tightly or loosely as is necessary to compete effectively in a rapidly-changing, customer-driven, competitive environment.

This decision is an integral part of the network strategy. Traditionally, it is an issue that has been addressed (usually in an ad-hoc and evolving, rather than in a planned, manner) only after the basic network or plant rationalization decisions have been made. The options here depend on process technologies, product technologies, information technology, and the key success factors in the business.

1. *Single-line or multi-line?* A process line here refers to a discrete production process for a product or family of products. The issue here involves duplicating production lines or plants in different locations to make the same product (for example, manufacturing frozen dough for rolls or assembling workstations in single or multiple locations).

2. *Single stage or multi-stage?* A manufacturing stage here refers to a part of the production process. A process line can be split into several stages, depending on the process technology and manufacturing requirements. For instance, semiconductor manufacturing is usually split into fabrication, assembly, and test. On the other hand, owing to FDA requirements and the constraints of the process flow, a pharmaceutical company manufacturing tablets in a clean environment probably cannot split the line into separate stages beyond the active ingredient manufacturing stage. The decision involves concentrating all stages in a single location (even though the company may have several plants) or splitting the stages, as is often done in the semiconductor and computer industries.

3. *Single, consolidated distribution center versus multiple distribution centers versus satellite distribution centers?* Distribution centers can be either:

• Service distribution centers (full or partial service), performing order taking, filling, and management, with full or partial product lines, and maintaining inventory and/or safety stock to service demand.

• Break-bulk distribution centers, performing unloading/loading, warehousing, routing, some order filling, and maintaining some inventory as a buffer

The distribution centers could, additionally, be national (servicing the country), regional (servicing a particular geographic region), or satel-

FIGURE 3–2
Process Line

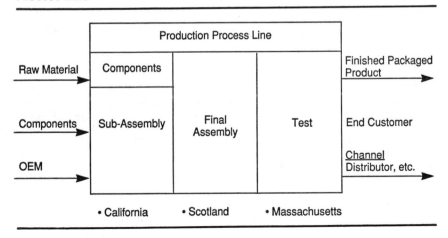

lite (servicing a small geographical area and, in turn, being serviced by a regional distribution center).

There are several options that a firm can adopt based on market requirements. For instance, strategically locating a combination of satellite warehouses serviced by a major distribution center would increase customer service levels at the cost of higher inventory levels and greater warehousing expense. Again, the selection of a particular configuration will also affect transportation costs (more links increase costs, while greater customer order consolidation reduces them). The point here is that every combination of distribution center type, scope, and location involves trade-offs in cost, sales, investment, and customer service levels. These trade-offs and relationships are shown in Figures 3–3 and 3–4.

This is not a necessary relationship, however, given the current operations of many companies. If the current processes are less than efficient or have reached a plateau where incremental improvements are minor in nature, redesigning the business processes can reduce total costs while improving customer service. Business process improvement and redesign are discussed in a later chapter.

Figure 3–5 shows these multiple stages in manufacturing and distribution as part of a logistics supply chain.

The single/multi-line and single/multi-stage network decisions are, of course, interrelated, and revolve mainly around total cost and customer service and response considerations. The various options have several inherent advantages and disadvantages. Some of these are outlined in Figure 3–6. As can be seen, the benefits and disadvantages range along a continuum, and need to be weighed against the objectives of the overall strategy.

One method to analyze process staging is to build a cost-cycle time model for the various stages along the value chain, building from raw material and components stages to delivery of the finished product. This model demonstrates the individual contributions and cumulative impact of the various stages on the overall cost and cycle time. Next, evaluate these stages against the qualitative and quantitative objectives of the logistics strategy (Figure 3–10) to determine whether it is desirable and feasible, from the perspectives of cost, proximity, time to market, and customer response, to:

Split the stages

FIGURE 3–3
Relationships and Trade-Offs Total Costs, Inventory, and Number
of Stocking Locations

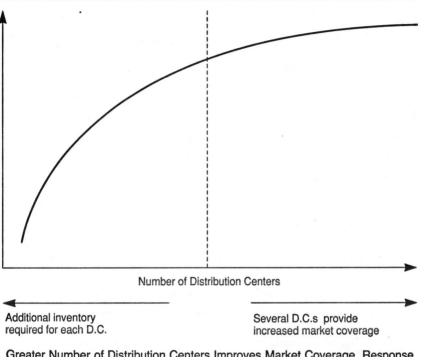

Number of Distribution Centers

Additional inventory
required for each D.C.

Several D.C.s provide
increased market coverage

Greater Number of Distribution Centers Improves Market Coverage, Response
Time, and Service Levels But Increases Overall Costs

Source: Gene R. Tyndall, "Logistics Costs and Service Levels: Evaluating the Trade-Offs," *Journal of Cost Management for the Manufacturing Industry*, Vol. 1, No. 1, 1987, Warren, Gorham & Lamont, Inc., New York, N.Y.

Accept low volumes/economies of scope, to allow smaller facilities
to be duplicated in different geographical regions

Identify the volume/demand and product life cycle stages at which it
becomes feasible to split the process

An analysis of process staging also provides the company valuable
information in two major decisions that are an integral part of the manufacturing strategy and have major implications for the configuration strategy (see Chapter 2, Table 2–1 for manufacturing strategy components
and their impact on logistics).

FIGURE 3–4
Relationships and Trade-Offs Sales, Costs, and Customer Service Levels

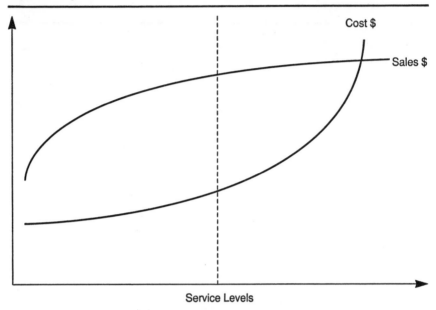

Optimum Service Levels Balance Sales $ Increases with Cost $ Increases

Source: Gene R. Tyndall, "Logistics Costs and Service Levels: Evaluating the Trade-Offs," *Journal of Cost Management for the Manufacturing Industry*, Vol. 1, No. 1, 1987, Warren, Gorham & Lamont, Inc., New York, N.Y.

1. *The make versus buy decision.* Cost and technical analyses may indicate that it is less expensive and more flexible to farm out a particular stage of manufacturing. For instance, several semiconductor companies farm out the fabrication stage but perform the assembly and test stages in-house.

2. *Positioning the order penetration point (OPP).* This is the "point where a product becomes earmarked for a particular customer". In Table 3–1 Zinn and Bowersox identify five types of postponement and their attendant costs (Walter Zinn and Donald J. Bowersox, "Planning Physical Distribution with the Principle of Postponement," *Journal of Business Logistics*, Volume 9, No. 2, 1988, pp. 117–136).

Determining the OPP for a given product line can have a significant impact on the location of process stages, the roles of the distribution centers, and on any value-added type of investment outside the manufac-

FIGURE 3–5
Multiple Stages in a Logistics Value/Supply Chain

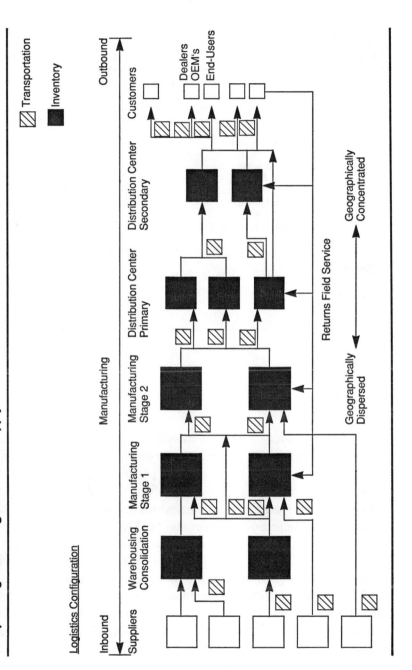

FIGURE 3–6
Single/Multi-Line and Single/Multi-Stage Advantages and Disadvantages

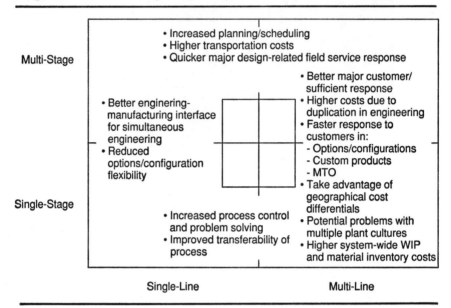

turing facility. Process staging analysis allows management to evaluate the trade-offs and costs associated with postponement. Traditional logistics network analysis has ignored the manufacturing process, treating it much like a "black box". Analysis often focused on the inbound and outbound aspects, arriving at conclusions that recommended location of plants or rationalization of plants and product lines with little consideration of the characteristics of the process. This situation is, however, rapidly changing. There is a strong trend toward integrating the organization "silo" functions of manufacturing, procurement, and integrated logistics and placing them under the broad umbrella of operations or supply-demand management. The advances in product, process, and information technology allow the process line to be decoupled or coupled to achieve customer service and total cost objectives. The issue here is not so much "should we?" but "when should we?".

Figure 3–7 provides some decision guidelines to address the process staging issue, provided it is technologically feasible.

TABLE 3–1
Postponement Types and Costs

Postponement Type	Costs
Labeling	Inventory carrying costs Warehousing costs Processing (labeling)
Packaging	Transportation Inventory carrying costs Warehousing costs Processing (packaging)
Assembly	Transportation Inventory carrying costs Warehousing costs Processing (assembly) Costs of lost sales
Manufacturing/ Fabrication	Transportation Inventory carrying costs Warehousing costs Processing (manufacturing) Cost of lost sales
Time	Transportation Inventory carrying costs Warehousing costs Cost of lost sales

Time/Proximity

The previous section—process staging—addressed the role of the manufacturing process in the configuration strategy. This section deals with the role of key processes in determining configuration—the most important characteristic of which is time. Given the fact that, in most companies, the effective time taken by a process is related to proximity with other cross-functional activities or external stakeholders, it is difficult to discuss time and proximity separately. Most key factors in business also depend on geographical distance (Figure 3–8 illustrates these dependencies).

Time is the new battleground of the business world in terms of new product development and introduction and product phase-out (before it becomes a cash and resource drain), and in terms of responding to and anticipating customer demands. This differentiates the corporate winners

FIGURE 3–7
Single/Multi-Line and Single/Multi-Stage When?

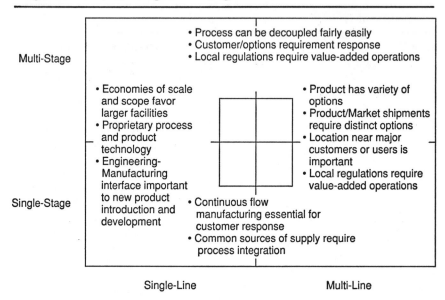

and losers, and calls for new processes, organization, and ways of doing business. In particular, it calls for multi-disciplinary teams and integrated operations. The benefits far outweigh the short-term costs and redundancies involved. Figure 3–9 outlines these time/proximity factors and processes and the corresponding logistics value chain activities. These processes are crucial to a firm's success and to its survival in the marketplace. The issue of proximity must, therefore, be addressed early in the configuration strategy process—whether the issues involve new plants, expansions, or plant rationalization. Among the key processes are:

Concept to manufacturing process design. This involves the frequent interaction among the following:

- Marketing
- Product engineering
- Process engineering/manufacturing engineering
- Production
- Purchasing

FIGURE 3–8
Key Factors, Their Functions and Geographical Dependencies

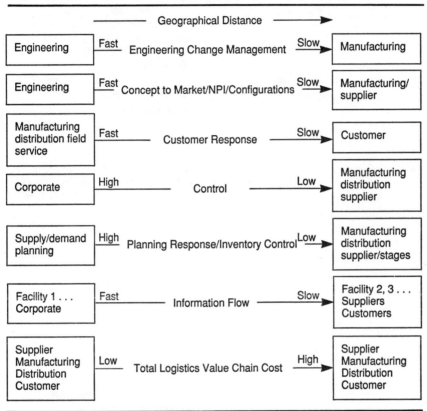

- Packaging
- Finance
- End customers

Production ramp-up to customer. This involves:

- Process Engineering/Manufacturing Engineering
- Physical Distribution—Warehousing, Transportation
- Supply-Demand Planning
- Purchasing
- Production (including Quality Control)

FIGURE 3–9
Time/Proximity Factors—Processes and Value Chain Activities

Time/Proximity Factors—Process	Value Chain Activities
• Customer order response time	Customer → order management → inventory management → manufacturing
• Customer option/configuration turnaround/response	Customer → order management → inventory management/OEM's → manufacturing
• Design iteration/variation time	Process engineering → product engineering → manufacturing → purchasing

• Engineering to manufacturing
  • Engineering/process changes
  • Simultaneous engineering
	Process engineering → product engineering → engineering change management → manufacturing → purchasing

• Technology security	Design engineering → manufacturing stages
• Service response	Customer → DC → field service → manufacturing
• Total pipeline cost	Transportation and inventory management
• Planning/business control	Supply-demand planning → manufacturing → DC → inventory management
• Information flow	Communications/IS → functions/ users
• Supplier alliance/development/ linkages	Supplier → product engineering → process engineering → manufacturing
• Customer linkage/development/ alliances	Customer → product engineering → manufacturing → DC → inventory management

- Suppliers
- Engineering Change Management

Customer response and service levels. This involves:

- Order management and sales
- Inventory management/supply-demand planning
- Physical distribution

- Information systems
- Field service
- Production
- Options/product configuration management
- OEMs and suppliers
- Customers
- Technical support

Figure 3–10 shows a matrix used to evaluate these qualitative and quantitative factors from a process staging and time/proximity perspective. In this particular case, the issues, benefits, and costs associated with vertical integration across manufacturing stages, and co-location with manufacturing are examined.

It can be seen that proximity among these functions is important. This can be either physical proximity (locating facilities near major suppliers or customers, locating production next to design, etc.) or virtual proximity (using information technology to assure frequent, rapid interaction on managerial and technical levels). Location can be transparent and unimportant to the customer, provided a competitive high level of customer service is provided along all dimensions. Given the time/proximity factors discussed above, the issue now becomes that of information to link the customer to the supplier along the logistics value chain. The strategies and uses of information technology to achieve virtual proximity are discussed in a subsequent chapter.

Virtual Co-location

Information technology provides a means to enable "virtual co-location"—the co-location of *like* activities through information integration, information sharing, and communications networks. For instance, one major electronics company has located engineering design functions in California and in the Middle East. Through information technology (common applications, shared databases, and communications networks) and high coordination of activities, these dispersed design houses (10 hours apart) can work on the same design through a good portion of a normal 24-hour California day. Similarly, another California firm can view results of the day's production-shipment/distribution policies the very next morning at the beginning of the work day.

A third company, a major computer manufacturer, has software de-

FIGURE 3–10

Evaluating Quantitative and Qualitative Factors Process Staging and Time-Proximity Perspective

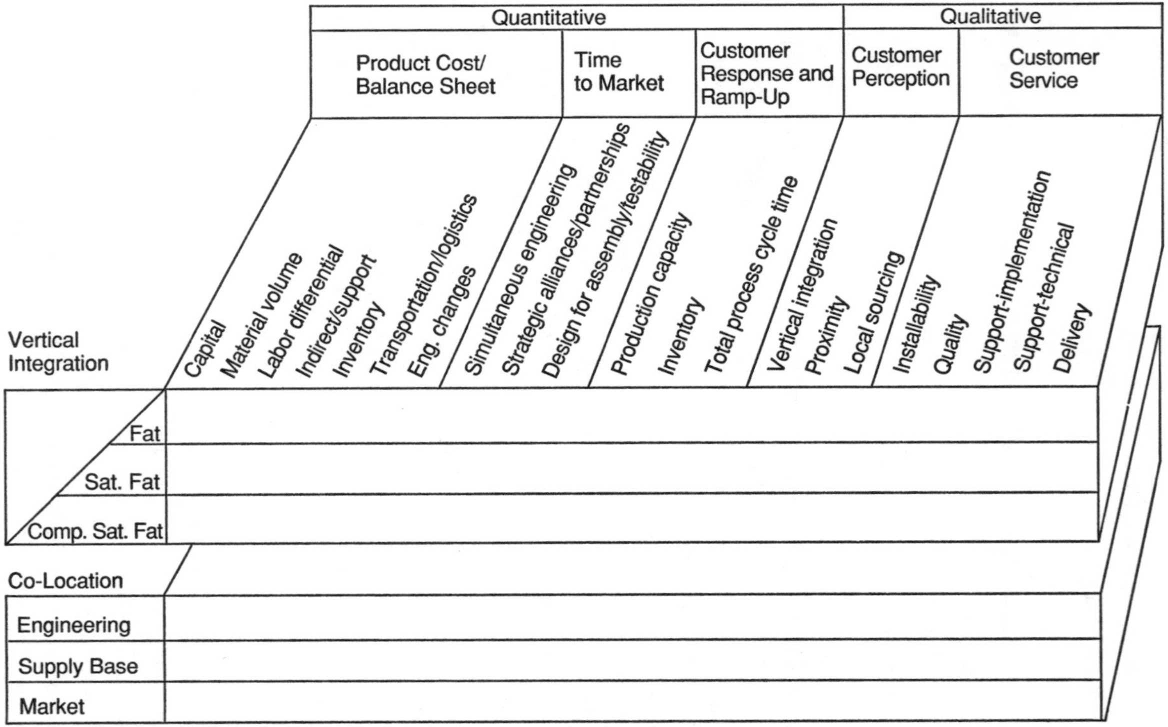

Source: Ernst & Young Center for Information Technology & Strategy.

velopment and design houses in the U.S. and in India (10 ½ hours apart) working on the same applications, thus ensuring 18 hours per day of development effort on the same applications. Conceptual designs are translated into detailed designs before the next U.S. working day.

The key here is the virtual co-location of like activities. Such virtual co-location is difficult for "sequential" or "rugby" functions such as engineering and manufacturing, particularly where the interaction is complex (versus simply assembly operations).

Process staging and time/proximity issues are management decisions that cannot be solved by any optimization/total cost model, simply because most of these factors are not quantifiable. They require careful consideration prior to developing an optimization model. Yet, the decisions made can influence the outcome of such total cost or service optimization analysis in a significant manner.

Market Preferences

Market preferences generally involve the following:

Delivery preferences. These include just-in-time, more frequent, smaller deliveries to the customer plant/distribution center; unitization for customer line use in lots that match the customer's production lots; and packaging for direct customer line use (for example, shipping semiconductors in tubes/cartridges that can be used directly on customers' automated insertion equipment).

Order preferences. These include rapid turnaround to orders (in effect, managing the customer's component/raw material inventory) and multi-delivery orders (a portion of the order must be delivered to a central distribution point and the balance to various user plants).

Major customer location. Sometimes the location of a major customer dictates the location of a plant/DC facility or field service center, economics notwithstanding. For instance, several automobile component manufacturers have located near a car manufacturer's plant far from the component manufacturers' Michigan home bases. Similarly, a major disk drive manufacturer chose to locate its new assembly facility in proximity to a major customer's facility in the Bay Area, although the economics of the decision suggested other areas.

Regional demand patterns. Regional demands vary considerably, and so do seasonality factors within regions. For instance, California is a huge market for high technology components and for ice cream. Within this market, some products exhibit some seasonality—in some cases, differently in southern California than in northern California. Locating a workstation assembly plant in Cleveland, for instance, may not be such a great idea. However, it may make sense to locate a full-service distribution center in Cleveland to service this part of the midwest.

Country-specific/region-specific characteristics. Individual countries have some unique characteristics in their logistics environment. Companies would do well to consider these in their formulation of logistics strategies. For instance, in Japan, customers expect same day or next day service. Planning to do less (for purposes of consolidation or inventory levels) would place the supplier at a competitive disadvantage. In some Far East countries, certain freight forwarders hold the balance of power and control the business. It is a necessity to identify and do business with them.

In Europe, transportation is expensive and trips take much longer than for comparable U.S. distances. Routes are frequently circuitous, not direct. Hence, highway mileages (as are often used in the U.S. to compute distances and fare structures) would have to be reconsidered in the European environment; it may be preferable to obtain quotes up-front from point-to-point for volumes and weights. Furthermore, transportation and warehousing are strongly regionalized and service is comparatively inconsistent.

As in most business situations, a competitive advantage may still be gained if the company is willing to do things differently—redesign processes instead of simply implementing the "accepted wisdom." J. H. Van Der Hoop identifies several key issues necessary for effective logistics configuration in Europe, including consolidation, commonality, customer service, centralized supply-demand planning, order postponement, centralized stocking, contract carriers, and distribution center location ("Geographic Perspectives of International Logistics: Europe," *Council for Logistics Management Annual Meeting Proceedings, 1987*, Volume 1, pp. 245–254). These appear to be very similar for manufacturers in this country.

Total Cost—Optimizing The Cost-Service Mix

There are several types of decision-support tools to assist management in the network design process. They typically include constructing a model and evaluating it for various strategic options and factors. The evaluation includes:

"What if" analysis

Sensitivity and flexibility analysis

An iterative approach to develop management commitment and "buy-in"

The evaluation seeks to minimize total network costs at competitive speed of response and customer service levels. It is at this point that the firm must analyze the impact of risks on strategies and options (see chapter two).

Modeling can be used to optimize either parts of the system or the entire logistics supply chain. Examples include product mix supply-demand modeling to balance global resources; local routing and distribution optimization; inventory deployment and customer service levels balance; and, total supply chain network configuration and flows.

The baseline for such a model is the "as-is" logistics environment defined earlier in the process. Additionally, it must include projected growth/demand rates, new product phase in/product phase outs, and projections of demand.

Modeling must be an integral part of the logistics strategy planning process, and not just an addendum to validate or justify current thinking. The advent of large-scale computing power, modelers who understand business operations and issues, and the total quality management philosophy of action based on data instead of instinct have encouraged this process.

A model can be developed based on the constraints and guidelines identified and prioritized earlier (process staging, time/proximity, market preferences) and the best options evaluated. An alternate approach used by some companies is first to develop a range of solutions and then to evaluate them based on the key drivers identified. There are different modeling approaches that can be used, depending on the complexity of the firm's logistics environment (product lines, facilities, markets, major customers, suppliers, etc.) and its size. These are discussed below.

Optimization Modeling

These are mathematical programming models that seek to optimize the network for minimum cost or maximum profit. They assist management to address a number of network configuration and rationalization issues and, through simulation, to determine the best network configuration and product mix/stocking policies within a series of cost and business constraints. They are excellent "what-if" tools and can prove extraordinarily useful in times of high capacity and resource constraints. Of course, this depends on the right package being selected, the model being set up correctly, and provision being made to handle the potentially tricky areas of semi-fixed and semi-variable costs.

Optimization models can typically handle more complex problems, and have the added potential advantage of uncovering options not readily obvious to logistics personnel within the company. There are several excellent modeling packages available on the market today to help in this process. They range from microcomputer optimization software to specialized logistics analysis and optimization packages, and usually employ mathematical programming. Such models can evaluate options and, within the guidelines and constraints developed earlier (process staging, proximity/time, and market preferences), can provide optimal solutions (in terms of total costs and service) to questions such as:

- How many distribution facilities/stocking locations are required?
- Where should they be?
- What product lines and product mix should be produced and handled at the various manufacturing facilities?
- What is the purpose (function and mission) of the manufacturing and distribution facilities?
- What are the optimum inventory stocking levels and safety stocks at each point?
- How should this inventory be managed and deployed, given changes in the product line and market demand?
- What combination of transport modes (rail, truckload, less-than-truckload, UPS, air cargo, sea) should be employed?
- What structuring is needed to make it economically beneficial to all parties to have customer pick-up?
- How should product and supply flows be managed?

- What is the cost to maintain customer service along various dimensions?
- What will it cost to improve customer service?
- What key sensitivity factors drive cost?
- What are the potential major risks ("what if") that can impact customer service and cost? What might be the extent of their impact?

The disadvantages of optimization modeling typically lie in their complexity to develop and maintain. While this in itself is not a major disadvantage, the problem is that they tend to require specialized resources from outside the firm. Again, the tendency exists to expand the model to cover too much detail and too wide a scope. Finally, it is difficult to model the proximity/time, process staging and market preference issues discussed earlier.

Heuristic Modeling

"Heuristics" are informed rules of thumb. These can include rules such as

All customers in the Bay Area must be serviced directly from the plant in Milpitas.

Heuristic modeling has its place in certain situations, but certainly cannot produce the range of solutions, or optimum solutions produced by optimization modeling. On the other hand, it can more accurately reflect the judgment of management, but has the disadvantage of using pre-determined rules, which may not be the most competitive or customer-sensitive.

Simulation Modeling

Simulation modeling, as the term suggests, simulates various scenarios provided by management. These scenario outputs can be compared for cost, profit, and, sometimes, time. As in heuristic modeling, a major disadvantage is that the technique accepts pre-determined scenarios and evaluates them.

In my experience and estimation, optimization models are the best suited to provide the necessary decision support in developing a configuration strategy. However, they are not sufficient by themselves. The constraints and ground rules must be established through the process staging, proximity/time, and market preferences analysis. Given these policies/ rules, one can then determine the best scenario that provides competitive service at the least total cost.

Typically, an "as-is" baseline model is first developed, and scenarios built on this model. Following this, the user generally performs "what if" and sensitivity analysis along a number of business, demand, and cost variables. The "as-is" baseline provides the company with a good knowledge of its business processes, its flows, performance, and costs. The performance measures must include customer-driven and financial (cash flow, costs by stage) measures.

Modeling/Decision-Support System Requirements
The general decision-support functions, and the attendant configuration/ rationalization and sensitivity analysis issues, are presented in Figure 3–11, which represents the very comprehensive functional requirements developed for a specific company. Figure 3–12 displays the plant—DC—customer/region mapping output for a model developed for a high technology firm.

Logistics modeling should conform broadly to these requirements. The model should be developed with some common sense—for instance, too much disaggregation (customer regions, SKUs) will provide little incremental benefit and probably require far too much cost and operational data. On the other hand, too much aggregation may not provide much of a solution or useful guidelines at all. The optimization approach is generally suitable for fairly complex logistics networks—those with a large number of demand and supply sources and complex delivery patterns.

The major constraints used by such an optimization model are typically the result of management decisions on process staging and proximity/time factors. It is imperative that these important decisions be made at the firm's senior management levels.

In-House Modeling Resources?
Given the specialization inherent in linear programming and the complexities involved in building a network optimization model, it is inadvisable for all but large companies with complex logistics networks to invest in the necessary talents and resources. This is particularly true since effective employees are required to be multi-functional, to have a broader perspective on the business, rather than focus narrowly on quantitative model building. The key ongoing resources required in a firm are those to

maintain the models on an ongoing basis, to use them, and to provide the necessary decision-support information to make network configuration and rationalization decisions. However, most companies should evaluate the several good packages already available, select one, and hire temporary resources to develop appropriate models. These resources are available at universities and at some logistics, software, and consulting firms. It is necessary that company employees work together with outside resources to develop the models, learn their use, and transfer that knowledge to the company.

Don't Underestimate This Task

The keys to developing and using such models are:

A firm knowledge of the company's costs and cost structure and how it behaves under volume conditions (for instance, many so-called "fixed" costs are really semi-fixed, and operate in a step-wise function with different volumes, technologies, and the particular phase in the plant's life cycle)

Data on its demand patterns, sources, and volumes

A fairly accurate allocation of direct and indirect costs to product lines

It is not often that a firm, even a larger, more sophisticated firm, has such data readily available. Some of it can be quite complex. Developing a cost structure for a reasonably complex outbound set of transportation and delivery links is difficult. One has to consider various modes (tractor-trailers, shipping, rail, air, route trucks) and their costs by volume or weight, their volumes (full truck loads v. less-then-full truck loads), multiple lanes, arcs, links, etc. In shipping some products, for example, one typically pays for a certain truck weight as the shipment weight approaches a full truck load—the rate is for 46,000 pounds but the shipment is only 42,000 pounds. Again, some states (such as Texas) impose a surcharge for intra-state shipments, and certain communities prohibit the pulling of "doubles" within their limits. Yet again, union work rules restrict driving hours to a certain number per week and no more. To add to this complexity, there are usually several types of delivery, such as direct shipments, consolidated shipments for routing stop-off or break-bulk, or customer pick-up—all with different cost structures. All these costs must then be traded off against frequent customer service and delivery prefer-

FIGURE 3–11
Decision-Support Requirements—Optimization Modeling Package

General Functional Requirements

Name	General Description of Module
Network Optimization/Rationalization	Optimization model to provide least total cost solutions/options under various changeable constraints through "what-if" and sensitivity analysis

Key Decisions	Information Required
• Manufacturing plant location and parameters (product mix/volume) • Distribution center location, type (service, break-bulk, etc.), parameters, products, stocking levels, throughput • Transportation flows (plant-DC, inter-plant, inter-DC, DC-customers/regions by product, source-destination links by product) • Plant-DC rationalization	• Production and distribution costs by product—direct/indirect and support • Demand volumes and customer/regions by product • Transportation data (lanes, modes, volumes/weights, rates, including overnight and 2-day air) • Delivery preferences and market data • Source-destination links and OEMs • Cycle times across supply chain • New product introduction/phase-out plans and projections

Critical Success Factors	Information Produced	"What-If" and Sensitivity Analysis	Technology Interfaces
• Accurate cost, volume, and projection data • Model parameters and constraints from senior management • Attributable product line cost allocation • Ongoing in-house use/maintenance know-how	Network: • Manufacturing plant/DC	Changes: • Demand and customer regions	• Costing system • Demand management/supply-

Constraints			
• Capacities • Throughputs			

Key Operating Issues	Technology Issues	Risk Management Issues
• Customer service levels/fill rates • Unique supply-demand regional characteristics • Source-destination links not permitted • Specialized storage/transport/plant/DC requirements • Product-process mix for plants • Unique proximity requirements • product mix and rationalization • Source-destination links (plant-DC-customer/region) • Graphical display—maps, lanes, distances Market: • Demand pattern analysis by order size, frequency, sales volumes, weights, cube, geography • Seasonality with flexible time buckets Financial: • Incremental cost differentials—one-time/ongoing • Link to plant level/corporate P&Ls • Total network costs by stages, source-destination links, fixed, semi-fixed, and variable costs • Warehousing and inventory costs	• Transportation rates • Operating costs and material costs • Source-destination links Products • Product mix by plant • New product introduction/phase-out Capacities Expansion—Plants/DCs Sensitivity Analysis • Demand • Cost v. customer levels • Cost v. stocking locations • Cost v. structures—key inputs	• demand planning system • Order management system • Marketing data systems (internal/external) • Production data bases • DRP system

Key Operating Issues	Technology Issues	Risk Management Issues
• Number and location of plants/DCs • Plant and DC parameters: Product mix and volumes, throughputs Inventory deployment Source-destination links (plant-DC-cust/region/product)	• Downloading/uploading of data • File compatibility	• Validate assumptions periodically • Run and evaluate model periodically for validation and changes • Track demand patterns for changes • Develop in-house logistics modeling capabilities • Ensure data accuracy, integrity

83

FIGURE 3–12
Mapped Network Optimization Outbound Primary Distribution Routes

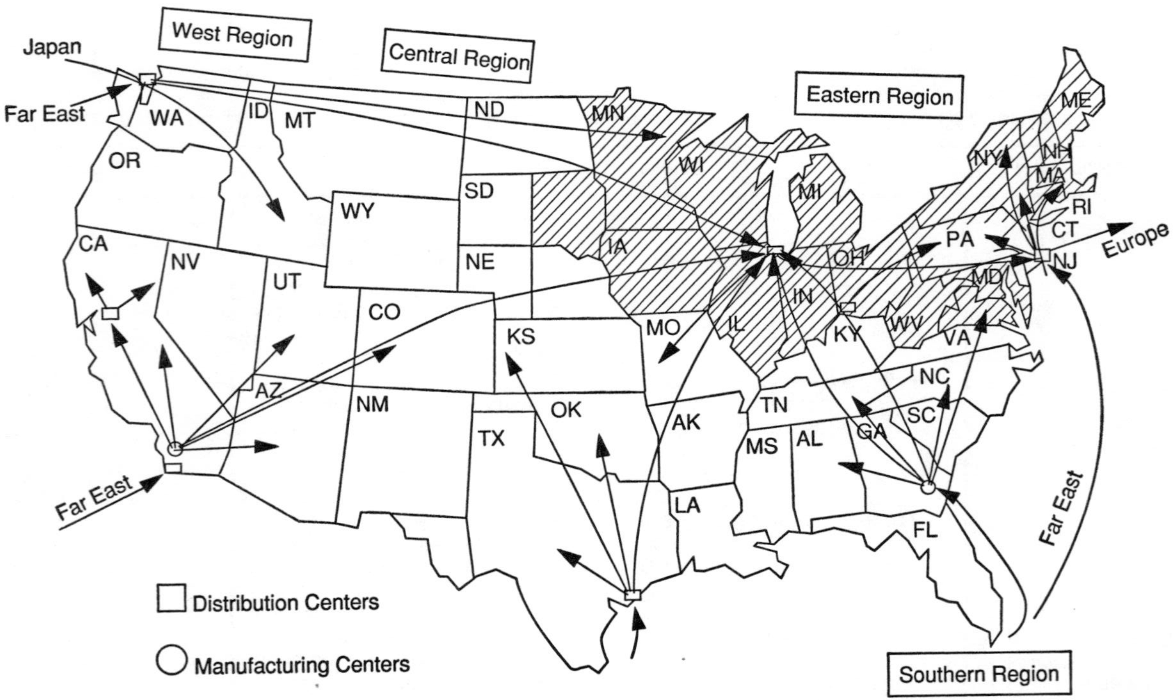
West Region
Central Region
Eastern Region
Southern Region
Japan
Far East
Far East
Far East
Europe
WA
OR
CA
ID
MT
NV
UT
WY
CO
AZ
NM
ND
SD
NE
KS
OK
TX
MN
IA
MO
AK
LA
WI
IL
MI
IN
OH
KY
TN
MS
AL
GA
FL
SC
NC
VA
WV
MD
PA
NY
NJ
CT
RI
MA
NH
ME
Distribution Centers
Manufacturing Centers

ences. In such complex cases, the use of an optimization program to consider the large number of variables and options can prove invaluable in determining the logistics network configuration.

In the absence of such detailed data, good approximations and estimates based on proxy indicators will provide a reasonable solution in some cases. In others, lack of such data could provide the impetus to start collecting good data, without which it is extremely difficult, if not impossible, to successfully manage the company and to control costs. In any case, a one-shot effort to collect such information will not provide any longer term benefits to the company short of the initial configuration and rationalization decisions, if provision is not made to collect the information on an ongoing basis, and this can be expensive. Detailed optimization modeling may not be necessary in a large number of cases, particularly where the company has comparatively few plants and distribution centers, uses distributors as major channels (less complexity and fewer source-destination links), has relatively few products, and is relatively small in terms of volume and transactions. In such cases, small microcomputer optimization packages or financial/operational modeling provides a reasonable alternative.

Microcomputer optimization packages are typically not as comprehensive as the larger ones. A significant amount of the data must be aggregated (mainly because of program and data base size limitations), and they thus lose some of the detailed analysis capabilities of the larger packages. On the other hand, they provide very good decision-support capabilities, and are easier to set up and maintain. Another advantage is the fact that employees can learn to set up, use, maintain, and modify them in-house with comparatively little training.

Financial/Operational Modeling

Financial/operational modeling is typically used when the scope of the network and problem is much smaller and more localized. This technique consists mainly of spreadsheet modeling, and requires a pre-selection of major network configurations and rules; hence, one term for them is heuristic/cost models. These configurations are based on market data and the knowledge and experience of management. The resulting scenarios are then modeled to provide the most attractive cost/revenue scenario. To be effective decision-support tools, they should provide a cash flow analysis along with a profits & loss statement for each scenario. As with any modeling technique, risks should always be identified and evaluated through "what-if" and sensitivity analyses on key variables. Obviously, the pre-selection of scenarios is very important (Figures 3–13 A–G show one such scenario).

The data analyses must be as rigorous as those required for a larger analysis, and should include:

Revenue estimates by customer segment, costs of lost sales, and increases from improved customer service

Inventory levels for demand patterns, including safety stocks

Incremental cost increases and decreases at various points in the logistics value chain

Capacity and throughput analyses for plants and distribution centers

The roles of the distribution centers

Capital investment, recovery, and replacement costs

Volumes of transactions, shipments, receipts

Transportation costs

These analyses are usually done off-line and the results input to the model. Alternatively, the model can often be set up to generate automatically alternative scenarios within pre-determined parameters and provide their costs.

As always, the first step is the construction of a baseline "as-is" model. Subsequent scenarios are built on this baseline in an incremental fashion. Finally, the P&L statements are compared and evaluated against qualitative factors. Such financial/operational models have proven to provide excellent decision support for smaller companies and to help with localized situations for larger firms (for instance, evaluating plants and distribution centers for a particular brand). It is certainly less expensive and can usually be performed in-house, which is always an advantage.

CONFIGURATION/NETWORK STRATEGY: PUTTING IT ALL TOGETHER

An approach to developing a configuration/network strategy is shown in Figure 3–14. Every step in the process is equally important. All too often, companies move directly to the modeling phase. The danger here is that serious flaws in determining time/proximity, market preference, and process staging will be institutionalized and acquire an air of respec-

FIGURE 3–13A
Financial/Operational Modeling and Analysis Cost Analysis Model of Supply Chain

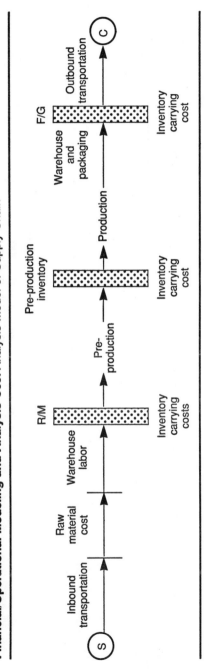

FIGURE 3–13B

Financial/Operational Modeling and Analysis Cost Model of Plant "A"

Inbound Trans.	*Raw Material Costs*	*Inbound Warehouse*	*Raw Material ICC*	*Pre-Production Costs*	*Pre-Production ICC*	*Production*	*Outbound Warehouse & Packaging*	*Finished Goods ICC*	*Outbound Trans.*
$4,051,000	$57,645,800	$210,000	$600,000	$6,100,000	$400,000	$7,500,000	$2,900,000	$900,000	$2,000,000

Stage 1	*Stage 2*	*Stage 3*
$68,606,800	$7,900,000	$5,800,000

Fixed Costs: People $4,000,000
Other $1,900,000

Source: Ernst & Young Center for Information Technology & Strategy.

FIGURE 3–13C

Financial/Operational Modeling and Analysis Cost Model of Plant "B"

Inbound Trans.	*Raw Material Costs*	*Inbound Warehouse*	*Raw Material ICC*	*Pre-Production Costs*	*Pre-Production ICC*	*Production*	*Outbound Warehouse & Packaging*	*Finished Goods ICC*	*Outbound Trans.*
$7,500,000	$130,500,000	$350,000	$1,900,000	$5,000,000	$550,000	$15,000,000	$6,000,000	$1,100,000	$5,000,000

Stage 1	*Stage 2*	*Stage 3*
$145,250,000	$15,550,000	$12,100,000

Fixed Costs: $15,000,000

Source: Ernst & Young Center for Information Technology & Strategy.

FIGURE 3–13D
Financial/Operational Modeling and Analysis Scenario I: Eliminate Pre-Production in Plant "A"

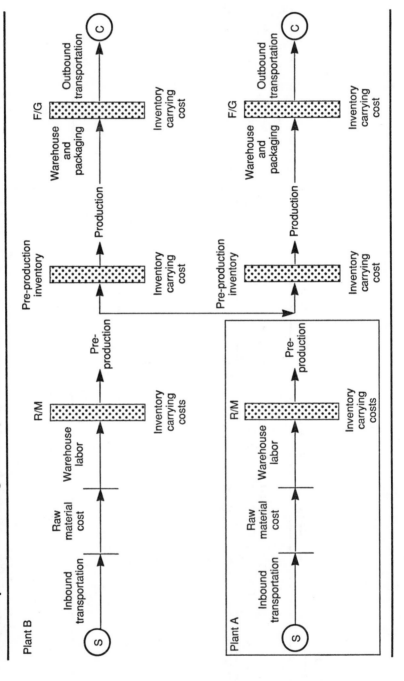

FIGURE 3–13E
Financial/Operational Modeling and Analysis Scenario II: Eliminate All Production in Plant "A"

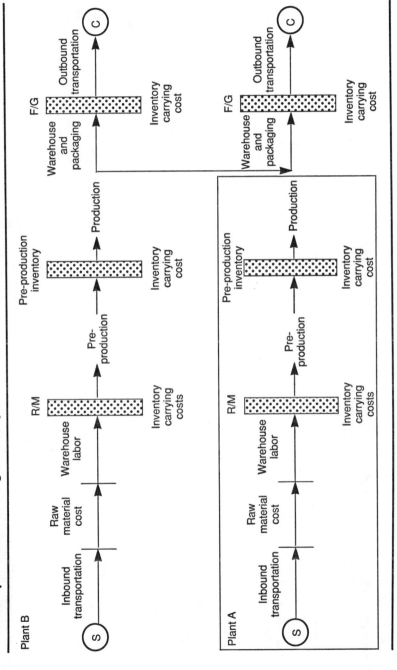

FIGURE 3–13F
Financial/Operational Modeling and Analysis Scenario I: Impact on P&L Statement

	1990	Incremental Cost Adjustments	Adjusted P&L
Sales Less:	$300,000,000	($4,050,000)	$295,950,000
Discounts	($4,000,000)	($90,000)	($4,090,000)
Freight paid out	($10,100,000)	($5,050,000)	($15,150,000)
Freight recovered	$9,005,000	$0	$9,005,000
Net Sales	$294,905,000	($9,190,000)	$285,715,000
Costs:			
Cost of sales	$260,450,000	$5,100,000	$265,550,000
Price variance	($1,050,000)	$0	($1,050,000)
Conversion variance	($5,510,000)	$0	($5,510,000)
Plant depreciation	$2,020,000	$0	$2,020,000
Total Cost of Sales	$255,910,000	$5,100,000	$261,010,000
Gross Profit	$38,995,000	($14,290,000)	$24,705,000
Operating Expenses:			
Commissions	$5,200,000	($69,000)	$5,131,000
G&A	$4,800,000	($290,000)	$4,510,000
Corporate G&A	$10,500,000	($160,000)	$10,340,000
Marketing	$8,200,000	$0	$8,200,000
Corporate selling	$12,900,000	$0	$12,900,000
Other	($240,000)	$0	($240,000)
Total Operating Expenses	$41,360,000	($519,000)	$40,841,000
Net Income (Loss)	($2,365,000)	($13,771,000)	($16,136,000)

FIGURE 3–13G
Financial/Operational Modeling and Analysis Scenario II: Impact on P&L Statement

	1990	Incremental Cost Adjustments	Adjusted P&L
Sales Less:	$300,000,000	($45,000,000)	$255,000,000
Discounts	($4,000,000)	($920,000)	($4,920,000)
Freight paid out	($10,100,000)	($1,300,000)	($11,400,000)
Freight recovered	$9,005,000	$0	$9,005,000
Net Sales	**$294,905,000**	**($47,220,000)**	**$247,685,000**
Costs:			
Cost of sales	$260,450,000	$54,100,000	$206,350,000
Price variance	($1,050,000)	$450,000	($600,000)
Conversion variance	($5,510,000)	$0	($5,510,000)
Plant depreciation	$2,020,000	$0	$2,020,000
Total Cost of Sales	**$255,910,000**	**($53,650,000)**	**$202,260,000**
Gross Profit	**$38,995,000**	**$6,430,000**	**$45,425,000**
Operating Expenses:			
Commissions	$5,200,000	($720,000)	$4,480,000
G&A	$4,800,000	($1,850,000)	$2,950,000
Corporate G&A	$10,500,000	($435,000)	$10,065,000
Marketing	$8,200,000	($320,000)	$7,880,000
Corporate selling	$12,900,000	$0	$12,900,000
Other	($240,000)	$0	($240,000)
Total Operating Expenses	**$41,360,000**	**($3,325,000)**	**$38,035,000**
Net Income (Loss)	**($2,365,000)**	**$9,755,000**	**($7,390,000)**

FIGURE 3–14
Approach to Configuration/Network Strategy

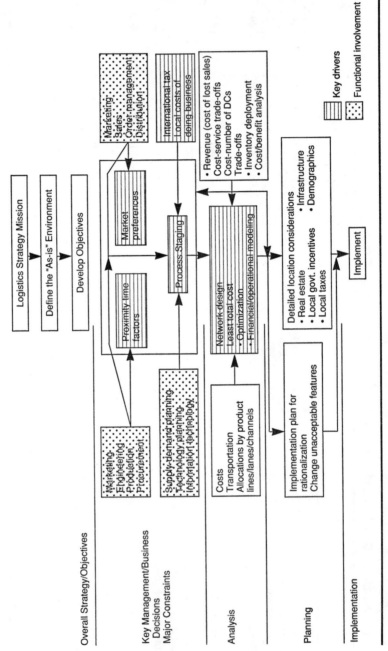

Source: Ernst & Young Center for Information Technology & Strategy. All rights reserved.

tability through a series of numbers and charts. Mistakes in network and location strategies can be very expensive, and management decisions in the "qualitative" aspects of configuration strategy are crucial—*the quantitative analyses are driven from these qualitative decisions* to refine and set implementation parameters.

Figure 3–15 provides a useful checklist of key structural factors along the logistics value chain (a similar chart is provided in Chapter 1). It is important that these be considered when developing and implementing a configuration/network strategy.

Essentially, developing a configuration/network strategy consists of 5 phases.

Phase 1:   The overall logistics strategy and objectives (covered in chapter 2), and driven from the corporate, marketing, and manufacturing strategies.

Phase 2:   Key management and business decisions involving proximity/time factors, market preferences, and process staging—providing the firm structural parameters, rules, and major constraints within which the analyses and trade-offs will be performed.

This process must be multi-functional, as each major customer service function has its own priorities, which are often conflicting. Marketing, for instance, seeks to maximize sales, provide very low levels of stockouts and backorders, and maintain a high degree of production flexibility. Manufacturing, on the other hand, seeks predictable demand, reduced overall set-ups and set-up time, and decreased unit cost. Procurement wishes to provide its suppliers with long lead times and demand, and to deliver material in a consolidated fashion. Finally, finance seeks to minimize inventory levels (investment and carrying cost) and to consolidate facilities to reduce capital needs.

The multi-functional approach is necessary to determine trade-offs and to provide the requirements for analysis. All these functions are interdependent—a change in any one process or function influences the others. Attempts to optimize a particular function performed in a vacuum often adversely impact other functions (for instance, minimizing inventory levels could increase lost sales as well as unit manufacturing costs, as production endeavors to match production levels to demand without the benefit of level schedules).

FIGURE 3–15
Key Factors in the Logistics Supply Chain Configuration (Network) Structural

Sourcing	Inbound Logistics	Manufacturing	Outbound Logistics	After-Sales Service
• Number of vendors per product • Vendor location(s) distance • Capacity allocated • Local regulations and tax implications • Local market implications • Local labor and material costs • Local technologies • Local economy • Political	• W/H location(s) (plant adjacent or remote) • Number of W/Hs • W/H size, capacity, and function • In-house fleet vs. contract carriers • Modes of transportation • Number of carriers • Local regulations and tax implications	• Plant location(s) • Concentrated vs. dispersed manufacture (plans per product line) • Single plant or plants at different stages of manufacture • Level of technologies • Capacities • Manufacturing flexibility (dedicated vs. flexible) • Local regulations and tax implications • Local market implications • Local labor and material costs • Local economy • Political	• DC location(s) and functions • Number of DCs • DC size and capacity • In-house fleet vs. contract carriers • Number of carriers • Modes of transportation • Local regulations and tax implications • Political	• Number of service centers and functions • Service centers location(s) • Size and autonomy of service centers • Local demand and market implications

Phase 3: Analyses targeted toward minimizing total cost while providing competitive customer service levels across all major dimensions. This can consist of several iterations for making the necessary trade-offs, and the tools used can range from optimization models to heuristics and simulation models.

Phase 4: Implementation planning. In the case of a new facility, it involves detailed location considerations (real estate issues, local taxes and incentives, infrastructure—transportation, manpower, etc.—and demographics). In the case of plant rationalization, it involves planning for changes in distribution centers, plants, product mix, etc.

Phase 5: Implementation. This should consist of coordination/organization strategies/structure (discussed in the next chapter); risk management programs; time-phased action plans, schedules, milestones, and responsibilities; and timeframes for the development of customer service, inventory, and transportation strategies.

CHAPTER 4

COORDINATION/ORGANIZATION STRATEGY

The previous chapter addressed one of the two structural aspects of logistics strategy—configuration/network strategy. The discussion focused on the physical network vis-à-vis the industry, competition, customer service, and costs. Having defined the network, the next step involves determining the appropriate organization structure and processes necessary to manage effectively the integrated flow of material from supplier to customer. In his book *Competition in Global Industries*, Michael Porter defines this aspect of logistics strategy, coordination, as the

> linking of like activities along the value chain

This chapter examines the processes and issues involved in determining the appropriate aspects of coordination relevant to logistics.

Coordination: the global linkage of activities, enabled by information technology, to best meet market demands and competition.

An interrelated issue is the structure to formalize and manage the necessary coordination.

Organization structure: the roles and responsibilities necessary to effectively manage the supply chain.

THE VISION

> To paraphrase Stanley Davis, the virtual supply chain organization of the future is one that will provide the customer with anything he wants, any time and in any place (*Future Perfect* [Reading, Mass.: Addison-Wesley Publishing Company, 1987]).

Whereas this vision may be unattainable in its entirety in the near future by most organizations (though it has virtually arrived in certain industries), it is a goal toward which to work. The enabling factors here are formalization of logistics, the virtual supply chain, and information technology. Information technology advances have changed companies from their "always done it like this/management instinct" state to a data-driven state, and is currently changing them to an information-responsive state.

Bowersox, et al., based on their own research of leading edge logistics organizations, have put forward their own vision of the future, embodied in eight propositions:

1. Basic logistical requirements will increase.
2. Environmental factors will become increasingly restrictive.
3. Logistical solutions will become more sophisticated and more proprietary.
4. Focus will be placed on process accountability.
5. Competency will be increasingly viewed as a strategic resource.
6. Trading relationships will become more relational.
7. Functional execution will be dispersed throughout the organization.
8. Organization structure will become increasingly transparent.

The validity of these propositions for the future is borne out by the experience of leading companies using logistics to gain a competitive advantage.

As discussed in Chapter 2, logistics strategy and management is the integration between marketing, manufacturing, corporate strategy, and the customer. Logistics becomes Warren Bennis's demand-satisfying activity to marketing's demand-creating activities. If the firm is to succeed in defining the structure and processes in the organization, it must first identify the characteristics of the organization—those that encompass the competitive and industry trends, its core competencies, and Stanley Davis's "future perfect" vision.

There are three key questions that senior management must ask of itself:

1. What characteristics would best enable the organization to respond to and achieve the competitive imperatives being set by the marketplace?

2. What are the methods we use to incorporate such characteristics or changes?

or

What management structure, roles, responsibilities, and process linkages would best enable the firm to achieve its corporate objectives and strategy; manage the logistics configuration/network to provide best competitive customer service levels with minimum costs and maximum flexibility; use logistics to provide a sustainable competitive advantage; and link logistics strategy planning, execution and performance closely to manufacturing and marketing strategies and performance?

3. What are the technology enablers to achieve such an organization?

The major issues inherent in these questions are discussed below.

CHARACTERISTICS OF THE ORGANIZATION

Bowersox, et. al. have done a great deal of significant research on the practices of leading edge logistics firms, all of which are entirely compatible with, and satisfy, the vision of the future's highly competitive, customer-driven logistics organization. This is probably the first major piece of logistics research of strategic importance following "Corporate Profitability and Logistics" (Ernst & Whinney for the Council of Logistics Management and the National Association of Accountants, 1987). The research of Bowersox, et al. and that of others reveals that the following are among the key characteristics of the advanced, competitive logistics organization.

- *Flexibility*, which can be defined as:
  - Response to customer demands in product, options, and configurations
  - Response to changing orders, quantities, and delivery preferences (frequencies, lot sizes, unitization, and location)
  - Response to ad hoc and emergency customer requirements
  - Changes in product mix and system throughput
  - Accomodation to a variety of product flows, including returns, field service repairs, and spares
- *Process-based performance measures and monitoring mechanisms*, which are:

- ○ Focused on time, response, cost, customer service levels, and quality
- ○ Based on customer requirements
- ○ Tracked against competitive benchmarks—best in industry and best in class
- ○ Monitored and tracked as much as possible in real time
- ○ Consistent with corporate and logistics objectives

- *The use, and innovative development, of information technology for decision support, to link the virtual supply chain, to integrate the company's information needs and to manage its operations*

  - ○ This includes advanced applications such as expert systems and analyses packages.
  - ○ The organization of the information system functions to suit local needs as well as control corporate-wide standards.
    Many companies are moving toward becoming information-based organizations that no longer rely on the functional, information "silo" structures. Responsibilities, as indicated by Bowersox and his team, *are* becoming diffused, and activities are linked through information sharing and commonality.

- *The view of outsourcing, partnerships, and third-party alliances from a strategic perspective based on core competencies, cost, flexibility, and customer service*

  - ○ Stakeholders (customers, suppliers, warehousers, carriers, outside processors and finishers, etc.)
  - ○ Support services (information systems, specialized analysis, design alliances, project management, etc.)

- *Development of a virtual supply chain organization with a formal integrated management structure and process*

  - ○ Define roles, responsibility, and authority
  - ○ Provide the structure to enable the recognition and execution of opportunities in customer service
  - ○ Incorporate the continuous improvement philosophy to have an internal/external customer orientation (responding to our expectations of, and for, them) and redesign the process to meet changing, or major marketplace shifts

- ○ Establish investment decision power based on economic, value and strategic justification
- ○ Provide high-level executive responsibility and access to top management
- ○ Develop, through education, training, and rotation of personnel through the organization, multi-functional specialists with a strategic perspective
- *Utilization of costing systems that provide a real-time picture of true product costs by segment, links, and key success indicators*
  - ○ Based on activity-based costing principles
  - ○ Incorporating attributable direct, overhead, indirect/support, and semi-fixed/semi-variable costs
  - ○ Monitoring ongoing project costs, projected returns on investment, and asset management
- *Incorporation of strategic logistics planning within the formal business planning process, including an explicit recognition that logistics is one of the keys to achieving and maintaining a sustainable competitive advantage*
  - ○ Establish formal planning and update process
  - ○ Integrate with marketing and manufacturing

These characteristics form a continuous curve of evolution in most companies. Some companies, however, recognizing the imperatives of the industry, progress further down the curve in a quantum leap of policy and structure. It can be difficult for traditional functional departments, executives, and middle managers to move toward a new orientation and functional integration. (Line personnel typically have few problems readjusting and incorporating new philosophies—they probably see the necessities better than most.)

Most companies which have taken such steps preface their actions by thorough communication throughout the organization, since communication is the best preparation for change. Communication must include an explanation of the competitive necessity for the change to affected individuals, departments and the organization; the charter, explicit responsibilities, and operations of the new structure and roles; and the mission, objectives, and characteristics of the company. It is also important that the company provide team-building sessions.

In any event, it is strategically important for a company to adopt the characteristics listed above in its operating and structural philosophies—

the only question should be the speed of change. Experience shows that high technology companies, by virtue of their history, industry, and willingness to adopt new concepts, can move the quickest, followed in their pace of change by consumer products companies, whose success depends upon responding to the market. Companies in many other industries often require a market push. Of course, it is typical of leaders in every industry to be ahead of the others in implementing these characteristics within their organizations.

METHODS OF INCORPORATING AND INSTITUTIONALIZING THE CHARACTERISTICS OF COMPETITIVE LOGISTICS ORGANIZATIONS

There are three approaches—none mutually exclusive—all simultaneous and interdependent.

Coordination
Organizational structure
Continuous process improvement philosophy

Coordination

Figure 4–1 outlines the major logistics coordination activities—management of materials and information—along the supply chain. They include the following functions.

- *Marketing*
  - Planning of material for new product introduction and product phase-out
  - Demand management, forecasts, and changes
  - Intelligence regarding market and competitors' trends
- *Sales coordination*
  - Customer orders and quotes for delivery
  - Sales projections from the field
  - Intelligence regarding customer service levels and delivery preferences
  - Intelligence about competitors' actions and performance

- *Procurement*
  - Sources of supply and volumes
  - Volume projections
  - Delivery commitments and particulars (for example, supplier delivery versus source pick-up)
- *Manufacturing stages*
  - Product mix and capacities
  - Volumes and inter-plant transfers
  - Locations, process stages, and scope
- *Distribution*
  - Volumes and throughput
  - Functions, size, and location
  - Capacities
- *Inventory—raw material, components, work-in-process, OEMs, spares, semi-finished, and finished goods*
  - Status and visibility
  - Schedules and schedules v. actuals (stage ins, outs, and projected starts and outs)
  - Material requirements
- *Allocations*
  - Customer, regional, and segment allocations and policies
- *Customer service support*
  - Types and status of customer support (for example, strategic alliances, third party, field service, dealer support, etc.)
  - Requirements
  - Mean time between failure for products

The major issue here is that of centralization of responsibilities, central planning, visibility, and control *versus* decentralization and local planning/control. The trend in many industries, following *their* trends toward globalization and customer-focused supply chain activities, is toward increased centralization of many activities:

- Supply-demand planning to balance resources, optimize inventory levels, and use an enterprise-wide perspective on satisfying customer requirements
- Information technology strategy; integration requirements and justification; and common reporting requirements

FIGURE 4–1
Coordination of Logistics Activities

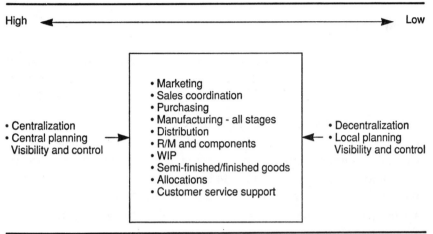

High ◄──► Low

- Centralization
- Central planning
  Visibility and control

→

- Marketing
- Sales coordination
- Purchasing
- Manufacturing - all stages
- Distribution
- R/M and components
- WIP
- Semi-finished/finished goods
- Allocations
- Customer service support

◄─

- Decentralization
- Local planning
  Visibility and control

- Corporate purchasing contracts to leverage volumes, reduce the number of critical suppliers, and effectively develop and manage them
- Network location, facility rationalization, and product mix management
- Global contract carrier negotiations and selection
- Global field service planning
- Product introduction/phase-out policies

In keeping with these trends, the focus of many successful companies is fast expanding beyond the boundaries of the firm, moving to the virtual supply chain and encompassing suppliers, customers, and other key stakeholders. This has resulted in the sharing of functional expertise, sensitive information, and schedules among business partners.

Coordination and organization issues must address these market imperatives as well as the structure and ability of the organization to respond to (and take advantage of) opportunities presented. This must result in the explicit charter of managers to spend more time interacting and working with the key stakeholders. It also raises critical issues regarding education, training, and a company's ability and willingness to radically improve or redesign the process managed. As business processes are so different from traditional, function-oriented methods, it is often necessary to redesign them to reflect coordination strategies.

Organizational Structure

Addressing the organizational structure requires a recognition of the key impediments to achieving this enterprise-wide, information-integrated perspective. Such impediments are mainly organizational, and include:

• The functional organization and structure
• Perception of the logistics functions and a lack of awareness of the strategic nature of logistics strategy and management (the competitive possibilities, industry, customer and competitor trends, best practices in other industries, leverage, benefits, and requirements)
• Conflict within the company due to traditional functional roles, conflicting performance measures, and charters

THE FUNCTIONAL ORGANIZATION AND AN ORGANIZATIONAL STRUCTURE TO MANAGE LOGISTICS: PERCEPTION AND LACK OF AWARENESS OF LOGISTICS

Functional Structure

Most organizations, traditionally, have been structured along functional lines (see Figure 4–2), with logistics functions fragmented and relegated to lower organizational levels. For instance, warehouse managers, traffic coordinators, purchasing managers, and material managers operated independently in an "over the wall" fashion. One result has been the development of functional "black boxes" where critical operations have been left to lower level managers who have little real authority beyond their departments. Such managers have typically acquired only narrow functional expertise and experience (often "one year twenty times over") in their respective areas, with little perspective on the total enterprise and its requirements. The dangers posed by functional "silos" to enterprise and information integration and customer service have been thoroughly discussed in the business press, and are sufficiently important to bear repeating here.

FIGURE 4–2
Functional Organization

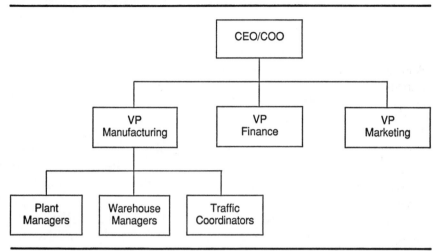

Source: *Corporate Profitability and Logistics,* Prepared by Ernst & Whinney for the Council of Logistics Management, 1987.

Logistics—Not Traditionally Glamorous

The functions involved in logistics have rarely been considered glamorous (except in distribution companies) and, consequently, have played a subordinate role in importance to such support functions as finance and information systems. This lack of recognition in many companies has been echoed in business schools. Very few have any logistics programs at the undergraduate or graduate levels. Many do not even mention logistics.

It is fairly obvious to most executives that, except for some advanced schools, few general management and strategy faculty members understand the strategic importance of logistics. Strategic management courses seldom mention logistics or manufacturing. Operations management courses focus on inventory and safety stock theory and mathematical programming. In some schools, a logistics course may be included as an elective in the marketing curriculum.

There are, however, bright spots. Several schools today are rising to the challenge with excellent programs, faculty, and doctoral research. Unfortunately, they are the exception rather than the rule. As a result,

"rising stars" have not, typically, been educated in logistics and its importance; they have not joined or been funneled through the logistics functions.

Accounting-Based Measures
One prominent educator and thinker stated, with great insight:

> Keep the accountants off the shop floor

Most line managers would wholeheartedly extend the invitation vis-a-vis
the supply chain pipeline. The classical budgeting process, with its breakdown of costs into narrow functional areas, has resulted in two types of
dysfunctional performance measures that *force* the development of functional "silos".

1. Cost control and reduction measures. Such measures (typically
percentages), provide incentives to maximize functional return on assets,
equipment utilization, and aggregate expenses per unit or dollar of output
(or as a percentage of cost of sales). At any rate, these measures have
rarely been tied to the internal or external customer, the key success factors of the business, or the process.

2. Volume-based measures. These measures seek to meet targets of
volume and shipments, number of orders filled per day, and emphasize
departmental or functional output rather than customer service.

The Evolution of Logistics Organizations
Logistics functions have, owing to these factors, traditionally resided
near the bottom of the organizational hierarchy (at one time surpassed
only by that of the manufacturing process). However, several factors
have prompted an increasing awareness of the strategic importance of
logistics: the globalization of world markets; competition and resources;
and advances in information systems, technology, and application. As a
result, the focus of logistics planning and responsibility is moving up the
organizational hierarchy. The perception of logistics in many companies
is evolving rapidly from that of warehousing and traffic management to
distribution management to integrated materials management (Figure 4–
3). This evolution has resulted in a move away from the functional organization to *distribution/organization*. Typically, a vice president of distribution is appointed to manage all aspects of distribution. In many organizations, the distribution function has its own information systems and

FIGURE 4–3
Perception and Trends

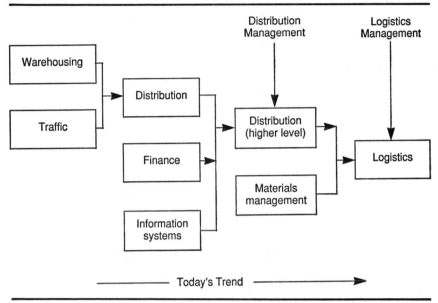

finance groups reporting to it. In others, these are dotted line relationships (Tyndall has depicted such an organization—shown in Figure 4–4).

The idea behind this structure is to elevate traditional distribution to a vice presidency level in order to emphasize its importance in the organization and to get its requirements and contributions taken seriously. Additionally, the vice president, a high-level executive in most (but not all) organizations, would ideally be able to coordinate and plan with his or her peers to provide an integrated, enterprise-wide perspective.

This happy situation has occurred only in some of the companies which have adopted this structure. One reason for the lack of success in others was that, in the final analysis, the vice president or director usually had a great deal of responsibility but little authority. In the words of James Heskett, the position requires "persuasion, negotiation and personal character"—not the most common of executive attributes ("Leadership Through Integration: The Special Challenge of Logistics Management," CLM annual proceedings, volume 1, 1988, pp. 15–21).

In some companies this structure has only resulted in the functional silos growing more vertical.

FIGURE 4–4
Distribution Management Organization

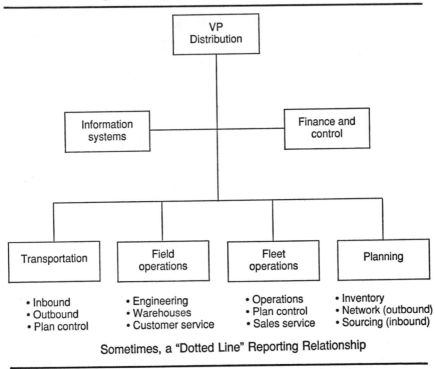

Sometimes, a "Dotted Line" Reporting Relationship

Source: *Corporate Profitability and Logistics*, Prepared by Ernst & Whinney for the Council of Logistics Management, 1987.

A more integrated structure adopted by many companies is the *logistics management organization*. Here, a high-level vice president of logistics has the responsibility and control over materials and distribution. In some leading companies, this control and responsibility extends to procurement and supply management. (Figure 4–5 depicts an example of this type of integrated organization). In this organization, functional boundaries become blurred. The supply elements of the supply chain conform to Warren Bennis's vision and become "demand satisfying activities."

These demand-satisfying activities include suppliers as well as procurement, manufacturing, transportation and inventory management. EDI and strategic alliances (which includes the exchange of status data, plans, schedules, and design information) are making this a seamless

FIGURE 4–5
Logistics Management Organization

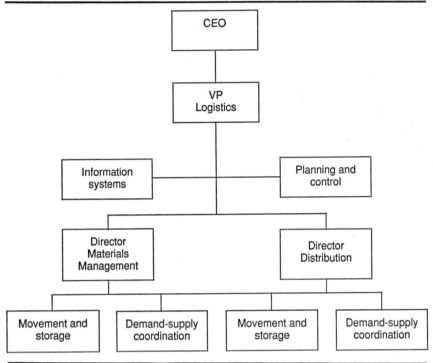

Source: *Corporate Profitability and Logistics*, Prepared by Ernst & Whinney for the Council of Logistics Management, 1987.

pipeline. Customers are linked into the chain—the "demand creating activity." The key integrator for the "virtual factory" is, and will increasingly continue to be, information, not material. Information hoarding (a characteristic in the functional organization) must give way to information sharing. The only ways for this to occur are through:

- A vision of the integrated supply chain
- Team and group-based performance measures
- Business process redesign, including information technology integration with the process
- Information technology strategy, its alignment with competitive strategy, architecture, and the applications to drive it

Designing the organization involves several organizational design and dynamics issues that are outside the scope of this book. Some of the issues and major steps (though not all) involved in classical organizational design should be mentioned, however. They include:

Division of work. Classical organizational design takes a ground-up approach, breaking functions into their constituent tasks, and further into constituent activities. Whereas this is a good exercise, implementing a radically different structure can be traumatic to an organization. It is worth remembering that, while many good people can cope with rapid organizational change, others may find it frustrating, and leave. The company should proceed carefully, making sure that appropriate communications are in place. Ways of breaking down work functions may seem elegant in theory, but may be difficult to implement smoothly.

Consistency of objectives. This has been discussed at length in an earlier chapter. It is crucial to the effective management of the organization.

Balance of authority and responsibility, and position definition. Position definition is important, and the issues regarding authority and responsibility have been discussed earlier. It is always worth reemphasizing that, while authority can be delegated, responsibility cannot, and that responsibility without authority will not accomplish much. Position definition should not be performed to the finest level of detail, but should, rather, evolve. It is difficult to envisage a new organization at the start. Furthermore, the necessity to remove responsibility or authority from a particular executive at a later stage, as a result of initial design not being the right one, can prove dysfunctional.

Span of control. It is essential to say a few words on the subject of the span of control required for logistics organization. Several organizations have appointed a vice president of logistics, have had a number of supply chain functions report to him or her, and have left it at that. In these cases, little reorganization was carried out, and the executive often ended up with an organization very similar to the previous one, with all the same problems of communication, integration, and multiple levels that filter and modify information flow to the top.

The trend in industry today is toward flatter organizations. Integrated organizations are characterized by an expanded span of control— the number of individuals that a manager or superviser can directly manage. Given the multi-functional nature of logistics management, it becomes impractical for a manager directly to control and micromanage subordinates. Not so many years ago, the qualification for a manager was that he or she excel in a particular function, resulting in the oft-heard assertion "I can do this better than any of my people, and they know it."

This really meant that subordinates had been relegated to the role of execution clerks. Total quality control philosophies, information technology, the new strategic imperatives, and multi-functional requirements have changed the manager's role to one of facilitation and support. An enlarged span of control supports this role and enhances communication, unfiltered monitoring of results, and improved employee involvement in important decisions.

Conflict Management

A significant portion of the logistics manager's role revolves around managing conflicts in the firm. Essentially, it involves identifying, making, and managing the trade-offs between functional interests and their impact on the business.

The Ernst & Whinney Study (*Corporate Profitability & Logistics*, prepared by Ernst & Whinney for the Council of Logistics Management, 1987) identified examples of some areas of conflict among three major functions within the organization which impact the business and which need to be managed through the logistics function (Figure 4–6). It can be seen that the resolution of these conflicts directly impacts the firm's customer service levels, flexibility, and costs. For instance, sales & marketing in a firm wishes for a high degree of production flexibility and rapid turnaround (cycle time)—interests that focus on increasing customer service levels. Manufacturing, on the other hand, favors longer production runs, fewer set-ups, smooth schedules, and a balanced line—to favor production costs and per unit costs. These are the types of trade-offs that must be made from an enterprise-wide perspective. If not, less-than-optimal decisions will be made (often depending on where the power lies within the organization or which crisis dictates action) that will seriously impact the firm's competitive ability.

Identifying the impacts and making these trade-off decisions requires timely decision-support systems and an analytical capability that has traditionally not been present in many organizations. In fact, many companies lie on opposite ends of the spectrum. While some either never make these critical decisions, or make them by gut instinct ("I've been in the business for fifteen years and know it completely!"), others have swung the other way. They hire operations, research, and information

FIGURE 4–6
Conflict Management

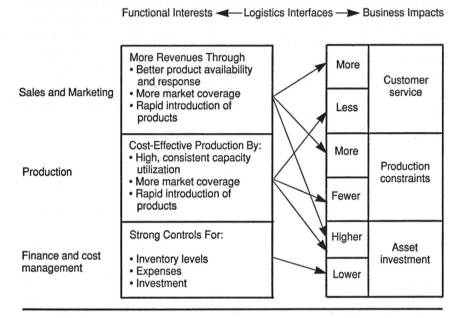

Source: *Corporate Profitability and Logistics*, **Prepared by Ernst & Whinney for the Council of Logistics Management, 1987.**

systems analysts who rarely understand business and the impacts of various decisions on business. What is called for is a combination of these two attributes—business knowledge and analytical capability.

Along with interpersonal skills, there are few better vehicles than data and analysis for managing conflicts and making trade-offs. Hence, an integrating and coordinating logistics function is necessary in today's environment for manufacturing companies.

Methods of Management

There are essentially three types of method used for managing logistics used in firms evolving toward (or which have evolved to) an integrated logistics management structure. Many firms use all three, whereas less-integrated firms typically use only one—the project management approach to logistics. Functionally-driven and structured firms often use none; they have no integrated logistics management. As firms evolve toward greater integration, their method of approaching and managing logistics also evolves, from project management to coordinating management and, finally, to line management.

Project Management. Typically this is used to analyze and to find solutions to particular problems, providing scenarios for evaluation or recommendations to management. Problems tackled this way include: capacity for new warehouses, local routing, collection of local government and freight rate information to help senior management make location decisions, analysis of various location and make versus buy scenarios, and similar tasks. Personnel from logistics are typically assigned to such project teams—in some instances, they even head them. However, experience shows that the scope of such project teams ends at making recommendations, not decisions.

Coordinating Management. This is a major stage in the evolution of logistics and integration within a firm. Senior management recognizes the strategic importance and integrative nature of logistics, but is hesitant to provide direct authority to a single person for traditionally functional roles. A senior title does not necessarily provide authority (except usually for traffic and warehousing) but often provides responsibilities for coordinating the different functions whose goals and interests have traditionally conflicted.

The success of coordinating management depends on the interpersonal and communications skills of the executive, as well as his or her credibility in the organization. Outsiders brought into this role must have a good background to achieve this credibility. Despite the constraints of narrow scope and lack of integration authority, this approach has worked fairly often. (Of course, the people involved have usually been of a very high caliber.)

Unfortunately, one result is also gridlock, frustration, and ineffectiveness for the executive. This is frustrating for all parties, and no change results in the functional orientation for the company—internal costs, not the customer, remain the focus. This happened recently at a large electronics firm. The executive brought in was highly thought of in the industry, as well as a leading conceptual thinker. He was provided with responsibility, but little authority, over the line functions. None of these functions were reorganized, and the corporate staff opposed any attempt to change performance measures, functional control, or reporting structures. They fought suggestions that they relinquish any corporate role in determining logistics strategies. The executive left within two years, and the company is actually worse off in terms of customer satisfaction and costs.

Line Management. Obviously, this is the best management approach for integrated, customer and industry-driven companies. Such a position involves direct responsibility *and* authority for the full range of logistics functions. The role requires a different type of organizational person: there are several instances where the promotion of a director of traffic or materials management just hasn't worked. In fact, in one large firm, such an appointment resulted in management paralysis. The executive simply could not get his arms around the role and its scope—he did not have a strategic or customer-driven perspective. It required the hiring of a senior manager, experienced in integrated logistics, to report to this executive and to assume most of the responsibilities. The requirements for a senior integrated logistics executive are discussed later in this chapter.

Continuous Process Improvement Philosophy

This is not intended to be a detailed discussion of continuous process improvement. There are a large number of books on the subject, varying in degree of excellence, usefulness, and implementability. However, since it is such an important characteristic of today's competitive, customer-driven logistics organization, we believe that it is necessary to say a few words on its requirements and key components as they pertain to logistics. These include:

Communications
Organizational structure
Employee empowerment and involvement
The team approach
Performance measurement and reward systems
Internal/external customer orientation
Process improvement and redesign
Education and training

Obviously, all of these interrelated facets are important. Some of them are vital from a logistics perspective. Supply chain management, because of its scope and multi-functional requirements, requires a focus on:

- Performance and monitoring (performance measures and reward systems)

- Management and improvement of the process (process improvement and redesign)
- Philosophy, awareness, education, training in tools, and transferability of best practices (education and training)

Performance Measures and Reward Systems. It is important that performance measures reflect team performance and output, rather than individual ratings. Advanced companies allow teams to dictate many of their performance measures, giving the teams only their goals and objectives. As with any endeavor, people will behave according to the ways in which they are measured; it is an important motivational factor. Measurements must be integrative, while the reward system (compensation and otherwise) must be based on total performance, rather than functional criteria. The key measures should be based upon cycle time, responsiveness, quality, and cost.

The setting of objectives and measures has been discussed in Chapter 2. Among issues worth repeating:

Are the measures updated and valid?

Are we measuring the right things?

Are the measurements team-based?

Does achievement of the measures have a business impact? Are the measures relevant?

Are the measures based on updated benchmarking, and do they reflect new realities and business conditions?

The team approach inherent in continuous process improvement serves to increase job enrichment, owing to the variety and scope of work, and the opportunity to see direct results from individual and team efforts. Appropriate performance measures complement this facet of team dynamics. Performance measures and reward systems are vital parts of incorporating and perpetuating a continuous improvement philosophy within the organization.

Process Improvement and Redesign. The firm must create an environment and structure that encourages continuous process improvement. This necessity has been given great publicity in the trade press, but few companies have actually implemented the philosophy successfully. Those that have, have reaped the benefits in terms of process simplification, quality improvement, cycle time reduction, increase in responsiveness, and strong customer orientation.

FIGURE 4-7
Continuous Process Improvement and Business Process Redesign

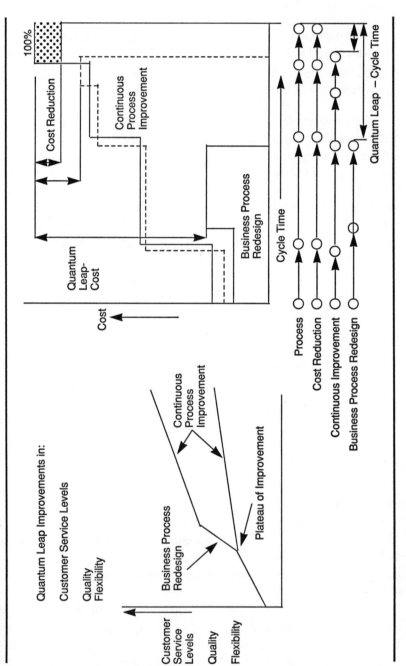

Source: Ernst & Young, Center for Information Technology & Strategy. All Rights Reserved.

The management and company focus must be on the *process*—the quality of the product depends on the quality of the process. Obviously, the people who execute the process know it best, and they must be empowered to manage, improve, and make key decisions regarding the process. There comes a point, however, where incremental improvement by line employees from within the process may not be sufficient to achieve a major competitive advantage or even to retain parity. In such cases, the process must be redesigned (the situation is shown in Figure 4–7).

Business process redesign involves re-engineering the process to achieve:

Integration with information technology

Competitive objectives and key indicators focused on cycle time, market responsiveness, flexibility, cost, and quality

A "pushing of the envelope" to obtain breakthrough processes, methods, and ways of doing business

The essential elements of business process redesign are shown in Figure 4–8. The steps required are:

- Development of a "vision" for the organization and the process
- Definition of the "as-is" state of the process
- Determination of process objectives and key indicators
- Assessment of current information technologies and relevant potential advances
- Process redesign—a "to-be" detailed picture of the process that explicitly views information technology as a driver
- Testing of the new process
- Implementation

Naturally, among the keys to business process redesign are employee involvement, and multi-functional teams and their input. Business process redesign can be a major undertaking and can also be expensive (in terms of money, effort, and the opportunity costs of employees' time). Additionally, it carries a certain degree of risk and can be somewhat traumatic in terms of developing the vision and assessing true current practice (during which industry analysis, customer surveys, and company performance can provide unpleasant surprises) and surfacing and testing assumptions (during which long-held and vested planning and operating assumptions may be discovered to be invalid and unimportant).

FIGURE 4–8
Business Process Redesign Integration of Process and Information
Technology

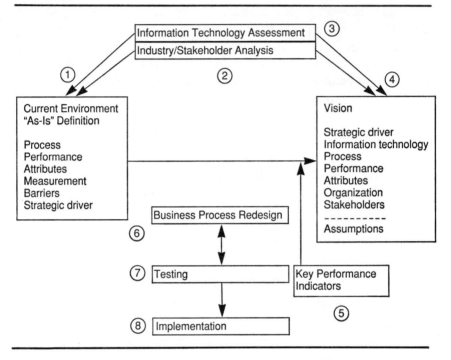

Business process redesign, nevertheless, is an immensely important tool for manufacturing companies, particularly to bring up-to-date processes which were designed with a functional organization and a different competitive marketplace in mind. Moreover, most business processes have evolved under the basic assumption that information technology was merely a support tool—an assumption that is clearly invalid today, when it is recognized as an integral part of the process. A quantum leap in performance is necessary to provide a sustainable competitive advantage.

Improvement Functions and Targets for Business Process Redesign. The following is a list of the major customer-oriented logistics functions. It is useful to keep this in mind when developing continuous process improvement programs and multi-functional teams.

- Transportation—inbound, outbound, intra-company
- Warehousing—plant-adjacent raw material and finished goods, field finished goods and spares, public and contract warehousing

- Inventory management—raw materials, work-in-process, finished goods, spares, OEMs/components
- Order processing—taking, management, filling, and invoicing
- Procurement and sourcing
- Supply-demand planning—forecasting, production planning, procurement planning, distribution requirements planning
- Information systems—planning, maintenance, justification, selection and acquisition, modifications, interface/integration, and implementation
- Customer service—spares, repairs, returns, field service, order fulfillment
- International logistics
- Engineering/packaging
- Carrier evaluation and selection process

On the other hand, those logistics processes which are typically major targets for business process design are multi-functional. Some of these are:

- Customer order receipt
  - Product delivery
  - Cash collection
- Supply-demand planning
- Forecast process cycle start to:
  - Production plan delivery to plants
  - Schedule delivery to contractors
  - Procurement plan delivery to suppliers
- Returns management/field service process
- Supplier certification process
  - Initiation to certification to delivery & usage

Education and Training. The challenge of the logistics organization of the future is to manage the change of both indirect and direct personnel into knowledge workers, and to provide them with the education, training, information, and tools they need to enhance their productivity and effectiveness. Skills required now, and those that will be required five years from now, will certainly be quite unlike the technical skills required a few years ago. A common set of educational requirements will revolve around process improvement and the incorporation of the continuous process improvement philosophy. The logistics manager of the future will require a different set of functional skills than has been required in the past (see Figure 4–9).

In many traditional organizations, two sets of skills were valued— those of the generalist and of the functional specialist. The generalist (typically an MBA with limited industry skills) knew a little bit about most things, generally at a top-side level. Generalists often found themselves in corporate and staff roles, and rarely had the experience to manage in the line organization. Consequently, they tended to focus on the common denominator for the organization—numbers. Functional specialists, however, knew a great deal about one function. They may have started out as generalists, but have typically spent a great deal of time in functional "silos." Together, these two types of managers have provided much of American industry with the finance-driven, functional "silo" per-

FIGURE 4–9
Human Resources—Employee Skills

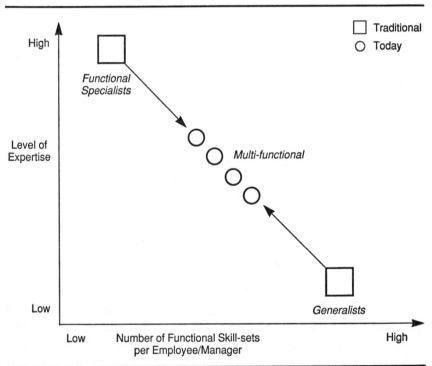

spective that has placed it at a serious competitive disadvantage. The logistics manager of the future (indeed, any manager in the organization of the future) must be a multi-functional specialist, capable of managing several key functions. A major path used by many successful U.S. and Japanese firms is rotation through several functions—lateral movement to gain experience. A "flat" organization cannot accommodate rapid promotions and advances through the organization as it did in the past. (This practice often resulted in senior executives who failed to understand the dynamics and needs of the industry and the customers, hence compromising the competitive futures of their companies.) Lateral movement is increasingly important in the development of multi-functional managers—

FIGURE 4–10
A Logistics Education Program

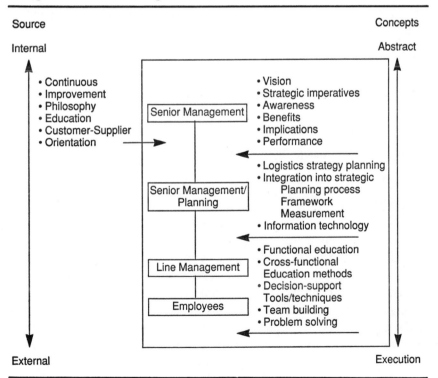

even more so because many business schools are busy turning out generalists or top-side graduates with little depth.

Planning and managing for a customer-driven organization which can use logistics as a competitive advantage, however, calls for additional education on several different fronts and planes. Figure 4–10 shows one such program used by a large electronics company. Among the more important issues stressed is *Awareness for senior management and other high-level functional executives*. Figure 4–10 also shows the strategic importance of logistics and the competitive imperatives of the marketplace, operational effectiveness, and the cross-functional usefulness of logistics. Also vital is *Education for senior management*. This should incorporate logistics into the strategic planning process along with marketing and manufacturing. *Education is also a factor for line management and employees*. It should deal with logistics management and requirements; negotiation and team-building skills; cross-discipline education; using decision support tools; and functional rotation.

Education programs such as these can achieve several objectives. They can:

• Help senior management appreciate the importance of logistics as a strategic component in the firm
• Provide a structure and guidelines for developing and implementing logistics strategies
• Enhance the integration efforts of the firm
• Develop line management and employees for the future

AN APPROACH

Figure 4–11 pulls these concepts together in an approach to developing coordination/organization strategies. A point to note here is that this is not a static, one-off, one-time process, and must be reviewed on a periodic basis. Whereas continuous process improvement is, by definition, an ongoing process, an organization structure, roles, and coordination must be refined periodically to accommodate market changes and compensate for miscalculations in initial organizational design and personnel appointments.

Major organizational changes should not be frequent—the old warning against institutions reorganizing merely to provide an illusion of pro-

FIGURE 4–11
An Approach to Developing a Coordination/Organization Strategy

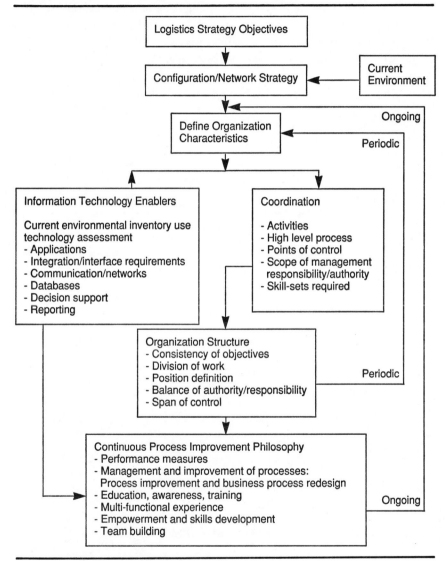

gress still holds true. There are few greater demoralizing actions in a company than frequent reorganizations. Unfortunately, frequent reorganization is, too often, a ploy by senior management to attempt to focus blame for poor performance on the structure, and to deflect it from the basic strategic, process, and leadership issues facing the company. Organization and coordination are just one aspect of a company's competitive posture.

CHAPTER 5

CUSTOMER SERVICE STRATEGY

DIMENSIONS OF CUSTOMER SERVICE AND COMPETITION

History and Definition of Customer Service through the Ages: toward a Definition of Customer Benefit

Modern definitions of customer service have their roots in the Industrial Revolution (as illustrated in Figure 5–1), when the invention of the power loom created a demand for mass production of clothing. The feudal aristocracy emerged as the first customers, as we know customers today. A critical shortage of goods to support the rapidly growing population, denial of land ownership, the Enclosure Movement, and mass migration to the cities resulted in an uneducated and unskilled labor force to operate the newly invented looms to produce products for the aristocracy. The result of poor customer service sometimes ended with the "customer" sending the manufacturer to the gallows!

As mass production was refined, the trend developed to combine land, labor, and capital to provide income to the peasants. During this period, two concepts emerged:

Specialization of labor. This concept simply stated that people should specialize in products that they were most efficient at producing, and buy goods to meet their other needs.

Interchangeable parts. This process allowed for standardized parts and the easy repair of broken goods.

As time went on, the concept of mass production improved to the point where factories could produce much more product than they could sell. This increased capacity, in the face of increasing competition, caused management to seek new ways of getting large amounts of product to distant customers—thus, the development of product promotion and the concept of customer accessibility, or distribution.

FIGURE 5–1
History of Customer Service

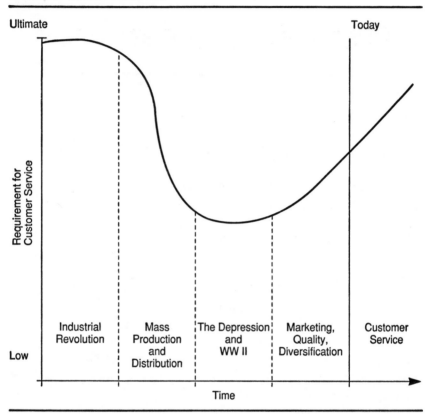

The arrival of the Depression slowed the development of sales and promotion advances in selling and delivering factory goods. World War II required so much productive capacity to meet military consumption that production of consumer goods was also curtailed. Following the war, consumers had many unfilled needs. Factories were unable to satisfy demand, which caused companies to expand their capacity. History repeated itself later when factories were again producing more than they could sell. This time, however, products were easily accessible to the customer.

This caused companies to develop the "marketing concept." The direction of this idea was to change from producing what the company could make, to producing what the customer *wanted*. Also, in view of the fact that it was seldom that a single product could meet the needs of the masses, an industry was created to research trends in customer needs. Companies often found that diversification of current products was more costly than resulting profits warranted. Those companies who were unwilling to make this change devoted themselves to serving "niche" markets. The companies who invested in diversification found that new products had to be developed and introduced rapidly, causing a greater need for the engineering-manufacturing interface and design disciplines.

Over time, quality became the issue upon which customers focused. Given increased competition and greater credit availability, customers searched for products that were more reliable and dependable. Management had to enhance its focus on being low *cost* producer to include being highest *quality* producer. Some manufacturers soon realized that, by increasing the total quality of their products, they could actually reduce the cost.

We have now arrived at a new era in the business of providing goods to customers. Service has been added to companies' original base of simply providing goods. Customers have advanced to the point of demanding more than just product features. Customer benefits that become more evident in the purchase of a product include some new needs along with the strengthening of some of the historical service concepts.

Customer Benefits. Included in the benefits today's customer seeks in the purchase of the product are:

• *Convenience* in obtaining and using the product, including its packaging. Easy operation of the product, or "user friendliness" is also an important convenience, along with the ability of the manufacturer to service the product and/or the customer after the sale.

• *Flexibility* of the product and its value chain to respond to special needs of the customer is an important benefit. The ability of the value chain to alter a product's basic features and options enables it to reach a greater customer base. Rigidity in product design can cause customers to search elsewhere, simply because minor features or options are unavailable.

• *Responsiveness* of the product and its value chain leads to increased sales, repeat business, and customer loyalty. The value chain must be sensitive to the customer's need to solve related product problems in short order. It must, additionally, be able to meet changing customer buying patterns, ad-hoc purchases, and emergency demands. This task is the most difficult to embody in the value chain, as it requires significant changes to a company's basic structure, planning, and operating philosophy.

• *Packaging* the product, including clear assembly and operating instructions, benefits the customer by providing ease of operation and product storage. Every reader has, at some point, purchased a toy with "some assembly required" that lacked passable assembly instructions. Such a situation typically biases a customer against any future purchase of similar products because the assembly turns out to be almost impossible. Industrial customers often must unpack and repack products for their specific needs, following which they must "de-trash" packaging and dispose of it—an extra expense and a non value-added step in their operations— resulting from non-customer-driven packaging. Packaging should also prevent damage to the product, damage that can further inconvenience the customer, and can result in greater order processing expenses and in returns.

From this brief historical perspective, a definition of customer service can be derived which applies time-tested concepts and common sense extensions to a basic produced good. For many companies, this is revolutionary. For other leading edge firms, it is a way of life.

> *Customer Service*: the activity of providing desired goods, quality, and total support to benefit every aspect of product use at a competitive price and in a timely manner.

Management and Measurement of Customer Service

The management of customer service has been defined earlier as

> exceeding customer expectations of service while minimizing total overall cost and maintaining response flexibility to changing market conditions

Figure 5–2 outlines an approach to managing the key elements of customer service. Primary to success, management must integrate these elements and approaches in its logistics strategy—they will ultimately decide success or failure in the marketplace. Most of these elements have been addressed in previous chapters. It is worthwhile, however, to refocus attention on their role in providing customer satisfaction.

Philosophy of continuous improvement. This involves a culture change within the organization, with shared values and norms that often differ quite significantly from traditional ones. It includes the concepts of internal/external supplier-customer orientation (addressed later in this chapter); the institutionalization of an ethic to improve continuously the process under control or influence; problem-solving methods at all levels; common goals and objectives cascading from corporate goals; cross-functional operations; and clear, two-way continuous communications. Hewlett-Packard, already cited as a company leading in excellence, is an example of such a culture. Its break-even time (BET) measurement exemplifies cross-functional striving toward a common competitive goal. The incorporation of a process on continuous improvement is a prerequisite to servicing the customer effectively.

Measure our performance against that of competitors, "best in class" companies, and customer requirements. It is essential that we know ourselves and our current performance—the basis for improvement strategies, whether continuous or quantum leap. (Elements of this have been addressed in Chapter 8.) Key elements include identification of customer service requirements and the performance of others through benchmarking techniques, which are briefly discussed later in this chapter. Customers (and companies) often define their requirements as those needs or perceived needs within their current line of sight. Identifying customer requirements involves "visioning" to identify those trends and requirements that will be in the line of sight over the next few years, and to prepare our response.

Identify and eliminate performance gaps. As performance gaps are identified in comparison to "best in class" companies, business process redesign methods can be applied to improve organizational effectiveness, inventory policies, manufacturing processes, and operational performance. Only after the business process redesign has been accomplished should a company apply information technology to close the performance gap. Simply stated, a company should improve its business process before making any attempt at automation or integration of information.

Analyze total cost-service level trade-offs. Few companies can satisfy every need or perceived need of customers without running out of resources. Customer service management involves a series of trade-offs and negotiations that provide service at *strategically profitable* levels. The bulk of these trade-offs involves inventory availability and packaging convenience. It may also involve undertaking those processes traditionally belonging in the customer realm but now deemed non-value added. For instance, many customers are moving toward outsourcing functions such as purchasing for non-critical items; managing inventory

FIGURE 5–2
Elements of Customer Service Management

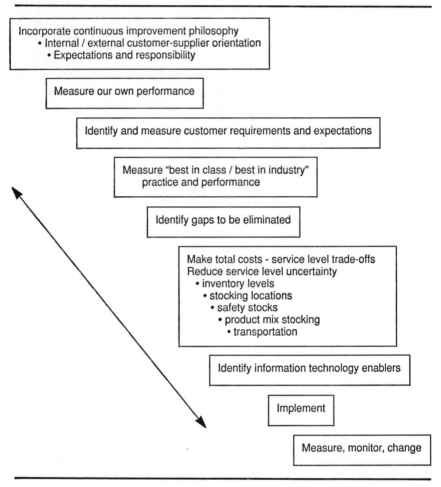

between dock, stock, and production floor; and invoicing. Suppliers must be prepared to take over and manage these functions for customers if it is required to gain a competitive advantage and to establish a long-term strategic partnership (see Figure 5–3). Strategically profitable customer service involves looking at the long term. Just as the experience curve dictates that pricing below current cost can increase volume and make a profit over the long term (while driving competitors out of business), we,

FIGURE 5–3
Customer Service as a Competitive Weapon Co-opting the Customer into
the Value Chain

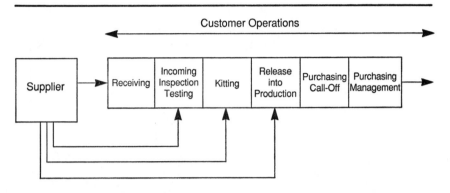

Stages of Assuming Customer Functions:

Stage 1: Shipping to customer
Stage 2: Shipping straight to customer incoming inspection
Stage 3: Shipping dock-to-stock through quality/testing certification
Stage 4: Shipping direct to customer point-of-use/line
Stage 5: Delivering to replenishment levels at customer's stock
Stage 6: Procuring other components for customer–"one-stop shop"

as companies competing on a business battlefield, must be prepared to
ignore the current costing system and provide services that will prove
profitable over the longer term (as shown in Figure 5–4).

Identify information technology enablers. The era where information
technology was viewed as a tool has passed. Today, information technology is an integral part of the process, along with people and equipment.
For competitive advantage through excellent customer service, information technology must be viewed as an enabler and part of process improvement and redesign (see Figure 5–5). In other words, the role of
identifying information technologies has passed from the MIS department
to the functional users, with MIS acting as facilitator, researcher, and
expert advisor. The topic of information technology is addressed at
greater length in Chapter 7.

Implement, measure, and monitor change. None of the above will
be worth too much if the firm does not put its strategies into practice,

134

FIGURE 5–4
Strategically Profitable Services The Customer Service-Incremental Volume Relationships

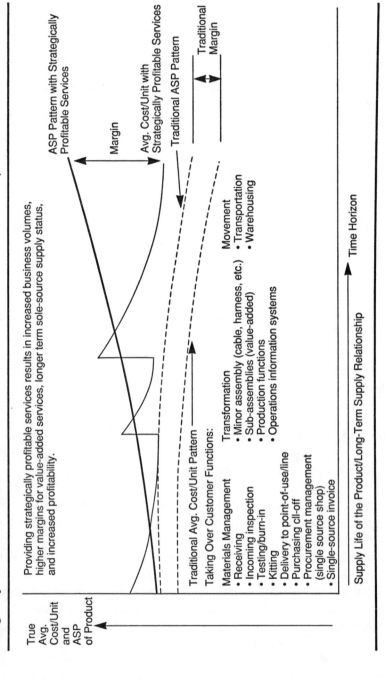

FIGURE 5–5
Information Technology Processes Today's Competitive View of a Process— *Integration* of Process, People, Equipment, and Information Technology

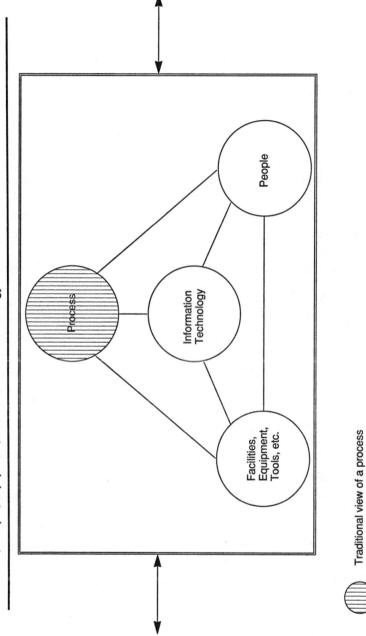

Traditional view of a process

measure their effectiveness, and refine them to reflect performance and changing market conditions.

Internal/External Customer Service Orientation

The philosophy of internal and external customers states that every individual or entity in the value chain has at least one customer and is a customer to at least one supplier. Each day, every person in a manufacturing environment assumes the role of customer. Each one knows his or her requirements and needs, and selects products and services which meet those needs. Typically, most view the customer as a consumer or end user of a product. However, customers are identified all the way back in the total supply chain.

Many companies have traditionally fostered a vertical approach to satisfying the external customer. Internal to the enterprise, value added elements focus on one organizational "silo" supplying the next organizational "silo" with some form of value added product until the product is in the hands of the final user. This approach to manufacturing and distribution causes several negative performance effects on the value chain, and leads to the institutionalization of resource-draining operating philosophies (the unwritten rules of a corporation). Such philosophies can destroy individual drive and lead to poor customer service, resulting in reduced corporate competitiveness in the marketplace. They lead to organizational inertia—movement arising from the weight of historical decisions, with no innovation or "hunger to succeed," two characteristics distinguishing the successful organization of tomorrow.

These operating philosophies will, doubtless, sound familiar to most logistics and manufacturing executives:

- "Black box" environment (typically, manufacturing, distribution, etc.)
- Functional "silos"—optimizing the parts rather than the whole enterprise
- "Over the wall" (usually, the hand-off from engineering to manufacturing)
- The feeling of, "I've done my job, now it's your turn."
- Detailed, precise, infrequently changed job descriptions which lock people into operating closets

- Performance measures which are based exclusively on efficiency and output
- Quarterback/running back/wide receiver analogies, instead of the team itself was the proper analogy
- The suspicion, "Those guys can't make/distribute/design (pick one) anything!"
- Individual/lone wolf/gunslinger/cowboy descriptions used admiringly—such people are long-term disasters in the making
- Narrow, one-dimensional training of personnel (or worse, no training at all)
- "End of the month/quarter hero" syndrome
- The complaint, "They never tell me what they want." (They often won't, if never asked.)

To resolve these wicked problems, management must adopt the horizontal view of the value chain and an operating philosophy based on:

- Talking frequently with customers. It would be well to remember that most of the hugely successful products have emerged from talking with customers, not from market research.
- Teamwork (horizontally and vertically, across all levels)
- Internal/external customer-supplier orientation
- Multi-functional skill-sets
- Viewing organizational output as a benefit to the customer
- Cross-functional operations
- Careful planning
- A coherent vision

The elimination of organizational "silos" will result in the transparency of the organization (viewed from the customer point of view, it looks like a single enterprise, not a collection of functions), and will lead to the integration of the horizontal supplier and customer relationships in the value chain. Problem solving will be refocused from the organizational hierarchy to the product/service itself. Change can then be identified and quickly implemented with management serving as facilitator and arbiter to ensure that changes are legal and are documented to eliminate future occurrences.

Figure 5–6 defines the customer service chain as a series of cus-

FIGURE 5-6
Enterprise as a Customer Service Chain

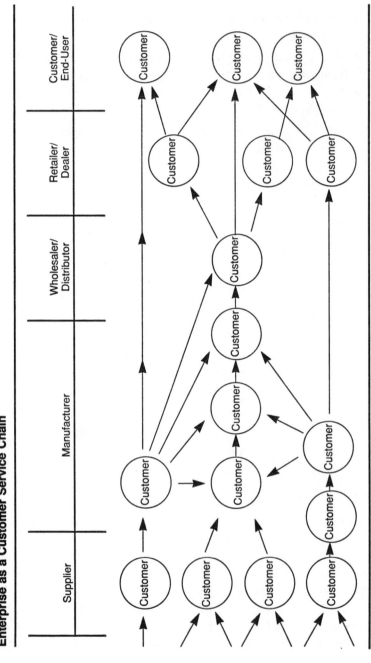

TABLE 5-1
Customer Expectations and Responsibilities

Customer Element	Expectations	Responsibility
Consumer/ End-User	• Immediate delivery of product • Product features • Quality of product • Functional adequacy • Best overall value • After-sale service/support • Convenience of purchase • Price	• Communication of requirements • Informed product knowledge • Competitive shopping • Communication of product/ service issues
Retailer/ Dealer	• On-time delivery • Accuracy of delivery • Undamaged goods • Vendor stocking • Packaging requirements • Emergency response • After-sale service/support • Cost/appropriate margins • Sales support	• Market forces/trends • Communication of sales plans/ partnerships • Concise ordering • Vendor/supplier knowledge • Understanding/communication of distribution requirements • Communication of product/ service issues
Wholesaler/ Distributor	• On-time delivery • Packaging • Reliable distribution network • Adequate inventory • Ease of material handling • Sales support • Cost/appropriate margins • After-sale service/support	• Location (between supplier and customer) • Bi-directional partnerships/ planning • Concise ordering • Product knowledge • Customer requirements knowledge • Supplier knowledge • Communication of requirements to supplier • Communication of product/ service issues

Manufacturer
  • Shipping/warehousing
  • Final Assembly/Test
  • Subassembly
  • Process
  • Procurement
  • Planning
    • Process
    • Material
    • Order
  • Engineering
  • Sales/Marketing
  • Management
	• Clear objectives
	• Concise strategies
	• Market/sales goals
	• Responsive product development
	• Best product solutions
	• Well engineered products
	• Stable orders
	• Quality materials
	• Well engineereed processes
	• Best suppliers at lowest cost
	• Quality parts and service
	• On-time delivery of material
	• Accurate equipment
	• Material handling
		• Vision
		  • Mission, goals, objectives
		  • Product requirements
		  • Design requirements
		  • Process requirements
		  • Customer service requirements
		• Realism
		  • Company capabilities
		  • Quoted time requirements
		  • Value-chain limitations
		• Continuous Improvement
		  • Assets
		  • People skills
		  • Process
		  • Product
		  • Customer service
		• Communications
		  • Employee involvement
		  • Strategic alliances
		  • Partnerships
		  • Customer issues

Supplier	• Good source of supply • Quality materials • Sales stability • Financial stability	• Vision • Realism • Continuous improvement • Communication

tomers requiring goods or services ultimately to benefit (as defined above) the end user or actual customer. In the case of many consumer goods firms, the end customer often means the retailer. It can be seen that each business is a supply chain consisting of many customers working toward a common goal.

Throughout the value chain, the internal and external customers have been identified along with their differing service expectations. This is not a one-way street. Flaig's "virtual factory" concept and our vision of the logistics enterprise of the future (chapter one) involve customer co-option and integration into the value chain. This implies that both suppliers and customers have needs, expectations, and corresponding responsibilities. Table 5–1 depicts the value chain from a customer element perspective, to identify expectations and corresponding responsibilities. It is important that business come to the realization that, if customer responsibilities are not assumed by the customer, it is necessary, and incumbent on the supplier to foster them by means of incentives, alliances, strategic relationships, and measurement-action systems.

To complete the customer-supplier orientation and lead to the institutionalization of good management practices for customer service, the inverse view of the value chain must be explored. The supplier chain, in Figure 5–7, shows that every element of the value chain leads to the final satisfaction of the customer, consumer, or end user. This dictates the supplier responsibility to use innovation in providing the basket of products and services that make up the benefit to the customer.

In summary, all individuals and entities are both suppliers and customers in the value chain, with attendant expectations and responsibilities. Management of companies striving to meet total customer expectations views the customer and supplier chains as an integrated unit. While addressing the internal needs of all customer elements of the value chain, manufacturers must also meet the responsibilities of total customer service for the end user. Balancing these two perspectives is the responsibility of management thoughout the supply, manufacturing and distribution chain. Figure 5–8 revisits the basic value chain and integrates the supplier and customer chains, with a representation of the activities required to serve the customer.

Customer Buying Criteria

During the sale process, the customer is driven by four obvious purchase criteria:

FIGURE 5-7
Enterprise as a Supplier Service Chain

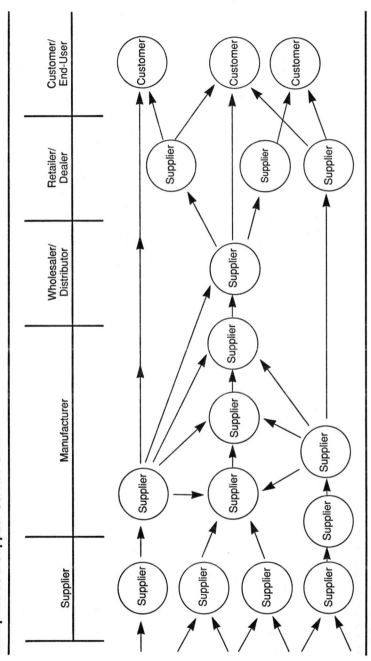

141

FIGURE 5–8
The Value Chain Enterprise as a Supplier-Customer Chain

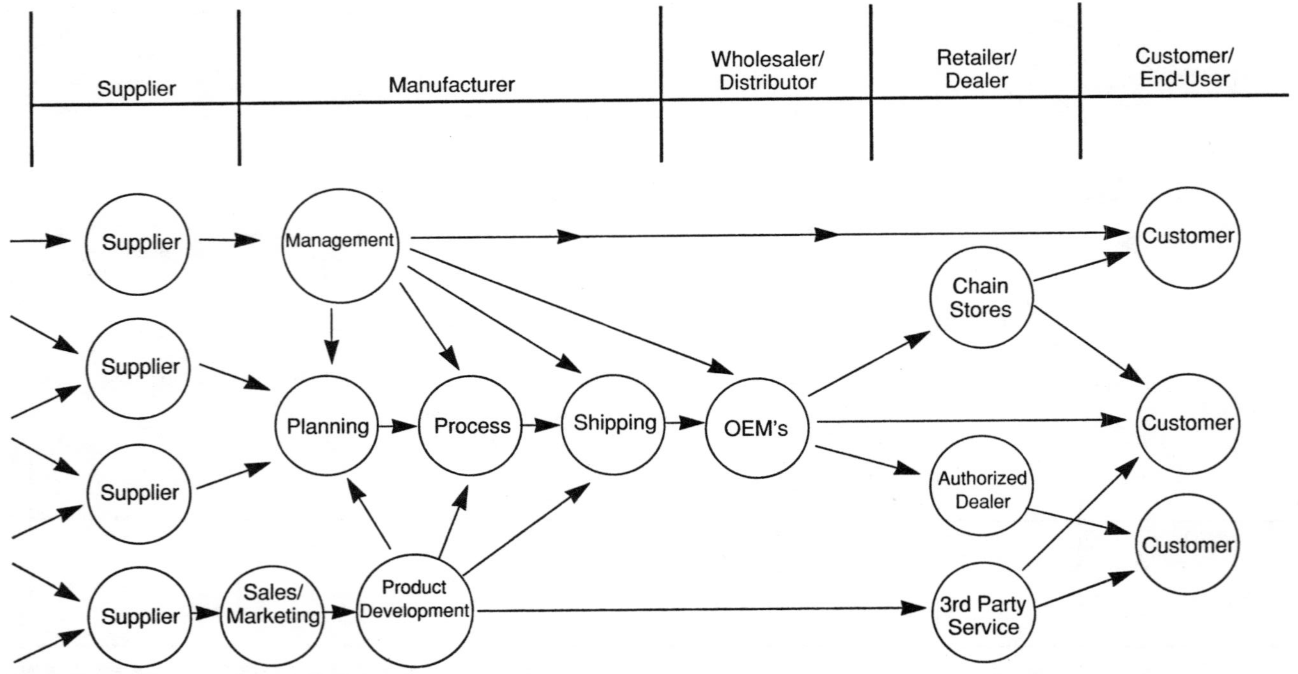

Price

Product features and options

Quality and reliability

Customer service

A fifth criterion, availability, may sometimes negate the other four. Managing availability involves inventory deployment, which is discussed in chapter six.

Research has shown that, from the customers' viewpoint, product features and quality are equally important sales components, as illustrated in Figure 5–9. Price, although an important component of the sale decision, is not the leading differentiator. Increasingly, the key factor in closing a sale is the service performed by the company in support (before, during, and after) of the goods purchased.

In order to sell the product, management must present the highest possible product performance elements to the customer. Product features, options, and price are tangible components of the entire sale equation. Quality and reliability can be proven statistically (even in the case of new products) through customer-supervised testing/burn-in for certification, publication of performance data, third-party reliability and comparison testing, and analogies with previous products.

Customer service very often becomes the differentiating means by which the purchaser will make the buying decision and has also been, until very recently, the least tangible of the sale components. Unfortunately, it is also the component most likely to cause the customer to undo the purchase and to look elsewhere, breaking the long-term relationship. Customer service has several quantifiable elements which management can track to measure their importance to the customer, and the company's performance against competitors.

Not all of these are applicable in every situation, but together they form a comprehensive picture of customer service requirements.

• *Order fill rate (by item)*. The rate at which purchase order line items are satisfied at point of sale

• *Order accuracy (by order)*. The rate at which purchase order items are accurately filled and delivered to the customer

• *On-time delivery*. The rate at which product is delivered to the customer at the committed time to satisfy the customer's definition of on-time delivery (within the hour, shift, day, etc.)

FIGURE 5–9
Customer Buying Criteria—Components of a Sale

- *Total order cycle time.* The elapsed time from order receipt to product delivery (depending on customer expectations, this can vary from hours to days, and occasionally, weeks)
- *Response to emergency requirements.* The time required to respond to and satisfy unplanned and unforeseen customer needs
- *Damaged goods.* The degree to which customers receive product damaged during transit or installation
- *Presence (inventory distance to customer).* Geographic relationship of supplier to customer in time and distance—a managed expectation which can be diminished by response and on-time delivery
- *In-stock inventory levels/availability.* The immediate availability for the most expedient order filling
- *Order completeness (line items and quantities).* The degree to which product delivery to the customer satisfies purchase order requirements of time and item quantity
- *Customer access to inventory/order status.* The ability of the customer to view the supplier's inventory and/or the order status

• *Response to customer complaints/issues.* Quality and time of response required to recover adequately from complaint to satisfaction

• *Packaging convenience.* The function, features, information, and quantities of product packaging needed for ease of shipment, receipt, storage, and use

Measurement. It is impossible for management to deal with problems without having adequate data upon which to base performance. Useful measurement systems for application across the entire value chain must focus on the following three activities and issues:

1. Definition of the customers' needs. This task is necessary to assess the real issues and requirements that will satisfy the customer with the purchase of the product and/or post-sale service. Some of the major issues and methods will be addressed in Chapter 8.

2. Creation of an appropriate and accurate system of measurement. This process and accompanying tasks must be performed with critical objectivity to be successful. The final goal is to create an integrated set of performance metrics of customer and internal value chain issues. The metrics must be accurate; communicated in a timely and frequent manner, and available, within reasonable limits, to the major stakeholders. Such a process is sometimes termed "measurement by objective and process." Measurement is a thread that runs through this book, and has been addressed in Chapters 2 and 4.

3. Benchmarking of products, processes, and the business that supports them. This process is designed to compare internally and externally the company's product(s) and processes against those of the competition. It is also designed to compare the products' supporting value chain against practices internal to the enterprise, best practices in the industry, and "Best of the Best" and World Class performance objectives.

The process of benchmarking is both cultural and methodological. It is often very difficult for companies to justify the time and cost of taking an introspective look at their operations. After all, "the business has always performed well in the past," and it is difficult to allocate internal resources to accomplish this task. Yet, as leading corporations have shown, it must be an integral part of the management process. In several companies there has been a groundswell of support for better measurement systems: operating managers and supervisors have very often taken the initiative to try to incorporate change from below (change without an executive "champion" or group of "champions"). Sometimes such change percolates to senior management but, in most cases, such an approach is unsuccessful in institutionalizing the practice.

Some of the reasons why this may be true center around the greater knowledge of the industry and competition at lower management levels. Changes in the attitude and practices of these individuals can be attributed to several factors.

The information explosion. The proliferation of trade journals and awareness seminars has increased awareness of the possible. Many managers read journals and attend seminars seeking ways to improve their jobs and remove some of the daily "headaches" of their responsibilities. Most good seminars related to new methods result in a rush of energy and excitement after communicating with industry peers who appear to be spending more productive hours in their jobs.

Competitive awareness. Most managers realize that the products offered by their company are only as good as the value chain producing them. They have probably seen, and may have been a part of, a company which lost its competitive edge. They have more than likely witnessed or experienced cutbacks and, perhaps, the demise of businesses similar to their own. This "survival of the fittest" reality often causes these individuals to take matters into their own hands: they realize that if cutbacks are required, they will probably suffer before the executives responsible for the malaise.

Restructuring. Leaner organizations have forced managers to look for new ways to increase productivity and to do business. A prerequisite for this is change—something that many people resist. Those individuals who are able to accept change will survive. The lower levels of the organization, in many cases, are more amenable to change.

In many other companies the opposite situation exists. Management executives have directed their people to start the process of incorporating change into the tactical aspects of the operation. Many of these efforts have not produced the all-important true "champions" at sub-levels in the organization. Many line managers, in these cases, are too involved in the daily firestorms to want to accept additional responsibilities.

In both of the above cases, the result is often the same—frustration, and failure to institutionalize the process of change. In fact, change initiatives which lack the full support of the entire organization can have an adverse impact on the effectiveness of the business. For this reason many companies have incorporated methods for change that create a plan from the "top down" and specify implementation from the "bottom up". Consistency throughout all levels of the company and the value chain can be achieved only with planning and implementation activities shared with the major stakeholders of the enterprise. Companies which are successful at the art of change and performance measurement work very hard at building a championship *team* instead of relying on *individual* champions.

The accomplishment of change in the enterprise, however, must be measured and controlled to maintain the original plan and to adjust to the reality of everyday problems. It is important that all levels of the enterprise be involved not only in the planning and implementation of change, but also in the creation of a system to measure the effects of change. Many managers have taken the risk of providing an umbrella for their subordinates in terms of measuring according to non-traditional indicators. Measurement, and benchmarking to set targets, are critical components of the change process. Many traditional methods of measurement focus on the efficiency of labor, rather than on moving material along the value chain more rapidly and with greater quality.

Measures must focus on the customer to be effective. One set of customer service measures that were developed for the supply chain in a company included:

Backorders as a percent of total (dollars/unit sales/total orders placed)

Planned versus actual customer service levels (fill rates by line item/ order)

Actual inventory turns versus planned

Actual "days" of inventory versus planned

Turnaround (order cycle time, invoice cycle time)

Delivery performance and reliability

Errors in paperwork

Demand fill rate measured by dollars demand shipped/dollars demand ordered

Quality (damaged and inaccurate shipments)

Customer feedback and complaints (response time on first call)

These measures were benchmarked against the competition and against customer needs. The company was surprised to find that, while it appeared better than its competition in terms of satisfying customer needs (also meeting most customer expectations), its inventory levels were the highest in the industry by a considerable amount—the company was buying customer satisfaction at a high price. Additionally, its performance was not consistent across geographical regions and product lines. Stepwise improvement targets were set based on customer feedback, competitor performance, and the performance of companies considered "best in class".

Some of the improvement projects that resulted were:

- A forecasting process, and a process to match demand projections and history with inventory stocking levels
- Information systems integration of planning, forecasting, and inventory visibility
- Automation of the invoicing function and cross-checking of order information with the goal of eliminating the invoicing function altogether

Competitive Benchmarking. For product-oriented enterprises to be successful, they must redefine the competitive battlefield. But, before any redefinition can occur, the existing battlefield must be mapped. Knowing what the competition provides to the customer is essential to provide strategic direction for the enterprise. Information about the operations (performance, process) of the competition can also provide the enterprise with valuable competitive objectives. There are some fairly simple ways of gathering this type of information.

- *Ask the customer.* This is probably the best way to benchmark product and service performance. The customer is the most important stakeholder in the enterprise, often with explicit expectations of the enterprise's product and service compared to the competitors'. These expectations involve perceptions of both service and quantifiable objectives. For instance, one major computer company defined its on-time delivery requirement from suppliers as $-1 + 0$ days to committed delivery date (one day early and no days late). A survey of suppliers revealed that fully a quarter were confused about this requirement and were not aware of its very high relative importance in the supplier evaluation process.
- *Ask the Suppliers.* This is probably the easiest way to benchmark the enterprise against the industry. Suppliers, as stakeholders in the business, want and need the company to succeed. Soliciting their perspective vis-à-vis the competition and the industry is a valuable exercise. In fact, their customers may, and probably do (if this is a world class supplier), include

the competition. For instance, one company learned from a common supplier that a competitor asked for kitted components in a single "pop-open" package in lots to be delivered every day. The empty packages were returned through backhaul for reuse. The supplier, while not including a discussion of price (they often do not), implied that the price paid by the competitor was higher. A computational analysis revealed that the competitor probably enjoyed a 5–7 percent advantage in purchased material cost, since some of the components were expensive. The company, thus spurred, began redesigning its processes and reorganizing, to achieve a process to provide superior results. It consolidated suppliers into "one-stop shops" (the new set of suppliers included the one that provided the intelligence), and reconfigured its production lines for just-in-time to handle smaller, more frequent lots.

• *Survey the industry's published best practices.* Human nature encourages the publishing of details regarding successful ventures. Almost all industries have an association of manufacturers, suppliers, and academic experts who publish information on successes and trends. Some industry associations, like the American Electronics Association (AEA), publish metric tables listing actual performance levels of the competition and other industry comparables. These, and other secondary research (trade journals, etc.) are excellent sources of relevant information.

• *Survey industry experts.* There are many individuals, consulting firms, and academicians who can be very useful to the intelligence gathering toolbox. An important factor here is that the firm must understand its objectives. If the objectives are not clear, these experts could provide misleading trend information and advice. It is important to manage these relationships carefully in terms of objectives, expectations, time, and money.

• *Ask the employees.* Empower employees, as the most concerned stakeholder group, to benchmark the enterprise. Their interests are tied in with the success of the business. They are also the first line of defense against stagnation. Keeping them involved as active participants in the strategic vision is important, because they are the tactical implementors.

The processes of benchmarking and measurement are interdependent, as shown in Figure 5–10. Benchmarks establish the criteria management needs to compare the enterprise with the competition and to set world class targets. Information systems and decision-support tools, (addressed in chapter seven) are available to give management an instant picture of

FIGURE 5–10
Benchmarking and Measurement

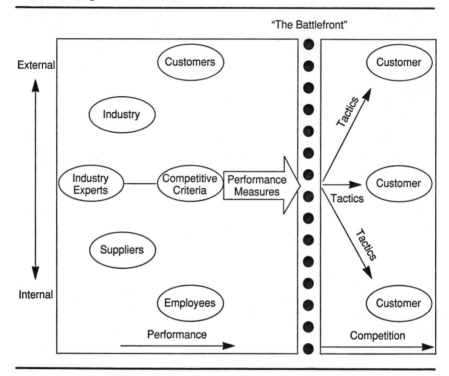

the enterprise's performance on the competitive battlefield. Used together, they provide management with the concrete information and market imperatives needed for better direction of the supply chain to focus on a delighted customer.

David T. Kearns, CEO of the Xerox Corporation, has defined benchmarking as

> . . . the continuous process of measuring products, services, and practices against the toughest competitors or those companies recognized as industry leaders.

Figure 5–11 illustrates the benchmarking steps that Xerox has used in its very successful attempt to be the competitive leader in its industry. We highly suggest you take the time to read *Benchmarking: The Search for Industry Best Practices That Lead to Superior Performance* (Milwaukee:

FIGURE 5–11
The Benchmarking Process Benchmarking Process Steps

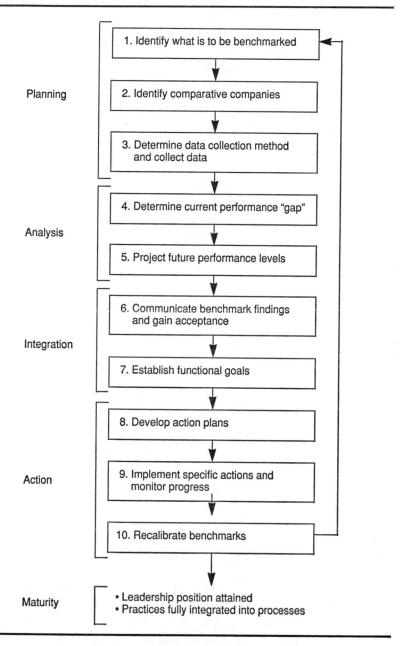

Source: Robert C. Camp, *Benchmarking* (Milwaukee: ASQC Quality Press, 1989).

ASQC Quality Press, 1989). Authored by Robert C. Camp, this book explains the benchmarking process in detail.

Today the manufacturer's president does not have to pay the ultimate personal price for poor customer service, as in feudal days. However, the enterprise will ultimately pay the same price if customer delight is not achieved. The excellent competitors of the future will see to it.

COST-SERVICE TRADE-OFFS IN CUSTOMER SERVICE MANAGEMENT

To be a viable competitor in the customer service era, an enterprise will be required to commit some capital. If a strategy for customer service and a performance measurement system has been adopted, the customer service trade-off parameters and requirements will be known. When combined with a cost management system that provides a true cost picture of product lines (by attributable cost based on cost drivers, not allocations based on labor or equipment utilization), management will be able to respond quickly and favorably to changing conditions.

Leading companies have instituted strategies and measurement systems that can capture the true costs of selling and servicing the product. Several factors become important in being able to measure, determine, and control an optimum balance between cost, potential sales, and customer service. Just as in the benchmarking process, an information-gathering system and decision-support tools are necessary to report and analyze performance and cost of the customer service strategy. Some of the cost factors involved in these trade-off decisions include:

- *Material cost*. The cost of the materials used in the product build
- *Packaging cost*. The cost of packaging throughout the supply chain
- *Marketing/sales cost*. The cost of initiating sales and leads, developing customer requirements, and processing orders
- *Product development cost*. The cost of developing and designing the product, in terms of expended cost and time to market cost.
- *Overhead costs*. The costs associated with the manufacture of the product—tooling, capital equipment, facilities, utilities, etc.
- *Transportation cost*. The cost of the means to move the product from the last production process to the customer

- *Storage/inventory costs*. The costs of storing and handling in-process and finished goods
- *Service cost*. The cost of providing customer satisfaction through after-sales service and support
- *Indirect costs*. The costs of indirect and support functions that assist in the non-direct tasks of transforming, storing, packaging, and moving the product.

It is the explicit responsibility of for-profit businesses to be profitable: there is really little other rationale for their existence. Today, with increasing customer expectations, it is obvious that customer service is not free. For instance, if inventory is maintained at a high level to service the customer through all possible demand fluctuations and operating uncertainties, the results are significant downside cost ramifications. However, if inventory is maintained at a low level, the penalty may be lost sales or customer dissatisfaction.

As sales and market penetration increase, the cost to maintain optimum service levels also increases. The important task for management is to maintain the balance between sales and optimum service. Figure 5–12 illustrates the point that there is an optimum level of customer service to be achieved between the sales dollar and the cost of servicing the sale.

Providing optimum service levels may require increased levels of capital and working capital, but the benefits in terms of improved customer service and sales can be significant. Table 5–2 shows some of the potential cost trade-offs. Areas of improved resources may include one or more of the following:

Facilities
Inventory deployment
Product/process design
Communications
Information systems
Personnel

The issues involved have surfaced through a series of questions inherent to logistics strategy. Many of these have been addressed in other chapters of this book, but it is important that they be highlighted here, in their role as fundamental issues of customer service management. Management can make some of the major trade-offs necessary by analyzing

FIGURE 5–12
Logistics Management Cost Trade-Offs

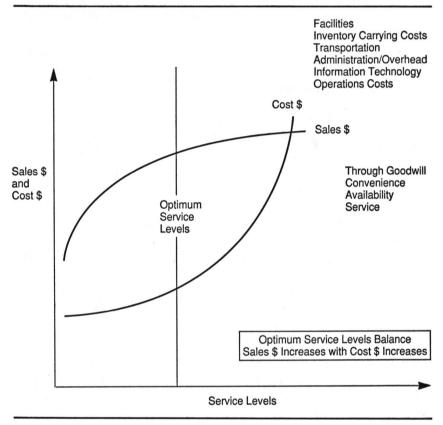

Facilities
Inventory Carrying Costs
Transportation
Administration/Overhead
Information Technology
Operations Costs

Cost $

Sales $

Sales $ and Cost $

Through Goodwill
Convenience
Availability
Service

Optimum Service Levels

Optimum Service Levels Balance
Sales $ Increases with Cost $ Increases

Service Levels

Source: From Gene R. Tyndall, "Logistics Costs and Service Levels: Evaluating the Trade-Offs," *1987 Journal of Cost Management for the Manufacturing Industry,* Vol. 1, No. 1, Warren, Gorham & Lamont.

the inventory, processes, distribution, transportation, customer service, and information needs of the entire supply chain. Figure 5–13 shows the major cost trade-offs for computation and analysis, while Figure 5–14 outlines methods used to make cost trade-off decisions. These tools and techniques have been discussed under different contexts throughout this book. Their applicability ranges from local analysis to global and system-wide analysis, and they can be used for "point-in-time" analysis as well as "what if" and sensitivity modeling. Safety stocks, for instance, have been addressed in chapter six, while financial and optimization modeling are integral parts of chapter 3.

TABLE 5–2
Cost Trade-offs: Potential Cost vs. Benefit

Resource	Potential Cost to Value Chain	Benefit to Value Chain
Facilities	• New facility 　Manufacturing 　Distribution 　Sales/service 　Suppliers • Re-aligned facility use 　Rearrangement • Co-location • Warehousing	• Improved response time • Order accuracy • Simplified material 　management
Product/Process Design	• Product introduction teams 　Design for 　　manufacturability 　Design for distribution 　Design for customer 　　satisfaction • Organizational realignment • Policy changes • Equipment changes	• Incorporated "voice of the 　customer" 　Product loyalty 　Problem solving • Reduced cost 　Manufacturing 　Distribution 　Service 　Engineering change • Involvement 　Value chain entities
Communications	• Network architecture 　Satellite 　WAN/LAN 　Telephone/FAX 　Mail handling 　EDI • System integration	• Real-time response • Customer contact • Data accuracy
Information System	• System analysis • Strategic information 　planning • Enhanced system design 　New systems 　Reverse engineered 　　systems • System implementation 　Hardware/software 　　procurement 　Software modification 　Education and training	• Decision support • Accurate data/order 　accuracy • Improved response time • Communication • Control
Personnel	• Organizational realignment 　Customer driven • Education and training • Empowerment	• Employee involvement • Improved communication • Customer relations • Problem solving/decision 　support
Inventory Deployment	• Stocking points • Stocking levels 　Taxes 　Carrying cost	• Customer satisfaction • Accessibility

FIGURE 5–13
Making Major Trade-Offs: Areas for Analysis

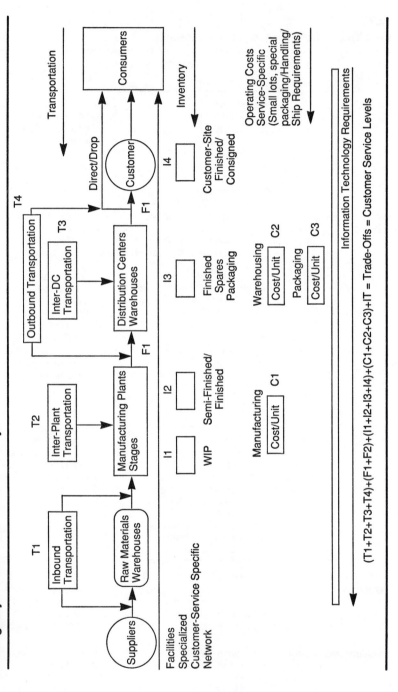

$$(T1+T2+T3+T4)+(F1+F2)+(I1+I2+I3+I4)+(C1+C2+C3)+IT = Trade-Offs = Customer Service Levels$$

FIGURE 5–14
Making Cost Trade-Offs: Methods for Analysis

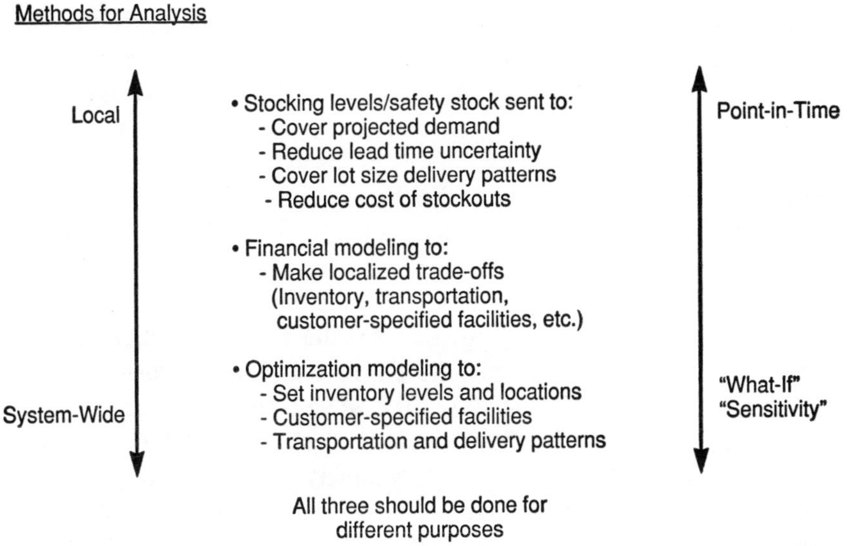

Methods for Analysis

Local — System-Wide

• Stocking levels/safety stock sent to:
  - Cover projected demand
  - Reduce lead time uncertainty
  - Cover lot size delivery patterns
  - Reduce cost of stockouts

• Financial modeling to:
  - Make localized trade-offs
    (Inventory, transportation,
    customer-specified facilities, etc.)

• Optimization modeling to:
  - Set inventory levels and locations
  - Customer-specified facilities
  - Transportation and delivery patterns

Point-in-Time

"What-If"
"Sensitivity"

All three should be done for
different purposes

It is important to realize that all these analyses really have the same
goal—the optimization of the customer service level—cost mix,
whether the costs are associated with facilities, inventory, or
technology.

Facilities

Customer service-driven strategies require that the enterprise audit the
real estate and network issues of the existing value chain for "gaps."
These issues should include:

Location of suppliers to manufacturing and customer(s)

Flexibility of suppliers to support multiple manufacturing sites

Co-location of engineering and manufacturing

Multiple site and stage production strategy

Warehousing and distribution center strategy

Product return and service strategy

Sales office placement

Defining and locating the network has been addressed in Chapter 3—Configuration Network Strategy. Network strategies are very costly. Since land purchase, lease, and construction are capital-intensive undertakings, management must proceed with the knowledge, based on analysis, that customer service will indeed be improved. Also, management needs to know the cost trade-offs associated with the customer service levels desired. For instance, if the customer is satisfied with a three day delivery lead time, it would be imprudent for the manufacturer to build a dedicated distribution center local to that customer.

Management must maintain its integrated business plan perspective of the entire supply chain in order to make the best customer service facility decisions. Two basic facilities-related questions should be asked, to aid in this decision-making process: Are the current facilities adequate to support the enterprise in embarking on a new level of customer service? If not, what facility aspect(s) of the value chain are lacking?

Subsequent questions should include those associated with configuration/network strategy: Should the company own distribution centers, contract, or rent public warehouses? What are the trade-offs? Can a single manufacturing facility meet the customer's needs, or are multiple sites required? What are the trade-offs? Are suppliers located close to the manufacturing facility and the customer? What are the trade-offs? Are the sales/support/service centers integrated and close to the customer? What are the trade-offs?

Essentially, questions regarding facilities revolve around geography. If one of the goals of improved customer service is the shortened elapsed time from raw material to product delivery, then strategic geographic location becomes an imperative.

Product/Process Design: Velocity and the Value Chain

Internal aspects of the manufacturing enterprise need to be addressed in the same manner. It has been noted that 80 percent of the manufacturing cost of a product is "sunk" at the time of design release. This cost is reflected in several ways. Materials management, quality, process, and in some cases, distribution costs are beyond the individual control of the value chain entity.

In recent years, several companies have embarked on design for manufacturing initiatives to improve their ability to introduce new products into the manufacturing environment with greater speed and lower cost. This has been accomplished by using product introduction teams to nurture a product from concept through the sustained manufacturing process. This is a good first step, but attention to the entire value chain must be maintained. The nurturing of new products must be a process that includes *all* "customers" in the value chain. The reasons are readily apparent. The computer industry was among the first to experience what can be termed "the product introduction avalanche": product life expectancy was reduced in several cases to a matter of months. To remain competitive, management had to focus not on the *speed* of the new product introduction, but on the *velocity* with which products were introduced. Recalling high school physics, speed is the relative quickness in which an object moves through space. Velocity is the speed and direction in which an object moves through space. If an enterprise controls the velocity through the value chain of new product introduction, it will produce products at a known time and cost to the customer. The customer must be an involved stakeholder in the process if there is to be optimization of overall customer service.

Communication

Effective communications throughout the value chain significantly affect total costs. The ability to communicate quickly the needs of all customers in the value chain will greatly reduce the time required for the product to traverse the value channels. Again, unique situations must be considered when choosing the most appropriate means for communication lines. The two questions one must ask are:

> What do customers want to communicate, and how do they want to communicate? Can new methods of communication generate an advantage for the company with the customer?
>
> Are current communication methods adequate to satisfy the customer's current desires and possible future needs?

Communication methods usually translate into a capital-intensive, technology-driven initiative. Several alternatives exist for the enterprise; to choose the best alternative, a few questions should be asked:

> Does the customer wish to incorporate electronic data interchange (EDI) technology? Is the customer currently collecting point of sale information? What will the customer's needs be two years from

now? (With rapid advances in communications and network technologies, five years may be too long a horizon.)

How good is the communication between the sales force and engineering? Manufacturing? Customer service? The distribution centers? Key suppliers? The customer?

Do the suppliers have EDI capability? Are they planning to incorporate EDI in the foreseeable future? Is there any benefit to incorporating supplier EDI in the enterprise?

Does the company currently incorporate local area networks (LAN) into the information systems architecture? Wide area networks (WAN) to remote facilities?

Effective means of communication will greatly reduce the amount of confusion in transmitting the needs of the customer throughout the organization. Nowhere is this need more apparent today than in the supply chain—the "demand satisfying activity". It will also demonstrate to the customer that the enterprise is sincere about responding quickly to needs.

Several companies are incorporating such information technology and connectivity standards into their standard procurement/buying agreements. The "virtual factory" concept, shown again later in this chapter, demands such information linkages.

Technology alone, however, is not the answer. The enterprise should be prepared for all levels of sophistication in communications tools used by the customer from Pony Express through Star Wars technology. It is not technology, but its *effectiveness* that counts. One major Japanese multinational company defined its EDI strategy as simply "fax". Another company installed, at great expense, terminals and EDI hook-ups to the engineering department of a major potential customer. It believed that the customer's engineers would design its parts into the product (because they could place small engineering orders quickly without having to go through the corporate purchasing bureaucracy), and that it would emerge as the preferred supplier. The engineers complied, but large purchases for production were handled by the customer's procurement function, which put the orders out to bid. This investment did not pay off. The successful customer-focused enterprise must possess the ability to respond quickly, no matter what mode of communication is used.

Information Technology

Information is the thread holding the entire value chain together. Enterprise management should view the methods and procedures of collecting, organizing, and dispersing decision-enabling information as the most valuable weapons in its competitive arsenal. The "virtual factory" framework (Figure 5–15) illustrates the role of information technology in achieving the competitive imperatives of the market. Information is the linking factor.

It is important that management be rational and careful when determining the most appropriate system to best serve its customers. They must provide an information support system that adds value to the product from the perspective of customer service excellence. Important customer-driven questions must be posed: Is the customer dependent upon enterprise supplied information for proper and continuous use of the product? For ordering and managing inventory? What type of information (and in what form) will best serve the product and customer? Are the current information systems and technologies adequate to meet customer and product requirements? In five years? In ten years? Chapter seven will address the information strategies and technologies required to meet customer service needs in a competitive and cost-effective manner. It is safe to say in general that a good customer and management decision-drive information system is one of the key enablers of competitive customer service. The costs and benefits cover the entire spectrum of operation.

Personnel

Managers cannot forget that the customer is human, and that human beings are the first link in the communications network. As discussed through this book, operating in the customer service era requires that management personnel adjust their attitudes toward themselves, their suppliers, and their customers. The value chain is made up of people who are both customer and supplier. The questions that the enterprise must ask itself concerning its people, therefore, revolve around motivation, empowerment, and training: Are employees satisfied and confident in themselves, the product they represent, their management, and their company? If not, why? Do customers feel that their needs are being met in a friendly, professional, and timely manner? If not, why? Are employees

FIGURE 5-15
Information Technology and the Virtual Factory

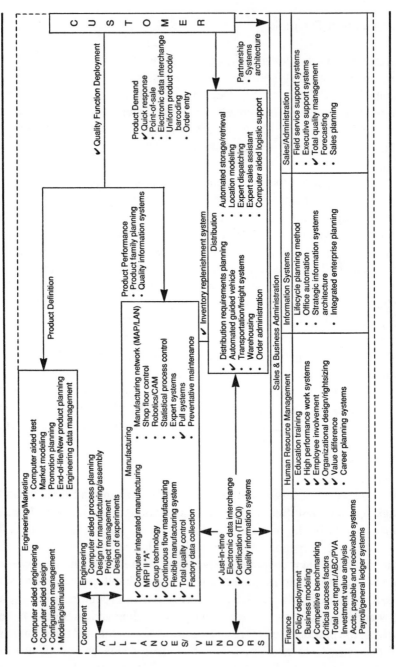

Source: Scott Flaig, Ernst & Young Center for Information Technology & Strategy.℠ All rights reserved.

162

willing to go the extra mile to ensure customer satisfaction? Does management allow them to do so?

People—the customers—judge people. Management must recognize that products and services are an extension of the personality of the enterprise. Chapter 4 addressed the organizational and structural issues necessary for ensuring a continuous improvement, customer-supplier-oriented culture. It is probably this facet of customer service management, more than any other, which determines an enterprise's success.

Managing the Next in Line—The Retailer

It is necessary, as part of this discussion of the enterprise as a supplier-customer chain, to address the all-important issue of managing the retailer. There may be problems at the retail level. As an example, a manufacturer has been doing all the right things to improve operations and customer service levels. The product, however, is delivered to the shelf of a retailer which has done little to improve *its* service to the customer or to ensure that product is always displayed. A situation arises where a product is out of stock or a store employee with a poor service attitude alienates a potential customer: the customer leaves the store without making the purchase. As a result, every stakeholder in the enterprise is a loser. This is a very serious issue today for most consumer products and electronics companies—the retailer decides the sale to a considerable extent. Figure 5–16 illustrates the issues mentioned in the above example, and some of the methods used in their management.

Many consumer products companies spend a great deal of money researching the end customer—how to "pull" him into the store. Yet, as illustrated in Figure 5–16, the channel can really decide the fate of the sale and, ultimately, market share. This is a problem that has yet to be resolved through an effective set of solutions that work across the board. It is an area where "break glass" thinking, problem resolution, and supply chain integration strategies must be developed. To manage this, companies use a number of methods, as outlined below. (This is by no means a comprehensive list, and varies in effectiveness).

• *Education of Retailers.* Several manufacturers have joined with retailers in providing technical education, customer-orientation, and satisfaction education—a joint education partnership. This is essentially true in the world of personal computers. Compaq Computer, for instance, is

FIGURE 5-16
Issues, Effects and Management of Channels

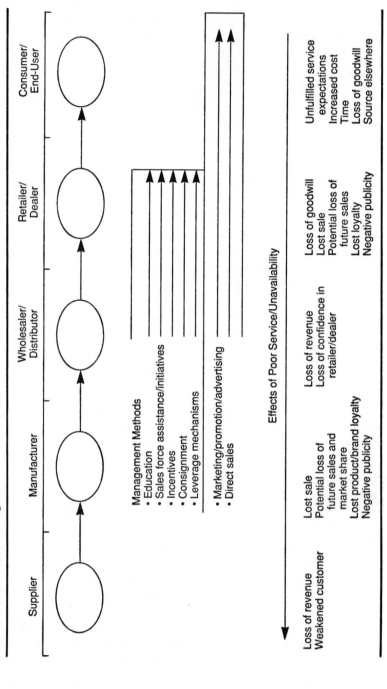

attempting to fight the highly trained sales engineering forces of its major competitors by training part of its dealer sales force in technical issues.

• *Manufacturer Sales Force Assistance/Initiatives.* Many consumer goods companies use field sales personnel to assist retailers in setting up displays, in checking, and in calling for replenishment of, stocks on the shelf.

• *Incentives.* Consumer products firms routinely provide money incentives and dealer discounts to encourage point-of-sale promotion and price reductions of their products.

• *Consignment.* An indirect method to provide financing and monetary benefits involves sending goods on consignment to distributors and retailers. In the electronics components business, this "ship from stock and debit" syndrome results in overall higher prices as manufacturers assume the risk of inventory and, as the practice is industry-wide, provides little advantage to the individual manufacturer.

• *Leverage Mechanisms.* The most direct and expensive method of influencing retailers, this involves issues such as ownership and financing. If a significant portion of the channel's sales are from the manufacturer, this can provide the volume leverage necessary to force customer-oriented change.

Ultimately, the actions of supply chain representatives impact the ability of the enterprise to compete. Every member of the enterprise has the responsibility to ensure that a positive attitude is embodied in the end product and service. It is management's responsibility to ensure that this happens as a prerequisite to competitive success.

DEVELOPING A CUSTOMER SERVICE STRATEGY

Figure 5–17 depicts an approach to developing a customer service strategy within the overall logistics strategy planning framework. While the configuration/network strategy details the facilities, and the coordination/ organization strategy maps out the organization structure, roles, responsibilities, and coordination of like activities, the customer service and integrated inventory strategies are interrelated—they deal with the costs and achievement levels of customer service. They follow directly from the structural decisions made in the configuration/network and coordination/organization strategies.

FIGURE 5–17
An Approach to Developing a Customer Service Strategy

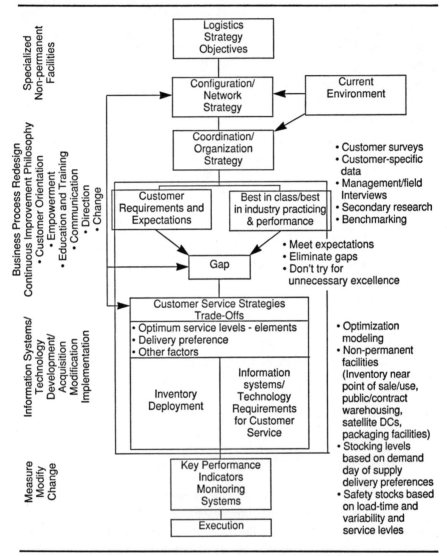

FIGURE 5–18
Evaluating Response to Customers—Order Turnaround Lead Times

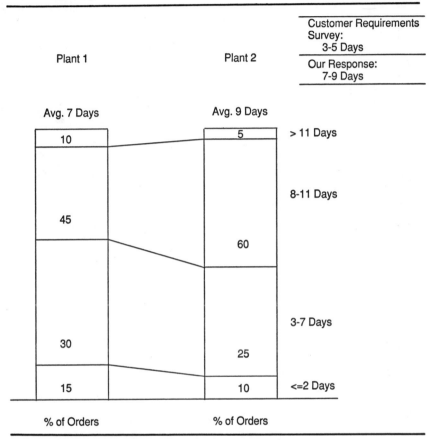

The first step involves determining customer requirements and expectations, using methods such as customer surveys and interviews, interviews with line management and field sales/service personnel, etc. (This will be addressed in some detail in Chapter 8.) The next involves setting targets by benchmarking for best performance, practices, and processes against the industry, best in class, and best of the best.

The "gaps" between company performance, practice, and targets are then identified. The object is to eliminate these strategic gaps, not to try to achieve unnecessary excellence which can lead to expense without

FIGURE 5-19

Trade-Offs in Customer Service Levels—Inventory Costs Modeling Results: Reduction in Service Levels Can Result in Significant Cost Savings

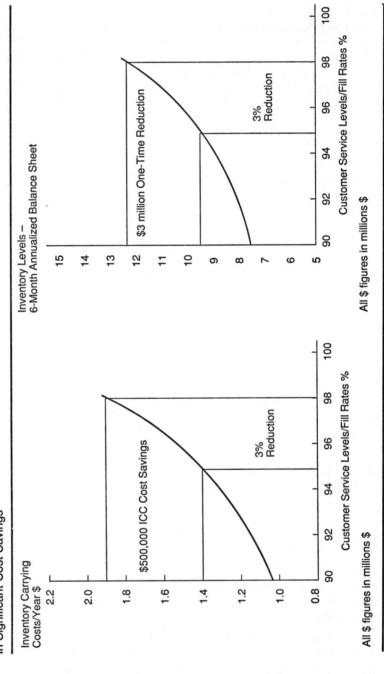

return. The gaps are then addressed in terms of improvement programs—continuous/incremental improvement targets (increasing order accuracy and reducing paperwork errors, for example); discrete projects, such as developing new customer-directed packaging and material handling equipment requirements to automate; or business process redesign, such as sales order to collection, forecasting, and supply-demand planning. For example, a consumer products firm discovered that, while a survey of a particular class of customer required order lead times of three to five days, their plants provided an average of seven to nine days. (See Figure 5–18.) This led to a redesign of their process to meet market expectations. Many of these solutions call for information technology enablers and integration—issues typically addressed by multi-functional task forces with some MIS representation.

Having set customer service levels and determined customer expectations, the next step is to make the necessary trade-offs between service and cost. This addresses the ongoing management of customer service in terms of policy and inventory deployment. For instance, one consumer products company, in evaluating some of these trade-offs, found that, if it was to *reduce* its service levels by 3 percent, it would realize a $500,000 ongoing savings and a one-time balance sheet reduction of $3 million in inventory costs (see Figure 5–19).

Service trade-offs include availability/fill rates, delivery preferences, and turnaround/response times to customer needs. Costs include facilities, packaging, transportation, storage and inventory levels, and carrying costs. The tools and techniques have been addressed in Chapters 3 and 6 and include:

• Optimization and financial modeling
• Evaluation of non-permanent facilities (for instance, inventory near point-of-sale/use, public/contract warehousing, satellite distribution centers, downstream packaging facilities, etc.)
• Stocking locations and levels using customer service levels and fill rates from a product line–customer segment analysis, and based upon projected days of supply and delivery preferences. (This also includes safety stocks to cover uncertainties in demand and operations.)
• Information technology requirements necessary for customer service and communications. The next major step is to identify key customer service performance indicators and develop measuring and monitoring systems.

FIGURE 5–20
Field/After-Sales Service—Alliances/Outsourcing Options

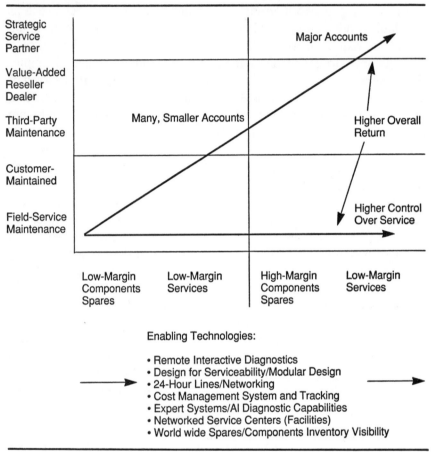

Customer Service Orientation—Integration into Operating Philosophy

There are three operations-oriented areas where the philosophy of effectively managing customer service must be incorporated into the firm's operating philosophy. They have been discussed in more detail at various points in the book, but it is necessary to highlight them again because of their critical importance in customer service management. They are the "envelope" surrounding the approach presented in Figure 5–17. They include:

Alliances and outsourcing
People and functional integration
Planning
Execution—measuring and monitoring

Alliances and Outsourcing. The common link through the "virtual factory" is the working relationship between external organizations in the value chain and internal functional entities. In the past, enterprises looked upon relationships with these internal entities only as short-term, cost-controlling efforts. In the customer service era, however, they are changing this approach drastically to create close partnerships with all value chain entities, both internal and external. Alliances are being developed, and functions unrepresentative of core competencies are being outsourced throughout the value chain. This is the basic theme behind the "virtual factory" concept presented in Chapter 1 and earlier in this chapter. The alliances and outsourcing efforts include suppliers, contract manufacturers, distributors, transportation companies, brokers, and customers. The operating criterion is a win-win effort to enhance customer service.

Figure 5–20 illustrates some of the trends in field and post-sale service. Briefly, the variety of alliance and outsourcing options ranges from strategic partnership to third-party maintenance agreements, while the products and services offered range from high margin to below-cost. The trend is moving away from the management of after-sales service on a response basis to integrated, coordinated planning and strategy, with the goal of integrating after-sales service into the logistics planning framework. This results in:

• Integrated service, spares, and peripheral planning leading to coordinated and proactive response to customer problems
• Focus on servicing major accounts and cost-effective management of other accounts to provide a high level of customer satisfaction
• Ability to target repeat sales to accounts which are profitable to serve
• Integrated product design (design for serviceability) with field service for improved servicing and reduced problem resolution turnaround times
• Perception of after-sales service as an integrated part of the value chain,

one that is a cornerstone of cost-effective customer service and makes money for the enterprise

People and Functional Integration. Integration within the enterprise is the theme of this book. Partnerships within the firm are ways of moving towards this integration—the interdependencies of various functions, their success or failure tied to that of the enterprise. It is here that the measurement systems are necessary, and they must focus on the supplier-customer relationships in the value chain. Measurements cannot be fragmented: they must be integrated in a focused customer service strategy.

Every aspect of the product channel must be driven by the needs of the customer. This raises the issue of "The customer is always right." Response to this issue depends on the identification of the customer—consumer, retailer, or the next functional entity in the value chain. Based on this, and the determination of the customer's needs, every person and link in the value chain must set aside traditional excuses and rationales for poor customer service performance—an attitudinal change. This change, however, can only be accomplished through the willingness of management to empower employees to focus on high cost-effective levels of customer service.

Such a change contains some inherent risks, but management can reduce risk by becoming a champion for customer service through a series of interdependent actions. These should be the bases for a philosophy of continuous improvement and a supplier-customer orientation. Though addressed in chapter four, they certainly bear repeating in the context of customer service strategy:

• *Responsibility for actions.* Employees should have the ability to act on problems as they arise. It is the responsibility of management to provide the necessary knowledge and tools to employees. Accountability is key—employees can assume responsibility for decisions and actions without stepping into a functional "silo."

• *Establish philosophies for education and training.* By providing education and training, management can promote and institutionalize a supplier-customer orientation. Consistent and assertive management can then create an environment of mutual trust between management and employee.

• *Communicate—share the wins and losses.* "Experience is the best teacher" is an excellent axiom and, when done effectively, the sharing of a team's wins and losses with the entire organization can be a powerful motivating and involvement factor. The process, however, must respect the rights of individuals to make mistakes as long as a lesson has been learned.

• *Set the example for customer service.* Management must ensure that actual customer service is consistent with the espoused—the concept of "Do as I say and Do". Until management sets examples and takes risks, the concept of customer service will be nothing more than just that—a concept—to employees. Managers cannot expect employees to be "guinea pigs" in what is essentially a risky process organizationally. What is more, should an employee be placed in a new situation and operating pattern, it is the manager's responsibility to share the burden of a potential mistake and set-back.

• *Better the company's chances in the future.* Every employee is entitled to mistakes and set-backs, when they are the consequences of rational decisions backed with sound problem analysis. The caveat is that employees should learn from, and not repeat such mistakes. This attitude is what informed risk-taking is all about. No organization can maintain a sustained competitive advantage for long if its members are risk-averse to the point of always staying with the status quo. A management attitude which provides empowerment and accountability, coupled with a tolerance for failure as a learning tool (again, provided it was the result of an informed decision based on analysis and multi-functional input), can generate a healthy risk-taking and energetic culture.

• *Planning.* A major tenet underlying Tom Gunn's world class manufacturing framework (see Chapter one) is the incorporation of a planning philosophy. A key task of enterprise management is the development of a vision for the enterprise. This involves the visioning process—painting a detailed picture of the future operation and thrust of the organization, planning strategy, and providing a tactical plan for implementation. This vision and plan must be communicated throughout the organization. By placing customer service as one of the important elements of the vision, management can successfully undertake the planning task and process (determining the needs of customers and other stakeholders in the enterprise). This can become a major strategic weapon in and of itself. The message telegraphed to the customer is one of concern for him as a major stakeholder.

Given a valid, unbiased analysis, the planning task should become an exercise in determining the best alternative for the enterprise. This is an iterative process, sponsored by management but driven by the major stakeholders, and involves communication with the stakeholders. The most important stakeholder in the dialogue is the customer. Such a planning-based dialogue closes the planning loop with the customer that began with the original voice of customer analysis.

• *Execution.* Execution of the plan must be swift, responsive to outside influences, flexibile in the face of change, and measured. Management must be proactive during every phase of implementation, and continue to analyze potential opportunities, technologies, and weaknesses. Customer service will cease to be a strategic weapon if management permits to lapse (by neglect or default) the disciplines inherent in the continuous improvement philosophy.

CHAPTER 6

INTEGRATED INVENTORY STRATEGY

INVENTORY AND CUSTOMER SERVICE

The previous chapter addressed the importance of all customers in the supply chain, and outlined an approach to developing customer service strategies and objectives and achieving customer delight. Integrated inventory management is the mechanism for achieving this customer delight, consistent with the firm's strategies. There are three critical aspects of inventory strategy and management needed to achieve these objectives:

Market coverage and inventory geography

Integrated materials planning and management

Inventory deployment: Location and stocking levels

The classic management dilemma in integrated inventory management revolves around the trade-off between inventory availability and cash flow. Now, in the customer service era, another dimension has been added to this mix—customer satisfaction using inventory management to increase profit. This is what Ian Mitroff and Richard Mason term a "wicked" problem, and can result in a variation of the "third" type of error—solving the wrong problem (*Challenging Strategic Planning Assumptions* [New York: John Wiley & Sons, 1981]). The wrong inventory on the shelf can cause customer dissatisfaction and result in decreased profit. Given that inventory is money, and that inventory is needed to satisfy customer demands in an increasingly short period of time, the enterprise must focus on keeping the right inventory on the shelf.

A need, by definition, is a condition that requires relief or satisfaction. The responsible customer initiates a process of identifying a product and/or service solution for this need. In most cases, given the highly competitive nature of today's marketplace, more than one solution is likely to be found. The process continues as the customer performs a competitive value analysis of the comparable products—formally or informally. As discussed in the previous chapter, this value analysis includes product characteristics and service. The customer also weighs several other factors in evaluating the solution for the need condition. These are shown in Figure 6–1 and include functionality, aesthetics, quality, price, availability, and service. The optimum trade-off that matches customer need must be found by the manufacturer: this is the challenge of integrated inventory management and development. When describing this inventory-customer service concept and trade-offs to executives in manufacturing firms, it is often useful to offer the following two examples, which are rooted in everyday life.

Our first example involves the buyer. Every consumer has probably had the experience of defining a need for a large appliance—for example,

FIGURE 6–1
Customer Buying Factors—The Trade-Offs

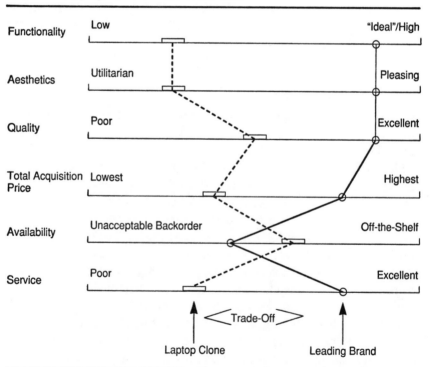

a new premium quality stereo system for the home. The following series of activities is quite typical, at the business or individual consumer level. The available products and options are first researched by a variety of methods—product brochures, store visits, conversations with colleagues, reading *Consumer Reports*, etc. The component products for the system are then analyzed and, almost immediately, conflicting priorities begin to emerge. One person wants a compact disc (CD) player to be part of the system, another wants a cassette player, while a third wants headphones. The buyer wants a good pair of speakers.

Buying all of these components at a time can add significantly to the bottom line price. Of the products that potentially fit the budget, two are chosen as finalists from a features and perceived quality standpoint. The next step is to visit competing retailers to determine the best source and product, to clarify features or quality issues with salespeople, and to examine floor models on display for aesthetics and ease of use.

After the buyer is satisfied that the best offer has been obtained from the first store, the process is repeated for the second product and, perhaps, at another store. The buyer discovers that the first store has the lowest price and returns there to make the purchase.

A *mismatch of expectations* may cause problems at this point: the purchase is initiated and the customer is ready to carry away the purchase, but the store does not carry that particular product in stock. What is the result? Backorder? Lost sale? Loss of goodwill (future sales)? The buyer is informed that the system will be delivered to his or her home in three weeks.

The second example involves the seller. In this case, it is the employee responsible for finding the product and placing it on the delivery truck to be delivered to the home of the buyer. The customer service representative (CSR) works for the manufacturer and handles direct-to-customer shipments. Unfortunately, she receives the order two weeks later. She then determines the inventory visibility/status: during the picking activity, she finds that the CD player is not in stock, and that the headphones are the last pair in stock but that the carton is damaged. She pulls the rest of the system and places it in a hold location.

The CSR's performance is measured according to the number of complete shipments made without damage to the product or container by the committed ship date. This now places her in the role of an internal customer of the supply operations. To expedite the shipment, she immediately calls the production control department to see when she can expect the missing items to be replenished. She finds that the headphones are due in Finished Goods in three days, but that the CD player is a purchased item and not due for two weeks. She must ship now if she is to meet the promised due date.

To attempt to coordinate *supply-demand*, the CSR pulls the headphones in the damaged carton and delivers it to the packaging department to be repackaged. Unfortunately, the packaging department lacks the proper materials to execute this; however, the good news is that a shipment is expected by the end of the business day: she could have the replaced carton by tomorrow morning. One of her needs has been satisfied, but the larger issue (non-availability of the CD player) is still looming over the horizon. At best, she may still be a day late. The CSR calls the purchasing department to determine whether the CD supplier can rush either a lot shipment or a single unit to her within the next 24 hours. The immediate response is negative, but the buyer pursues the matter and finds that the supplier could "overnight" the CD player—at a premium—to arrive within 72 hours.

While this was an improvement, it would inconvenience the customer by requiring the customer to stay at home to receive deliveries on two consecutive days (the transportation company would be able to deliver the shipment 48 hours after loading). The CSR called the purchasing department again to coordinate the delivery of the CD to correspond with the rest of the shipment. She then asked the sales department to contact the retailer where the stereo system had been purchased, to advise the salesperson of the actual delivery date, including the fact that there would actually be two shipments arriving. The salesperson, in turn, passed on the information to the customer. Both shipments were received, three days later, and only one day later than the original promised date, thanks to the vigilance of the CSR, internal customer.

This very real example demonstrates some customer service strategies through the supply chain, but it also illustrates the absence of some critical success factors of excellent customer service. The process is shown in Figure 6–2. By focusing on the supply chain entities, we can evaluate some of the strategic realities of these two examples. Table 6–1 illustrates some of the cause and effect relationships of these strategic realities.

The simple (but not simplistic) stereo example illustrates several factors about customer orientation:

FIGURE 6–2

"Stereo Example: Inventory–Customer Service"

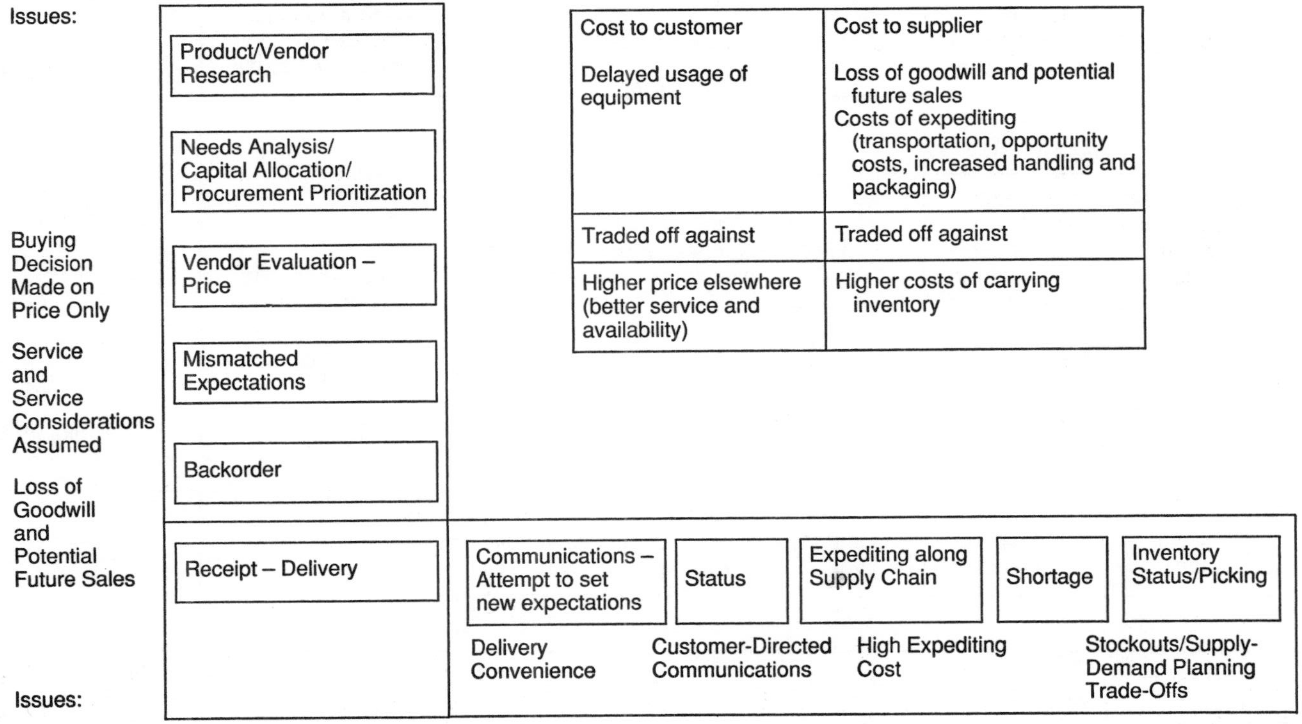

Issues:

	Cost to customer	Cost to supplier
Product/Vendor Research	Delayed usage of equipment	Loss of goodwill and potential future sales Costs of expediting (transportation, opportunity costs, increased handling and packaging)
Needs Analysis/Capital Allocation/Procurement Prioritization		
Vendor Evaluation – Price	Traded off against	Traded off against
Mismatched Expectations	Higher price elsewhere (better service and availability)	Higher costs of carrying inventory
Backorder		

Buying Decision Made on Price Only

Service and Service Considerations Assumed

Loss of Goodwill and Potential Future Sales

Receipt – Delivery	Communications – Attempt to set new expectations	Status	Expediting along Supply Chain	Shortage	Inventory Status/Picking
	Delivery Convenience	Customer-Directed Communications	High Expediting Cost		Stockouts/Supply-Demand Planning Trade-Offs

Issues:

179

TABLE 6–1
Strategic Cause and Effect—Lessons from the Stereo Example

Value Chain Entity	Strategic Issue	Effect on Potential Customer/Entity	Corrective Action
Consumer	Assumed availability	Last purchase flexibility Inconvenience/unfulfilled expectations Extra pre-procurement costs	Supplier/product evaluation and pre-procurement availability check Supplier service reference check
Salesperson —Supplier	Total product value description	Inconvenience/unfulfilled expectations Mistrust	Up-front discussion on product availability, plans, features Ask critical profile questions/ask the customer for his requirements Act on customer dismay
Retailer	Management policy Stocking policy	Salesperson: Limited availability to sell Lost commission/customer conflict Loss in product/service confidence Customer: Mistrust/inconvenience Lost loyalty/goodwill	Stocking locations/stocking levels Supplier/OEM alliances Communicated inventory policy Proactive customer support/ empowered salesforce
Manufacturer	Management policy Stocking policy Customer/supplier alliances Stocking locations Stocking levels	Retailer: Lost sale/loyalty/goodwill Salesperson: Lost sale/commission/customer conflict	Alliances/stocking agreements Regional/distributed stocking/ forecasting Marketing/sales support Open, 2-way communication

		Customer: Lost sale/loyalty/goodwill Inconvenience	
Shipping Manager	As a supplier: Empowerment As a customer: Involvement	Proactive customer service orientation saved the sale and managed expectations Pursued an expedited-based response to satisfy customer need/company commitment	Service response and accessibility Rapid delivery/turnaround commitment—published Survey of customers for requirements/ expectations Reward from superior Knew and exercised the upstream supply chain entities for results (more formal mechanism would have proved more effective)
Production Control	Involvement— proactive problem solving	Incurred extra cost and effort for internal customer	Education/training, empowerment, proactive problem-management
Purchasing	Empowerment Involvement	Pursued alternate solutions to satisfy internal customer	More explicit, formal, internal/external customer orientation
Supplier	Customer alliance Inventory deployment Distribution policies	Responded well in this case	Prevention of similar crises in the future through communication alliances

- Appropriate performance measures can drive customer service.
- Expediting is a costly but legitimate method of product delivery—it is the flip side of inventory stocking.
- Inventory availability can be a driving factor in purchasing decisions, but can be offset by price.
- The manufacturer has little control over final delivery performance, and must achieve maximum flexibility to respond to such conditions.
- Managing customer expectations is important.
- The customer service representative (CSR) is due for a promotion because of her passion for customer service. With the aid of the purchasing department buyer, she prevented the delivery problem from getting out of control. Had she accepted mediocrity, the customer would have been denied receipt of the stereo for at least two weeks and two days past the committed due date. This would have made the total lead time for a stereo bought off the showroom floor almost six weeks—hardly a performance to be proud of in this era of customer service, *unless the trade-off decisions had been explicitly made at a strategic level.*

Figure 6–3 illustrates this cycle of customer service and inventory levels. Inventory deployment policy and management of inventory created a customer service problem affecting the entire supply chain in terms of response and additional cost. This example provides some indications to determine an integrated inventory strategy to achieve our customer service.

It is necessary that inventory strategies be consistent with the corporate strategies, and that they follow from the configuration/network and customer service strategies. The key factor in proving the enterprise's commitment to customer service, and to delivering customer service, is the integrated management of material and information. Strategic inventory trade-offs must be undertaken by senior management and visionary leaders within the organization to meet required customer service levels within the realities of available working capital. The characteristics of integrated inventory strategists and solution implementors (some of these were demonstrated in the above example) include:

Rigor in analysis

Innovation in determining new methods to satisfy customer demand

Persistence in implementation and enforcing discipline

Communication to the organization, third party alliances, and customers in a timely fashion

FIGURE 6–3
Stereo Example—Customer Service Profile

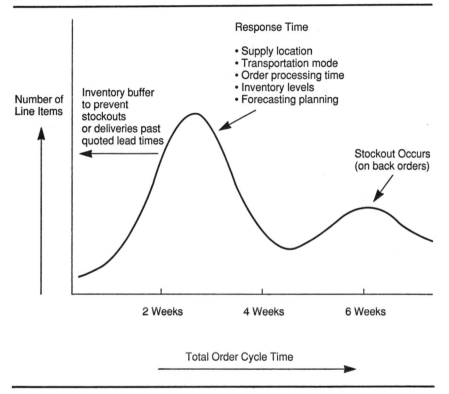

Companies are faced with several choices—innovative, traditional, and default—in achieving high customer service levels on today's competitive battlefield. One, therefore, must start at the enterprise level to understand external factors impacting product-market success. Marketing, typically, has the necessary market data to categorize demand in terms of geographical, channel, and use segments, as well as to identify the product-service requirements of those categories. Integrated inventory strategy in the customer service era builds on this knowledge base with robust inventory deployment strategies and initiatives, and effective management of material through the supply chain. The business issues of significant importance to the inventory strategist include:

- *Global markets and competitor strategies*
  - Customer identification and location

- ○ Engagement (or plans to engage) in multinational markets
- ○ Characteristics of foreign competition (price, service differentiator, price-performance-value)
- ○ Domestic supply for export purposes
- ○ Product proliferation and market penetration
- *Configuration/network strategies (covered in chapter three)*
  - ○ Configuration of plants, distribution centers, and their functions
  - ○ OEMs, third party contracts, co-packing
  - ○ Product mix and volume
  - ○ Source-destination links and points of supply
  - ○ Co-location of engineering and manufacturing, location—centralized or distributed
  - ○ Value of procured materials and value-added factors along supply chain
  - ○ Lead times, expediting lead times, and costs
- *Distribution/channel strategies*
  - ○ Channels used—retailers, wholesalers, distributors, direct, VARs, etc.
  - ○ Points of supply for various customer classifications
  - ○ Transportation modes, costs, and lead times (subcontracted, freight forwarders, or in-house)
  - ○ Spare parts and service functions strategies
  - ○ Maintenance of semi-finished stock for custom conversion, and location
- *Governmental regulations*
  - ○ Taxes on inventory, transportation, and transformation
  - ○ Co-production requirements and technology differentials among plants
- *Inventory environment*
  - ○ Finished goods—quantity, type (SKUs), location
  - ○ Work-in-process—state, quantity, location
  - ○ Raw materials/components, sub-assemblies—quantity, location, cost
  - ○ Inventory carrying costs
  - ○ Special handling/storage characteristics (refrigerated, frozen, fragile handling)
- *Financial strategies*
  - ○ Return on assets

- Profit requirements
- Working capital requirements
- Investment required to support customer service

Table 6–2 depicts several business issues that require strategic responses. It demonstrates the impact on an integrated inventory strategy of the various issues which must be considered in doing business in both domestic and global markets. As can be expected, all the issues impact all the strategies—the variable is the level of impact. This level of impact is the basis for making trade-offs. As discussed earlier in chapter three, geography is a critical issue. The larger the scope of the enterprise, the greater its impact. Geography (proximity/time) issues that are an integral part of the integrated inventory strategy include the relationships between:

Product inventory to customer

Sales to customer

Service to customer

Product availability at point of sale

Supplier to manufacturing

Manufacturing to distribution

Figure 6–4 shows the impact of such proximity issues on various system-wide costs related to inventory strategy. It also highlights the various strategic options that many companies adopt to ensure "virtual co-location"; to stay within their core competencies; to ensure flexibility of response without overextending themselves (financially or managerially); and to buffer the uncertainties inherent in customer demand patterns and operational variances. These strategic options include alliances; synergies through co-distribution, co-shipment, and co-packing; and outsourcing.

STRATEGIC INVENTORY MANAGEMENT

To best serve the customer and enable the enterprise to compete effectively, management must plan and control the flow of material and information along the supply chain. Material takes many forms as it traverses the supply chain—as each entity transforms, packs, or moves the material, additional value-added costs are incurred. Material typically accounts for 60–80 percent of the total cost of a product. This enormous

TABLE 6–2
Business Issues and Strategic Response—Relationships Customer Satisfaction and Information Technology Are the Highest Impact Issues That Span the Enterprise

Business Issues \ Strategic Response	Global Market & Competitor Strategy	Configuration/Network Strategy	Customer Service/Integrated Inventory Strategy	Distribution/Channel Strategy	Financial Strategy
Customer Satisfaction	High Impact	Medium Impact	High Impact	High Impact	High Impact
Product Innovation/Introduction	High Impact	High Impact Co-location	Medium-Low Impact	Medium Impact	High Impact
Information & Process Technology	High Impact	High Impact	High Impact	High Impact	High Impact
Labor Skills/Availability	Medium Impact	High Impact	Low Impact	Low Impact	Medium Impact
Material Cost	High Impact	High Impact	High Impact	Medium-Low Impact	Medium Impact
Transportation Costs	Medium-Low Impact	High Impact	High-Medium Impact	High Impact	Medium Impact
Manufacturing Costs	High Impact	High Impact	Medium-Low Impact	Low Impact	High Impact
Government Regulation Compliance	High Impact	High Impact	Medium-Low Impact	Low Impact	Medium-Low Impact

FIGURE 6–4

As Proximity Increases, Geographical Distance Decreases. The Likely Impacts on Cost Change. . . .

Proximity/Time Issues — System-Wide Costs	Product-Customer	Sales-Customer	Service-Customer	Supplier-Mfg.	Mfg. Plant-DC	Product Availability to Customer at POS	Additionally, Govt. Regulations Can Impact Costs. . . .	Leading to Strategies In
Expediting costs	→	—	→	→	→	→	—	• Inventory buffers/safety stocks
Transportation costs	←	—	←	→	→	←	←	• Alliances with transportation companies/freight forwarders
Communications costs (incl. customer)	→	→	→	→	→	→	—	
Cost of potential sales loss (goodwill)	→	→	→	→	→	→	—	• Field service strategic alliances
Cost of lost sales	→	→	→	→	→	→	←	• Customer alliances • OEM alliances
DC operating costs	←	—	—	—	→	←	←	• Channel alliances
Inventory carrying costs	←	—	←	→	→	←	←	• Co-packing
Sales force costs	—	←	—	—	—	←	←	• Co-distribution
Facilities capital costs	←	—	←	→	→	—	←	• Co-shipment and outsourcing
Service costs	—	—	←	→	—	←	—	
Field service center operating costs	—	—	←	→	—	←	—	

187

ratio dictates that management know the complete cost and operational structure of its current environment, including the best sources of supply; movement and packaging requirements; processes; and scrap, disposition, and storage costs. Of equal importance to these physical requirements are the cash and capital aspects that include *inventory carrying costs* and *lost investment potential*.

Inventory Carrying Costs

These are probably the most understated of all the costs of customer service. Many companies use their costs of capital as their inventory carrying costs. Cost of capital, however, is only part of the true cost. Inventory carrying costs include *all* of the costs of carrying an incremental dollar of the cost of the material, and include these elements (shown in the equation below as they interrelate):

- *Weighted average cost of capital or working capital line of credit rate.*
  - (depending on the method used to finance inventory) = C.
- *Holding Costs.*
  - Inventory taxes (varying by state) = T.
  - Insurance costs (typically corporate) = I.
- *Storage Costs.*
  - Warehouse costs (company-owned, contract, public, rented space, including ins and outs) = W.
- *Risk Costs.*
  - Shrinkage = X.
  - Scrap owing to damaged and otherwise unusable material (less recovery from resale) = (S − R1).
  - Obsolescence material (less resale recovery) = (O − R2).

Computing a highly accurate inventory carrying cost by SKU is a very tedious exercise and does not provide much incremental benefit. However, it is fairly simple to compute an aggregate carrying cost:

$$\text{as a percentage per dollar per year}$$
$$\text{ICC} = C + \frac{\{T + I + W + X + (S - R1) + (O - R2)\}}{\text{Annual \$ Material Cost}}$$

Another method, if nothing else is available, is to obtain and use an industry average (for instance, from Herb Davis's surveys). A good, highly conservative rule of thumb is to use an inventory carrying cost of 1.5 percent per month (approximately 18 percent per year). Various companies have computed their inventory carrying costs, and estimates range from 15 percent to 35 percent, depending on company and type of industry. One electronics company executive stated that his inventory carrying cost was 65 percent—if true, an enormous cost of customer service. In any event, the inventory carrying cost for a company (and it is a crucial component of computing inventory levels and setting deployment policies) is a good deal greater than the cost of capital.

There are two aspects to Integrated Materials Management: *setting (and monitoring) inventory policy and deployment* to best balance trade-offs between total costs and customer service and to ensure that customer service strategies (discussed in chapter five) are met; and *ongoing materials management* through the supply chain to best manage and control supply-demand planning and execute the planned inventory deployment. We shall examine both of these aspects below.

Inventory Policy and Deployment

The planning and management of inventory through the supply chain can provide a significant competitive advantage in terms of total cost. Few companies examine their total inventories through the supply chain to determine the carrying costs of their system-wide inventory; the opportunity costs in terms of alternative investments and net increases in sales required to generate this investment; or the true costs of unnecessary inventory and the costs of expediting required (over the planned level) to get it to the customer.

For instance, Figure 6–5 shows the various stages of safety stock and pipeline inventory in a typical semiconductor manufacturing firm. These are the key questions for the inventory strategist: What is the total inventory cost? Considering the various decision criteria—customer service levels, lead times and variability; demand variability; manufacturing yield and cycle time variability; and the variability of in-transit delivery times—is it a decision based on analysis, evaluation and an explicit strategy, or is it a default decision, a situation evolved over time through ad-hoc decisions and optimization of parts of the supply chain?

Figure 6–6 illustrates the inventory levels in a recent period (in terms of days in inventory) of the six largest semiconductor manufacturing companies. The difference between the company—Company two on

FIGURE 6–5
What is Your Total Inventory Costing You?

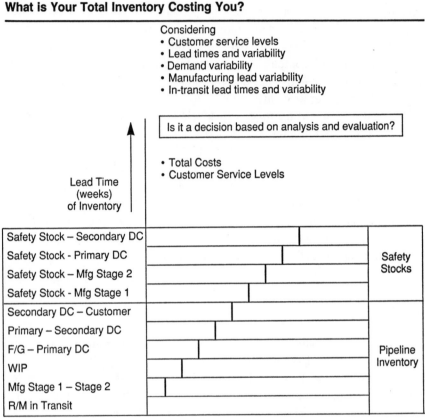

Considering
• Customer service levels
• Lead times and variability
• Demand variability
• Manufacturing lead variability
• In-transit lead times and variability

Is it a decision based on analysis and evaluation?

• Total Costs
• Customer Service Levels

Lead Time (weeks) of Inventory

Safety Stock – Secondary DC
Safety Stock - Primary DC
Safety Stock – Mfg Stage 2
Safety Stock - Mfg Stage 1

Safety Stocks

Secondary DC – Customer
Primary – Secondary DC
F/G – Primary DC
WIP
Mfg Stage 1 – Stage 2
R/M in Transit

Pipeline Inventory

Product Inventory Levels/Product Inventory Carrying Cost $ ——————▶

the chart—with the highest inventory levels (worst performance) and the average inventory level of the semiconductor manufacturing industry is 83 days. This translates to 4.2 percent of sales revenue for the firm compared to the 18 largest firms in the industry. In other words, its management of inventory through the supply chain has placed it at a significant cost disadvantage to the average player in the industry, leading to a high opportunity cost and potential vulnerability to a major economic downturn. Company two, by managing inventory to the average level in the industry, could achieve the same bottom line results as it could by increasing sales—at considerably less cost.

FIGURE 6–6
Inventory Levels and Ratios 6 Large Semiconductor Firms

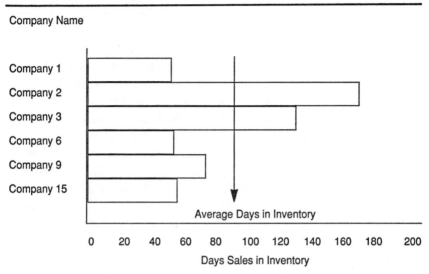

Company Name

Diff Ave – Lowest = 49 Days

= 2.1% of Sales
Ave – Highest = 83 Days
= 4.15% of Sales

On the other hand, the best performer—Company four on the chart—(lowest inventory) has inventory levels 49 days below the industry average, translating to 2.1 percent of sales revenues. This certainly has provided it with a competitive advantage! It is interesting to note that Company four has had a senior management level emphasis on logistics for quite some time, while Company two has only recently appointed a senior logistics executive to address the issues. Company four is also generally acknowledged to be one of the best managed and motivated companies in the industry, with a culture and operating philosophy of participative management and continuous improvement.

An Approach to Setting Inventory Policies
As with the other components of logistics strategy, integrated inventory deployment to meet customer service strategies is what Mitroff and

Mason term a wicked problem—it does not easily lend itself to comprehensive modeling and quantitative solution. It is an ever-moving target that must be evaluated periodically to ensure that changes are made to meet the dynamic environment of competition and customer expectation. We must, therefore, begin by determining the crucial qualitative factors involved—customer delivery preferences, the bargaining power of various customer classes and accounts (leverage), and our planned relationships vis-à-vis customers and products. We can then strike the customer service level-cost balance within these guidelines and constraints. Figure 6–7 illustrates just such an approach to setting inventory policy.

There are several components to setting inventory policies, derived from customer service strategies developed earlier in the logistics strategy planning process. In particular, key inputs to developing an integrated materials management strategy are these major trade-offs: delivery preferences; customer service levels for various service elements; other customer-specific service factors (such as very important status for long term relationships, testing sites, etc.).

Figure 6–7 is one approach to developing inventory strategies. It is customer-driven, as all successful approaches are, and seeks to balance customer service with cost. It involves, in the aggregate, the following steps.

Step 1: Analyze the current inventory environment to determine Product Classes and Customer Segments.
It is imperative that this classification be done with the active participation of sales and marketing. Interim and final classifications must have their approval—not only do they have the best base of knowledge regarding customers, but they are also most likely to be aware of future customer requirements.

Products can typically be classified into categories that parallel the product life cycle.

Phase-out. These products are at the end of their life cycle and are being phased out of the market and replaced by a new generation of products.

Ramp-up/introduction. New product introductions must be available in the target markets (in the case of computers this could mean national coverage) in quantities necessary to meet new product introduction and marketing objectives. *Mature*/ongoing products can fall into three classes based on their contributing margin per unit—low, medium, and high.

FIGURE 6–7
Setting Inventory Policies

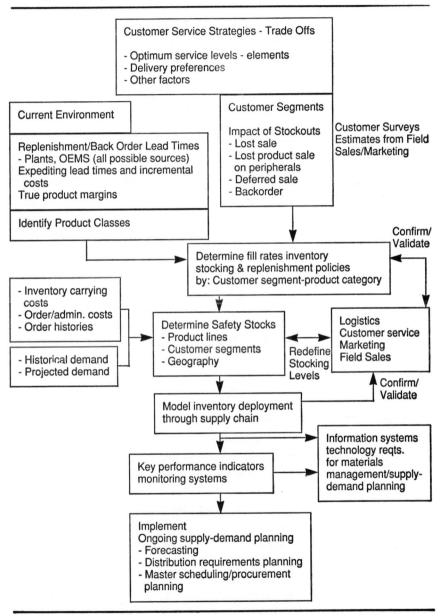

Customer Segments fall into two major categories—account segments (business to business) and mass segments (sales to a mass market). Account Segments can be either contractual or captive. Contractual segments represent customers that have a supply contract for delivery of product at a certain time and place at a given quantity, while typically in-house customers or business units within the same company are considered captive.

High and low leverage over customers. This includes factors that dictate the supply relationship:

• Percentage of total requirements from one source
• Unique product or manufacturing process/technology
• Financing relationships that enable one company to exercise supply leverage over the other
• Ownership factors
• Value-added services assisting in product design, performing pre-assembly, etc.)
• Information technology that has tied the customer or supplier to the company. (For instance, one electronics distributor is considering the installation of terminals and design tools to the design engineering group of a major customer, allowing engineers to transmit design parameters for ASICs through the distributor to foundries in the Far East. Another company provided EDI terminals, free of cost, to the design engineers of the customer—linked, naturally, to their own warehouses.)

Mass marketing—high and low competitive. These categories are fairly obvious and reflect product proliferation, price performance, absolute cost, and influence over buyers (for example, through promotion, advertising, or a hit movie or television show; or the fact that the components in personal computers have unchangeable replacement parts).

Step 2: Set Target Fill Rates and Inventory Deployment Policies.
Inventory policies depend upon the availability and use of information technology to develop the overall strategy. They consist of a combination of the following elements.

1. *Inventory levels.* This includes inventory levels to satisfy projected demand within replenishment cycles, as well as safety stocks necessary to hedge against uncertainties and variabilities in lead times, scheduling, quality, and demand fluctuations. Replenishment stock typically includes inventory necessary to cover projected product demand at the particular stocking location over the replenishment cycle time (the standard lead time to deliver an order/lot from the designated source of supply). If the standard lead time involves the entire supply chain, then, obviously, the replenishment stock will be high. Hence, the move by several companies to push the order processing point downstream and stock semi-finished goods for quick turnaround. Some of the strategic aspects of setting safety stocks will be discussed later in this section.

2. *Expediting.* This includes the incremental costs of moving materials quickly from one location to another (or producing it on an emergency basis) to ensure a certain fill rate consistent with company strategy. Costs of expediting include transportation (UPS, overnight airfreight, etc.), production (changeovers, scheduling, and order/requirements processing).

3. *Backorders.* The placing of the demand item in the regular production-shipping schedule when the item is not available at time of purchase is a backorder. Typically, the lead time is the standard quoted lead time through the supply pipeline. An incremental cost here is that of creating the backorder.

4. *Inventory carrying costs.* This has been discussed earlier in this chapter. These are the true costs of carrying an incremental dollar of inventory.

5. *Stockout penalties, including loss of goodwill.* The impacts of stockouts can be quantified to a certain extent. However, the underlying assumptions regarding impacts are merely that—assumptions. They are generally based upon customer surveys regarding customer behavior in the event of a stockout, and the best estimates from field sales and marketing. Figure 6–8 outlines the impacts and cost penalties of the various scenarios involving stockouts. Stockouts have broader ramifications from a profitability standpoint than the obvious ones of lost sales and others listed in Figure 6–8. Most significant is the generation of ill-will (or loss of good-will) which translates into potential losses for future sales.

6. *End-of-life (EOL) planning for phase-out products.* There are essentially four strategies possible for products that are being phased out (depicted in Figures 6–9A - 6–9D). The wrong strategy could lead to a heavy investment in inventory obsolescence or unsatisfied customers.

7. *Lifetime buy.* This involves a one-off buy or production run to cover the projected demand decline (Figure 6–9A), particularly where the incremental and opportunity costs of production until end of life (EOL)

FIGURE 6–8
Impacts of Stockouts

Impact	Penalty	
Lost sale	(Gross margin)	
Lost product sale + Loss on peripherals	(Gross margin of product) + (Gross margin of peripherals)	
Lost product sale + Loss of future dependent items (e.g., software)	(Gross margin of product) + (Estimate of future buys/item × gross margin)	× Frequency of occurrence = Cost
Deferred sales	Marketing/customer estimate of how many deferred sales before a product sale is lost (%) × gross margin	
Backorders	Cost impact of lead time before order filled (gross margin × discount rate) + incremental costs of creating a backorder	
	Cost of product substitutions including loss on margin of substituted products	

FIGURE 6–9A
Lifetime Buy
{Average amount in stock (D) × inventory carrying cost × time until EOL} v. incremental cost of producing until planned EOL (cost/unit × opportunity cost of capital × changeovers)

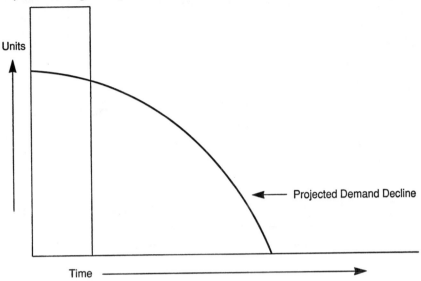

FIGURE 6–9B
Planned Phased Procurement/Production

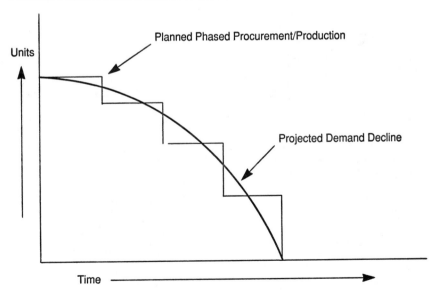

FIGURE 6–9C

Phased production/procurement to cover demand until new products take up slack

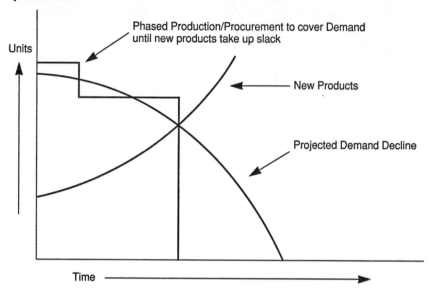

Phased Production/Procurement to cover Demand until new products take up slack

New Products

Projected Demand Decline

Units

Time

FIGURE 6–9D

Phased or one-time procurement/production while incentives depress demand and new products take up slack

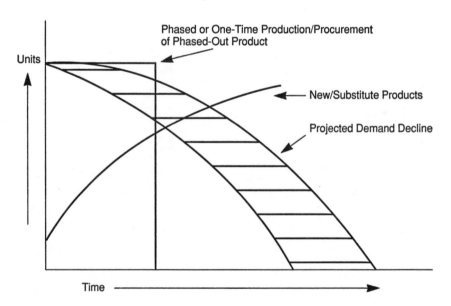

Phased or One-Time Production/Procurement of Phased-Out Product

New/Substitute Products

Projected Demand Decline

Units

Time

are high. This is especially important if a factory changeover from process and re-tooling is necessary for new products.

8. *Planned phased procurement/production.* This involves matching production or procurement to demand in a phased-out fashion until EOL (Figure 6–9B). This is feasible when the incremental and opportunity costs of product procurement (the supplier can run the product without special tooling or set-ups) and production are not significantly higher. A variation of this is to farm out production to a third party, including providing the process specifications and tooling necessary for product manufacture.

9. *New products.* This strategy involves phased production to meet demand until new products meet the demand for the phased-out product (Figure 6–9C). The key here lies in estimating the projected sales of the new product(s) that will take up the slack. A point to remember is that the complex, expensive models that predict such patterns are, in my experience, little better than the simple ones driven by a cooperative effort between field sales and marketing personnel.

10. *Substitute products.* This strategy frequently involves offering incentives to buyers to switch to a new product—in effect, hastening the EOL and depressing total demand for the phased-out product. The cost trade-offs here are the costs of incentives offered against the costs of producing, stocking, and servicing the phased-out product (Figure 6–9D). This strategy is useful when new generations of technology are being introduced. One computer company performing this analysis discovered it was considerably less expensive to offer attractive incentives to users to switch from the old computer generation to a new version. (The incentives included consulting in the transfer of files and databases.)

The setting of inventory policies must consider all these factors. Figure 6–10 provides some guidelines for setting inventory policy for various combinations of customer segments and product classes.

In general, the higher the profit impact of stockouts (particularly high in cases of product ramp-up/introduction), and the higher the probability of customers buying elsewhere, the higher the inventory levels maintained. When necessary, this also means a high degree of expediting to ensure product availability. In other words, fill rates need to be as high as possible. On the other hand, the lower the profit impact of stockouts and the lower the probability of customers buying elsewhere in the event of a stockout (high leverage over the customer), the lower the level at which inventory levels can be maintained. With these lower inventory levels, orders can be satisfied through a combination of backorders and limited expediting. Figure 6–11 illustrates this relationship.

It is worth noting again, however, that all these aspects of inventory order filling and availability policy are subordinate to marketing and field sales' determination of the delivery and order fill rate requirements for certain customer classes. The guidelines provided are just that—guidelines.

Step 3: Set Safety Stocks to Ensure Fill Rates Will Be Met at Certain Confidence Levels

The setting of safety, or hedge, stocks constitutes one of the oldest applications of operations research methods. Rather than discuss the computational details, we shall address the management issues inherent in the development of an inventory strategy. Safety stocks are essentially maintained to compensate for uncertainty while achieving customer service level requirements at a high rate of confidence and minimizing stockouts and lost sales penalties.

These uncertainties include:

Manufacturing lead time variability

Transportation/transit time variability

Trade procedures variability (customs, clearance, etc.)

Demand unpredictability

Manufacturing process variation (for example, yield variations)

Levels of confidence (as mentioned above) are set through customer service strategies, either by customer requirements or through a cost-service level analysis. The basis for inventory levels (replenishment stocks and safety stocks) can be viewed in three different ways for setting fill rates:

1. Percentage cycle: The average percentage of inventory cycles with no stockouts
2. Percentage demand: The average percentage of demand satisfied by off-the-shelf inventory
3. Number of bad cycles: The average number of cycles per year with stockouts

FIGURE 6–10 Guidelines for Setting Inventory Policies and Fill Rates by Product Class-Customer Segment Mix

Customer Segment	Product Classes	Phase-out	Mature/Ongoing — Low Margin	Mature/Ongoing — Medium Margin	Mature/Ongoing — High Margin	Ramp-up/ Introduction
Mass	High competitive	Bleed stock/ cover with NPI	Higher inventory Limited expediting	High inventory Limited expediting	High inventory Expedite	Highest inventory High expediting
Account	Low leverage over customer	EOL Planning	Make to order	Make to order	Low inventory Make to order	Higher inventory Make to order
Account	Contractual	Make to order	Make to order	Make to order		
Account	High leverage over customer	EOL Planning bleed stock	Low—higher inventory Limited expediting Backorder	Higher inventory Limited expediting Backorder	Higher inventory Expedite	High inventory High expediting
Mass	Low competitive	Bleed stock	Low—higher inventory Limited expediting Backorder	Low—higher inventory Limited expediting Backorder	Higher inventory Expedite Backorder	
Account	Captive	EOL Planning	Low inventory Limited expediting Backorder			High inventory Expedite

Customer Probability of Buying Elsewhere ↑

Profit Impact →

201

FIGURE 6–11
Determining Fill Rates

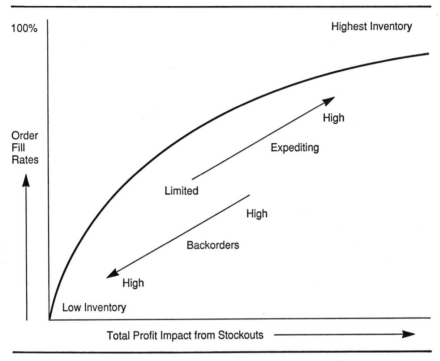

Safety stocks are set by determining variabilities of parameters (noted above), obtaining projected demand, and computing safety stocks by product/product group and by distribution center.

This latter computation is based on fill rates and confidence levels, order/administration costs, and order quantities (average weekly demand, economic lot sizes, ship lot sizes, multiples, etc.). It attempts to minimize total inventory costs. To estimate and evaluate total inventory costs from a particular inventory level and safety stock policy, we can use the following models, illustrated in Figure 6–12.

The Expedite Model (based on expediting to cover stockouts)

The Lost Sales Model (evaluating the impacts of lost sales due to stockouts)

The Backorder/ Non-expedite Model (based on costs of backorders)

FIGURE 6–12
Minimizing Total Inventory Costs—Evaluating Stocking Levels

Total Costs	=	Inventory carrying costs I.C.C. (average investment levels) + Administration costs per order placed $\left(\dfrac{\text{Total admin costs in product logistics network}}{\text{no. of orders placed}}\right)$ +
Expedite Model		$\left(\begin{array}{c}\text{Fixed expedite charge} \times \text{\% of stockouts per}\\ \text{order cycle} \times \text{avg. inventory per order cycle}\end{array}\right)$
Or		
Lost Sales Model		$\left(\begin{array}{c}\text{Estimate of lost profit penalty} \times \text{\% of}\\ \text{stockouts per order cycle} \times \text{avg. inventory}\\ \text{per order cycle}\end{array}\right)$
Or		
Backorder/ *Non-expedite* *Model*		$\left(\begin{array}{c}\text{Estimate of backorder cost/unit/period}\\ \times \text{avg. number of backorders}\end{array}\right)$

The underlying reasons for maintaining safety (or hedge) stocks at a particular stocking location are:

Poor forecasting

Poor supply-demand planning

Inaccurate and uncertain ordering process

Customer cancellations

Undetected changes in customer buying patterns

Poor engineering change control and implementation

Poor inventory visibility across the network

It is preferable to attack these process- and technology-related causes through a combination of analytical methods, assumption testing, continuous process improvement, and (where a quantum leap improvement is necessary) business process redesign. The alternative, and one that many companies use, is to slash inventory arbitrarily—a move that often adversely impacts customer service levels. An exception to this is inventory accumulation because of special promotions or new product introduction/ramp-up.

Step 4: Model Inventory Deployment Policies and Requirements, Refining Deployment Policies if Necessary

Modeling has been discussed in chapter three. We have found that the best techniques to model inventory deployment are optimization and simulation modeling. Figure 6–13 illustrates a network chain with the necessary parameters. The model should be able to perform "what-if" analysis on significant variables and provide solutions dealing with total cost. Again, the marketing/field sales guidelines on customer delivery preferences and fill rates for various product-customer classifications should provide the basic constraints. The results of the model should be used as a decision support tool to refine (or re-define) the inventory deployment policies. The requirements for a modeling package defined in chapter three fit such a purpose very well.

Step 5: Set Performance Measures/Indicators

As with every aspect of logistics strategy, appropriate performance measures should be defined to measure customer service levels (including fill rates, delivery performance, and backorders); total cost impacts (expediting costs, inventory carrying costs, transportation costs); inventory levels; and trends. These should be monitored periodically and be part of the executive reporting system. This performance data is essential for reviewing policy and adapting or changing it to meet customer and market needs.

Ongoing Materials Management through Supply-Demand Chain Management

To help management reduce its reliance on large inventories and better manage material in response to planned deployment strategies, we shall examine those aspects of demand management necessary to drive the process, focusing on the front-end drivers rather than on the tactical aspects of materials management. Figure 6–14 depicts the front-end of managing demand.

The demand management process consists of three distinct macro processes. They are:

- Product forecasting
- Supply-demand planning
- Master production scheduling/procurement planning

FIGURE 6-13
Inventory Deployment—Modeling the Network

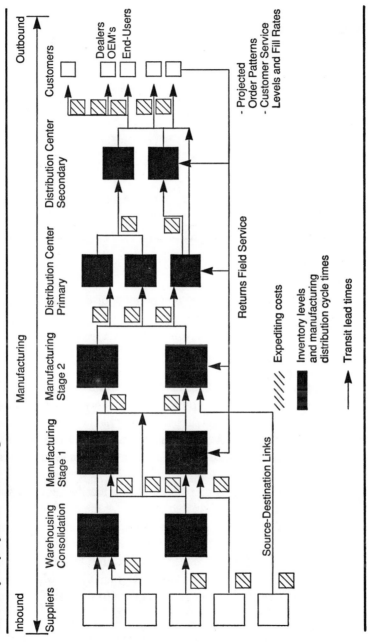

FIGURE 6–14
Demand Management

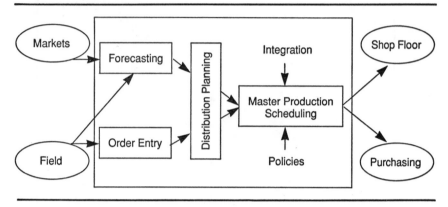

The first two are the key strategic components of demand management, and we shall focus on them for the remainder of this chapter. The third is more tactical in nature, and is driven by the first two. The demand management process, as depicted in Figure 6–14, typically follows the process described below.

Marketing identifies the markets in which the product can be sold. The focus is on product type, timing, and quantity, and on customer segmentation by major account, region, and channel. The time horizon can vary from a quarter to a year, or even three years, in some instances. This forecast is (ideally) based on historical demand patterns or analogies to history of like products (used particularly for new products with little or no sales history). Field sales personnel provide the regional input of their projections (firm and anticipated orders) for the coming time period. Service and spares requirements are also sent in from the field. This field sales input provides the added service of adding a dose of reality to the marketing projections. Firm orders are entered into the order entry/processing system, while projections are sent to marketing. Marketing then synthesizes these field projections with its own to generate its forecast.

At this point several things can, and do, happen:

• Management tempers the delta between the marketing and sales projections (marketing is typically optimistic and sales pessimistic). This provides some control against too much or too little material being purchased or product manufactured.

• The forecast is modified to reflect financial projections, marketing product projections, and sales quotas, and this can be done repeatedly at various levels in the organization before the finalized forecast is released to operations.

• Resource/capacity planning: in global supply-demand situations (discussed later in this chapter), rough-cut planning is conducted to determine schedule feasibility.

The forecast and firm orders are then entered (automatically or manually, depending on the level of information integration in the firm) into a distribution planning system, such as distribution resources planning (DRP II). Time-phased quantities (often lot-sized, based on pre-determined rules) are then generated for the various plants, distribution centers, and centralized procurement entities (corporate contracts or regional procurement), as in the case of semiconductor contracts for worldwide procurement. Such supply-demand planning is dependent upon manufacturing and distribution parameters (cycle times, yields, throughput); inventory deployment policies; and projected demand.

Master production scheduling translates this plant-level demand into plant loading schedules and plant-level procurement plans. The recipients of the build order are production control (short-interval scheduling) and buyers. We shall now examine the planning aspects of forecasting and supply-demand planning.

FORECASTING

Forecasting is often referred to as an art, and in some corporations it is. For instance, for a major manufacturer of a line of sump pumps for builder and consumer use, the single largest factor in forecasting sales across the country is the ability to forecast the weather accurately. Anyone who has watched weather reports on television knows how inaccurate weather predictions can be for the next 24 hours—not to mention six months out!

The success of any company is tied to its ability to predict the needs of its customers, their financial ability to buy, and the time frame for their needs to be satisfied. A forecast is a tool to match customer requirements against internal capabilities and external influences for a period of time somewhere in the future. Competitive advantage lies with the company with the right product and service available as the customer requires it.

A forecast can be made at several levels of aggregation and detail. The hierarchy of forecasts:

Market forecast
Product line forecast
Sales (SKU) forecast
Plant-level forecast
Distribution forecast
Delivery forecast

Depending upon the industry, company, and division, the level of disaggregation in these forecasts varies considerably. Many companies forecast at a great level of detail, usually by SKU. Ultimately, of course, every forecast must be broken down to this level of detail. Our experience has led us to believe, however, that enterprises that compete successfully at the global level tend to focus their forecast at an aggregate level, ensuring that the global nature of product demand will remain unstructured.

Forecasts depend not only upon the customer, but also on the ability of the supply chain to project and to respond to the product and service needs of the customer. Some internal influences to which the forecaster must be sensitive include:

Historical demand. Historical patterns, seasonality, trends, and the patterns of comparable products

Product designs. The structure and changing requirements (through engineering change notices and proliferating options) of the product's composition

Manufacturing processes used. Capacities and yields

Business strategies. Typically, the financial projections to which the forecast must conform (on a political level)

Marketing and sales strategies. Promotion of certain items, pricing-volume influences, new product introduction and ramp-up, and product phase-outs

Manufacturing strategies. Lead times, plants and stages, and their product mix

Inventory deployment. Stocking locations and levels to meet demand

While several of these factors do not play a part in the initial, "pure" forecast, they are all major factors during the forecast modification process. Equally important is the external environment within which the product and service are focused. External influences include:

- Customer needs and demand
- Climatic conditions (where applicable)
- Economics of a region (if the product-service is dependent on this)
- Regulations and laws (restrictions and constraints for certain types of products in certain countries and regions)
- Competitive forces, which serve to depress demand or counter planned promotions

Figure 6–15 illustrates these influences and highlights the characteristics of a good forecast and accurate forecasting function. Apart from these characteristics, every good forecast actively considers the internal and external influences, and is not generated in a vacuum. To ensure that an effective forecasting process is being used to generate an accurate forecast, management must be very disciplined in its focus. A degree in marketing only does not a good forecast make. After all, the forecast drives virtually all material and resource planning in the enterprise, and a poor forecast can have devastating effects on inventory levels, customer service levels, total costs, and employee morale.

The characteristics of a good forecasting process and a good forecast include appropriate forecasting methods and a stabilized forecast to allow for flexibility, require minimal amendment, and provide accuracy (to the extent possible, and continuously improving).

Too many companies use a standard set of methods to generate their forecasts. These are often based on the knowledge and comfort level of the forecaster with a particular method; the "we have always done it this way" syndrome; and lack of knowledge of forecasting methods, their applicability and uses, and the underlying assumptions and theory behind them.

Chambers, Mullick, and Smith addressed these issues in their landmark paper, "How to Choose the Right Forecasting Technique" (*Harvard Business Review*, July-August 1971, pp. 45–74). A single technique is not sufficient for all product categories—different categories demand different methods to predict demand as accurately as possible. Of course, it is a truism that there is no such thing as an accurate forecast, but there is such a thing as a better forecast and forecasting process. The various techniques available (from Chambers, et. al.) are:

FIGURE 6–15
Characteristics of a Good Forecast

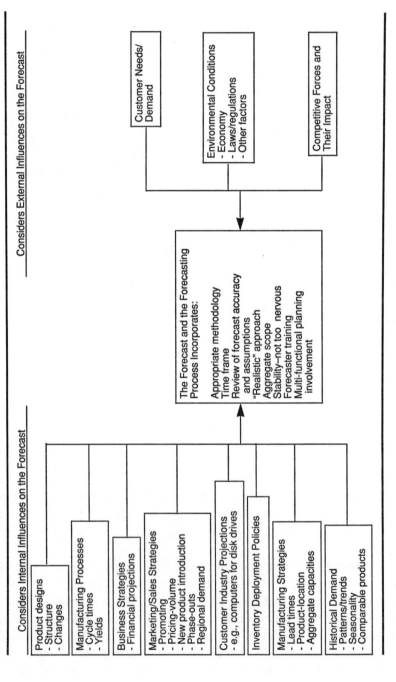

- Qualitative methods (Delphi/consensus, market research, analogies)
- Time series methods (moving averages, exponential smoothing and all its variations, Box-Jenkins, and other trend modeling and projection tools)
- Causal methods (regression and econometric models, input-output, and economic models to leading indicator analysis)

In any event, these methods are appropriate at different levels of aggregation and time horizons in terms of use (product forecasting to inventory modeling), accuracy, and amount of data required. One particular high technology company used a combination of regression modeling and "gut feel" for several years across all products, and were still surprised at a forecast accuracy (measured as the delta between forecast and actual over a quarter) of 60 percent or less. Another major electronics company used several techniques, but the results were modified at several levels to match senior management's financial projections. Forecast accuracy was less than 30 percent, wreaking havoc with plant schedules, inventory levels, customer service, and total costs.

This introduces another danger in forecasting—inappropriate processes and methods lead to frequent changes, or a "nervous" forecast. Nervous forecasts are translated into nervous production schedules and rapidly changing supplier requirements—again leading to higher overall costs. Figure 6–16 illustrates some of the costs associated with poor forecasting. A stable forecast and a stable forecasting process are essential to effective inventory and resource management. Stability can come only from a stable forecasting process that utilizes appropriate methods, involves the relevant functions, and monitors and tracks accuracy. Forecasting is the driver of the entire supply-demand planning process. Most line managers, on realizing the poor and nervous nature of their forecasts, build up inventory stocks to buffer their schedules, leading to higher system-wide costs.

Fixed time frame for forecasting: The forecasting time horizons should be consistent across product lines for effective global supply-demand planning. Inconsistent time horizons lead to problems with aggregate resources planning and cash flow/working capital projections.

Regular reviews with sales, manufacturing and purchasing. It is important that a committee composed of sales, manufacturing, and purchasing regularly review these aspects of forecasts:

FIGURE 6–16
Cost Impacts of Poor Forecasting Process and Forecasts

Symptoms	Impacts
• Nervous forecast (and production/procurement plans) • Poor forecast accuracy • Lack of involvement of manufacturing, purchasing, and sales **⟶** • Inappropriate methods • Excessive manipulation to match financial and marketing plans • Inappropriate levels of aggregation	• Excessive raw material/component, work-in-process and finished goods inventories • High levels of obsolescent inventory • Poor line management morale • High production changeover and expediting costs • Stockouts—loss of sales and goodwill • Poor customer service levels • Unnecessary capacity and resource investments • Quick turnaround penalties • Cancellation penalties

    Forecast versus actual

    Methodology review

    Assumptions

A "realistic" approach—not too aggressive or conservative is important. This is where the reality checks happen. Forecasts that are marketing-generated and presented to line management are often, in our experience, inaccurate and likely to be changed. They have little resemblance to reality, and have a strong relationship to marketing plans, financial projections, and product management goals. Forecast reviews with a forecasting committee composed of marketing, manufacturing, purchasing, and sales must be an essential part of the forecasting process, to review performance, appropriate methods, and their underlying assumptions (and change them when necessary).

Forecasting is the driver of the supply-demand management process. It should not, therefore, resemble a wish list or be a political tool. In one company, a rationale for a completely unreasonable forecast was that it served to set "stretch" objectives for the sales force. The sales force never did achieve the forecast over a three-year period, and the result was that the forecast was downsized each year in the final quarter to reflect reality. Meanwhile, the operating units continued to base procurement contracts, capacity, and resource decisions on the forecast-driven plan, resulting in high costs, excessive inventory levels, and poor morale among line management.

Forecaster training. This is a key element in the forecasting process. The forecaster(s) must be trained in the following:

- Forecasting methods, theory, and applicability (including the type, nature, and accuracy of the data required)
- Product-market characteristics (for instance, effects of price-volumes, analogies to comparable products, effects on related products, etc.)
- Challenging assumptions
- Improvement of the forecasting process

To permit a partially trained person to provide the basis for one of the most important pieces of planning information in the firm is exceedingly dangerous in terms of cost structure, customer service, execution of strategies, capacity and resource investment, and employee morale.

SUPPLY-DEMAND PLANNING

The goal of supply-demand planning is to supply the right amount of material at the right time to the right customer (internal or external). Prior to undertaking this effort, there are some strategic policies and parameters that must be defined by the enterprise. These include:

- *Design*
  Is the product highly engineered?
  - Unique for every customer, a standard across all customers?
  - High degree of options/configurations?
- *Product introduction*
  What is the rate of new product introduction and phase-out?
  - Number and frequency?
  - Ramifications to the manufacturing process?
- *Suppliers*
  What is the supplier environment?

- ○ Number of suppliers?
- ○ Substitutability?
- ○ Location and type of material?
- ○ Delivery policies?
- ○ Lead times?

- *Manufacturing process*
  - ○ Capacity?
  - ○ Product mix?
  - ○ Outside processing?
  - ○ Yield and scrap?
  - ○ Lead times?

- *Distribution center/warehousing*
  - ○ Capacities and throughput?
  - ○ Inbound materials sources?
  - ○ Shipment destinations?
  - ○ Location and number?
  - ○ Turnaround time?

- *Delivery*
  - ○ Lead times?
  - ○ Source-destination links?

- *Policy*
  What products are build-to-stock and build-to-order?
  Where are the order processing points in the process?
  What is the make versus buy policy?
  Is there a surge capability or policy (for example, co-packing, outside processing, or contract manufacturing)?

The enterprise in the customer service era should be looking for the inventory policy that is "just right". Figure 6–17 illustrates the extremes of inventory policy in the "build-to-stock" and "build-to-order" approaches. While the "build-to-stock" policy appears right in terms of customer response, it comes at a cost of inventory.

The supply-demand planner should have the "big picture" perspective while generating the plan. Hence, definition of the strategic parameters and policies listed above is essential, as is access to worldwide inventory status data.

Staged/decentralized and centralized planning. A number of companies use a decentralized planning process sometimes called "staged"

FIGURE 6–17
Impact of Inventory Policy on Schedule Response

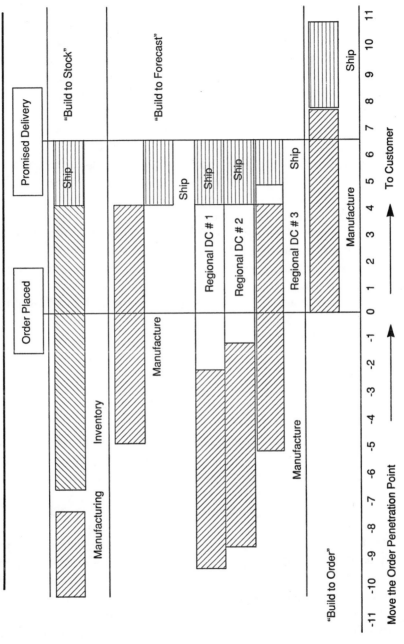

planning. In this process, the various components of supply-demand planning are distributed and treated as discrete planning exercises with input from the preceding stage. This often leads to multiple lead times, redundant safety stocks, inaccuracy, and sluggish response. Figure 6–18 depicts a staged, distributed, supply-demand planning process. As can be seen, there are several aggregation and disaggregation steps.

If we have a situation where uncertainty is introduced in terms of a poor forecast (frequently amended or grossly inaccurate), a ripple effect takes place, affecting all the redundant safety stocks and lead times. This results in sluggish system response to customer needs, and in a combination of high inventories (of the wrong product) and late deliveries or stockouts at the customer level (of the right product). This, additionally, leads to a lack of faith at the line level in the forecast, with the result that every entity maintains its own set of forecasts independent of the official marketing forecast. In one major electronics company, executives of the two major plants used the corporate marketing forecast only for tracking the forecast to actual sales, to send the results each month to corporate headquarters to demonstrate the poor job marketing was doing.

The decentralized process disconnects the various pieces of the supply chain (plants, stages, procurement, distribution centers) from the enterprise-wide customer service and inventory deployment objectives. This is illustrated in Figure 6–18. In this case, four different planning entities will each aggregate/disaggregate and develop lead times independently. They will, additionally, plan for safety stocks independently—in other words, each seeks to optimize its own planning processes without considering the global nature of the supply chain. This prevents effective global resource balancing for best asset utilization and customer satisfaction.

The current trends toward increased coordination and globalization, as well as our own work with several companies, have convinced us that a global supply-demand approach to integrated materials management is necessary for effective customer service and system-wide cost control. An integrated planning approach, as shown in Figure 6–19, will respond to customer needs from a total supply chain perspective.

A single, realistic forecast yields a single planning lead time for all associated master production schedules and purchasing plans. As discussed earlier, there are several external forecast influences that are specific to a region or a country. The planning lead time should, therefore, reflect regional constraints. The single lead time will allow all entities in

FIGURE 6–18

Planning Lead Times—Decentralized Staged Planning by Different Entities

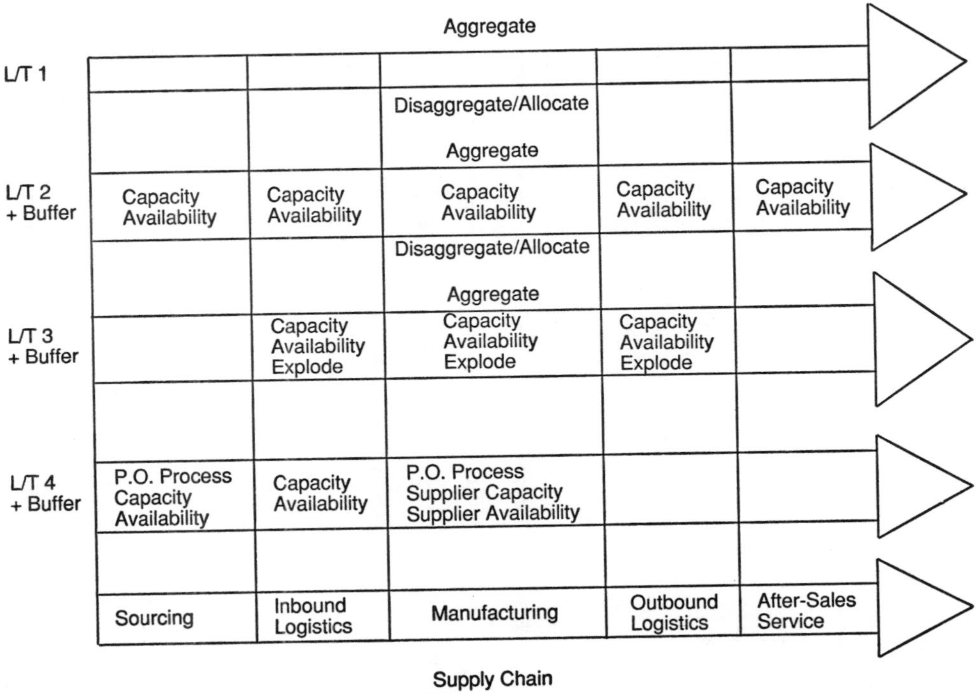

	Sourcing	Inbound Logistics	Manufacturing	Outbound Logistics	After-Sales Service
L/T 1			Aggregate / Disaggregate/Allocate		Aggregate
L/T 2 + Buffer		Capacity Availability	Aggregate / Disaggregate/Allocate	Capacity Availability	Capacity Availability
L/T 3 + Buffer		Capacity Availability Explode	Aggregate	Capacity Availability Explode	
L/T 4 + Buffer	P.O. Process Capacity Availability	Capacity Availability	P.O. Process Supplier Capacity Supplier Availability		

Supply Chain

FIGURE 6–19
Centralized Planning

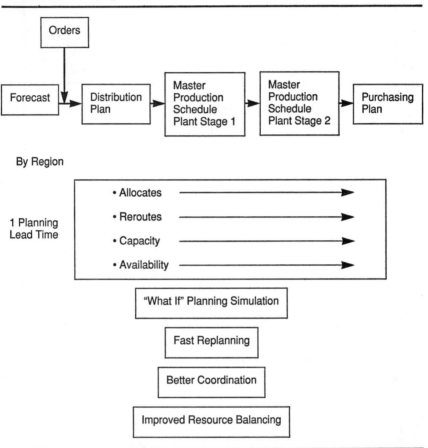

the supply chain to allocate capacity for planning and execution. In every case, supply-demand planning must be front-end driven. Figure 6–20 revisits the planning flow required to support the material flow in the supply chain, and highlights the key planning parameters at each stage.

Flexibility is required in a centralized planning environment to counter internal and external changes in the supply chain. Models can be created to conduct "what if" analysis and test the impact of potential changes on various scenarios. Such decision support tools will be able to replan quickly and coordinate the activities of downstream supply chain entities. These decision support tools include:

FIGURE 6–20
Centralized Planning Planning Flow to Support Material Flow in the Supply Chain

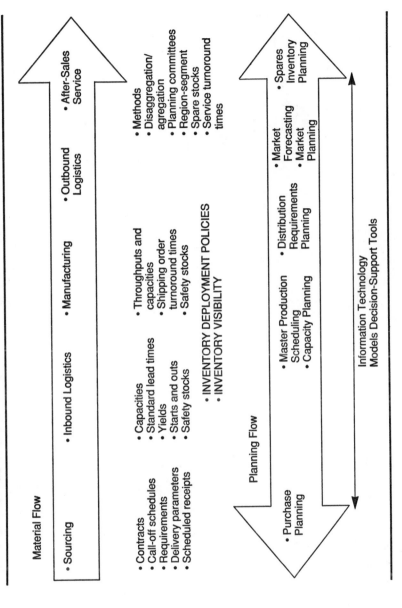

FIGURE 6–21
Global Resource Balancing

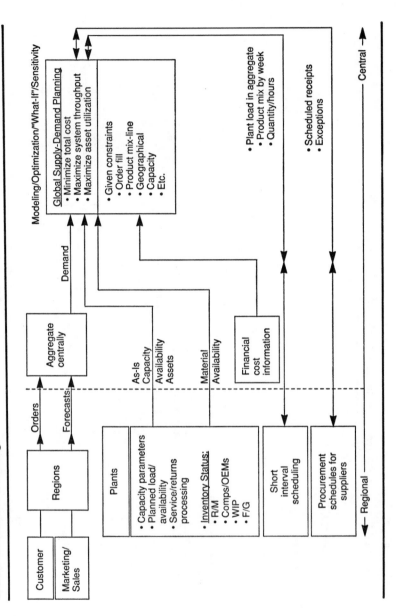

- Optimization models (discussed in Chapter 3) for resource/cost balancing
- "What if" simulation models
- Inventory/stocking computational support based on changeable decision parameters
- MRP II/DRP II systems that support planning scenarios
- Models to assess the impact of end-of-life (EOL) planning
- Models to assess the impact of new product introduction

The supply-demand planning process must include the use of these tools, as well as the frequent evaluation of their underlying assumptions and parameters.

Global resource balancing—a process. The essence of supply-demand planning is global resource balancing. Figure 6–21 illustrates such an approach used by some companies. Regional forecasts and orders are aggregated centrally. Then, based on the inventory deployment strategies developed, they are modeled either to minimize total cost or to maximize system throughput or asset utilization, depending upon the company's objectives. Parameters, inventory status, and financial cost data are uploaded from the plant level to the global supply-demand system for this planning effort. Aggregate plant and procurement schedules are then downloaded to the various entities. These are master-scheduled for capacity and material feasibility at the plant level and sent back up to central supply-demand planning to be refined. Finalized schedules are then downloaded to the plants for short-interval scheduling, procurement scheduling and execution. Progress and status are monitored against the schedules at central supply-demand planning, where they are tracked in terms of lots and customer orders.

The key to this effective planning is, of course, a good information system using networks and satellite communications. This will be discussed in the next chapter.

CHAPTER 7

INFORMATION TECHNOLOGY STRATEGY

THE ROLE OF INFORMATION TECHNOLOGY IN TODAY'S COMPETITIVE ENVIRONMENT

Information technology (IT) is the thread running through the enterprise—the true link across the value chain. It is the most powerful tool of the 20th century, and defines the competitive arena. The preceding sections, which addressed various aspects of logistics strategy, have described the role of information technology as the key enabler in developing and implementing logistics strategies and managing operations across a wide spectrum of technologies.

Philip Pyburn describes the development of information technology strategy as:

> (positioning) IT in a proactive role where the competitive strategy is not viewed as given, but rather as something that should be challenged, and perhaps modified, in light of emerging technologies and applications.

More significantly, perhaps, Pyburn states:

> Unlike some of the oft-cited examples of firms developing so-called strategic systems, our research suggests that the most effective and sustainable examples of IT use occur when IT is woven into the very fiber of the firm. In many ways, IT is most strategic when it is most mundane, having thousands of small impacts throughout the firm rather than one colossal and, often, easily duplicated success ("Redefining the Role of Information Technology," *Business Quarterly*, vol. 55, no. 3, Winter 1991, pp. 25–30).

This, then, is the theme of this chapter—information technology as an integral part of the logistics supply chain. There are two key concepts.

The first involves IT as an enabler to the management process (as is a specific process sequence of activities, or a strategic outsourcing decision). As defined in an earlier chapter, a process represents the integration of process flow, people, and information technology (see Figure 7–1). The successful company of the future will operate from a competitive basis of proprietary technologies *and* processes. The second concept involves the integration of IT with management methods (total quality management and continuous improvement, just-in-time, management through constraints, quick response, etc.) to address key business issues facing the company. These, discussed in chapter one, include growth, organization, globalization, cash management, and customer service and response.

In moving towards the "virtual supply chain" focus, three major IT-enabled elements will dominate management thinking:

Business focus on time/customer/process

Methods of improvement—business process redesign and continuous improvement

IT parameters for stakeholder/global access and communication networks

These aspects of IT do not involve "bits, bytes, feeds, speeds," but, rather, involve the application, integration, decision-support, and ability to resolve key business issues. It is fairly safe to assume that IT development will facilitate "seamless" enterprise and global systems over the next few years—indeed, many companies are moving toward this state. IT management in logistics today is analogous to driving a car—it is not necessary for a driver to know all about electronic fuel injection; he or she must, however, know how to drive, the rules of the road, and directions to the ultimate destination. Visualizing and deciding on the destination is probably the most important. Similarly, deriving a vision of how IT can be integrated into the key elements of the logistics process (process and management methods) for competitive advantage requires that managers "leave Kansas". It is important that they step beyond the paradigms of conventional IT thinking, and view information as an integral part of the logistics process. Following are examples of IT successfully used in the logistics process:

• A major medical products company extended its ordering process through its customers (health organizations) to its consumers

FIGURE 7–1
Processes—Integration of Process Flows, People, and Information Technology

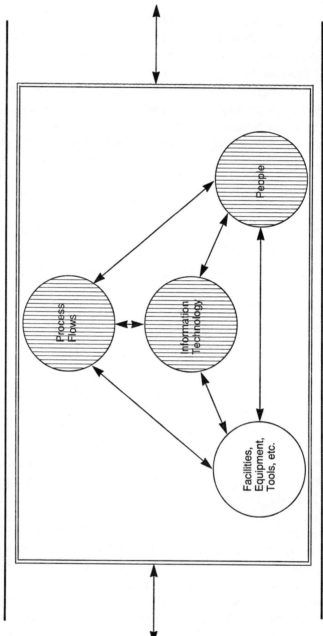

(physicians), allowing them to manage their own departmental inventories and to replenish directly when stocks ran low.
cians), allowing them to manage their own departmental inventories and to replenish directly when stocks ran low.

• A major computer company used Artificial Intelligence (AI) to extend its configuration/ordering process to customers, allowing them to configure systems for their own needs, and reducing the lead times and confusion involved in manually developing a configuration with the salesperson and a catalog.

• Several large semiconductor firms have extended their distributors' replenishment processes (and their own inventory management process) through information systems into the distributors' warehouses and procurement systems.

• One major electronics company is assessing the state of technology on the market and forecasting technological trends to determine whether key customer-oriented processes (the integration of flows, people, and information technology) need redesigning to provide a competitive edge in the next decade (see Figure 7–2).

• A large consumer products company replenishes its U.S. retail outlet customers daily, using satellite technology; it thus reduces pipeline inventory levels while eliminating stockouts.

Information as the Key Asset

In today's competitive quantum leap environment, information is increasing in importance as an asset of the company. Figure 7–3 illustrates this trend. As the relative importance of physical assets to the company is decreasing, the importance of information, processes, and people is rapidly increasing—a source of competitive advantage and management focus. Several companies have recognized the increasing relative importance of people as assets, but too many pay mere lip service to the concept. They make statements at management meetings and in annual reports; however, people are treated as basic productive resources, rarely consulted in major decision-making and problem solving, and laid off in times of economic downturn or mismanagement. Even fewer companies have recognized the increasing relative importance of information and processes as the major assets in the enterprise. Successful companies have done so, and have acted on this concept. While return on information is as yet a distant concept, that of return on management is gaining increasing acceptance, with "management" involving the managing of

FIGURE 7–2

Assessing Technologies for Customer-Oriented Processes

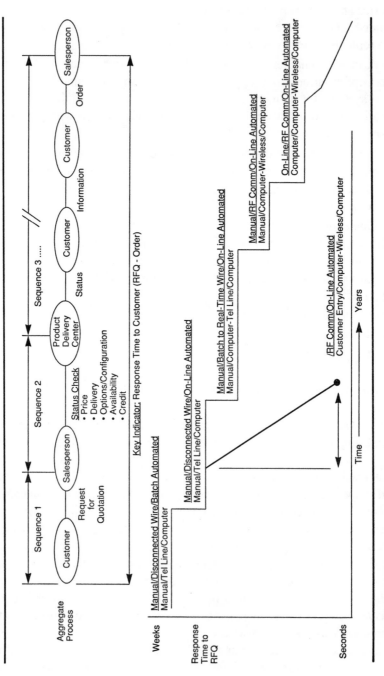

FIGURE 7–3
Trends—Relative Importance of Information as an Asset

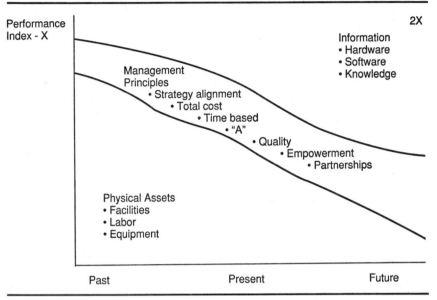

information, people, and processes to meet customer needs and to achieve a sustained competitive advantage.

Historical Shortfall in Projected IT Benefits

The promised benefits of IT have not materialized for many companies. Realization of the potential promised by vendors and MIS managers over the past decade has been disappointing in most firms (though some have reaped significant competitive benefits). Consequently, many senior executives are wary of projected IT benefits, and skeptical of the role of IT in their competitive strategies. This shortfall in projected IT benefits has several causes, the most important of which are:

- *The technology justification and capital allocation process*
  - Overly optimistic projections of benefits as part of the technology justification and capital allocation processes

- ○ Reliance on solely economic methods of evaluating costs and benefits, along with arbitrary hurdle rates of return
- ○ Focus on "invoiceable" out-of-pocket costs and cost savings, ignoring the actual and potential costs of time, response, customer service, and quality, and potential revenue enhancement benefits
- *Traditional IT relationships within the firm*
  - ○ MIS driving IT strategy, requirements, definition, and development
  - ○ The concepts of "MIS" and "users"
  - ○ The functional "silo" syndrome of developing all IT systems in-house, rather than evaluation of acquiring and modifying off-the-shelf packages or outsourcing design and development
  - ○ The all or nothing attitude of many firms towards centralization–decentralization issues of MIS functions
- *The traditional role of IT as a supporting factor to strategy, rather than as an integral part of the firm's competitive strategy*

The key issues, it can be seen, revolve around the organization, its perception, and the role of IT within the competitive environment. These factors will be addressed later in this chapter.

While this section addresses the development of an information technology strategy for logistics, it is virtually impossible to restrict the discussion of IT strategy to logistics alone. The approach and methods presented, therefore, are applicable to the development of IT strategies for the enterprise. Ideally, IT strategy development should be approached in an enterprise-wise manner. Given that this is not always organizationally possible or feasible, the major issues have been addressed from a logistics perspective.

IT Strategy and Strategic Alignment

It is worthwhile to distinguish between IT strategy and planning. The key differences are:

IT strategy defines the framework and expresses the firm's principles regarding IT and the business, with a time horizon of typically five or more years.

FIGURE 7–4
IT Strategy Alignment

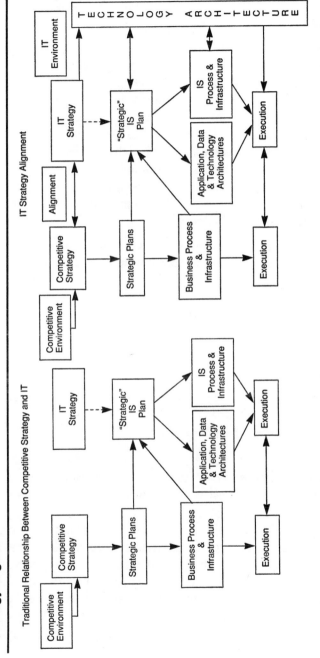

Traditional Relationship Between Competitive Strategy and IT

IT Strategy Alignment

Source: Philip J. Pyburn, "Redefining the Role of Information Technology," *Business Quarterly*, Winter 1991, Volume 55, Number 3, pp 26–27.

IT planning consists of a set of actions and plans, with a time frame of approximately two years.

Leading thinkers such as Pyburn, Henderson, and Venkatraman have emphasized that, if a firm is to be truly competitive in this information-driven competitive market, IT strategy must be aligned with the competitive strategy. Strategic alignment is the concept whereby the IT strategy is aligned with the business strategy in terms of resources and capabilities; consistency of rate of change and time horizon; and consistency of objectives and values. It requires that information technology be an integral part of the firm's total strategy, rather than, as has traditionally been the case, decisions that result from it. The differences are illustrated by Pyburn in terms of the planning process (Figure 7–4). He makes the point that an IT strategy

> helps managers define the decision making boundaries for future action, but stops short of determining the actions themselves. (This is where the strategic information technology plan takes over.)

Pyburn's work, liberally referred to here, provides an approach toward aligning IT strategy with competitive strategy. Briefly, the phases are:

Phase 1: Assess current alignment between IT and competitive strategies

Phase 2: Identify IT potential impacts on business strategy

Phase 3: Draft aligned IT strategy alternatives

Phase 4: Refine IT strategy

The dynamic nature of technology and competition make it imperative that the IT strategy be aligned with the competitive strategy. Given the IT strategy, which consists of a set of IT principles and directions, the information technology plan can then be developed. Logistics strategy, as part of the firm's competitive strategy, must include IT in order to be truly competitive and to reflect the dynamic technological and competitive environment. IT, traditionally viewed as an implementation tool, must now be perceived, planned for, and used as an enabler. Figure 7–5 represents Davenport's concepts of this shift, and illustrates the new competitive approach to IT.

The remainder of this chapter addresses the strategic information technology planning and application phases of the process, particularly as they pertain to logistics.

FIGURE 7–5   Strategic Perspectives of IT—Traditional (Implementor) and Today (Enabler)

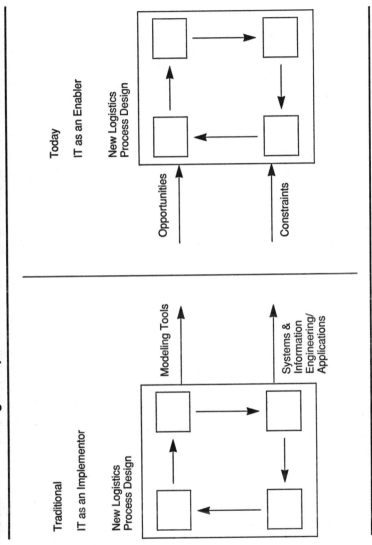

Information Technology Planning

Figure 7–6 outlines an approach to IT planning. This, and every other approach (they are all similar in concept), uses the strategic business plan as the baseline for IT planning. A major assumption at this point is that the business plan incorporates several aspects of good business practice. The focus of IT planning must be on process and strategy, not on methodologies or technology. Briefly, in order to ensure that the information needs of the value chain suppliers are aligned with the requirements of the customers, management must test the validity of the business plan against current, available, and modifiable systems. To achieve this end, the planning process must have an organizational "champion", must dovetail business and information needs, and should include the following steps.

Project Initiation
Initiate the planning process. This step must include a determination at senior management level of the mission, goals, and objectives of the business—the strategic planning process. Included in this phase is the creation of a project steering committee, organization, and review mechanisms. It should also include the identification of an empowered project team, including key representatives of alliance partners and customers, logistics management, logistics user representatives (these may change depending on the areas and applications being analyzed), and representatives from the IS department to facilitate the process. Additionally, the development of a detailed work plan is essential to establish schedules, attainable milestones, and responsibilities. It is often helpful to use this initiation phase as an opportunity for planning team formation and building exercises—team dynamics is an important component of the IT planning process.

Current State Analysis
Review the business strategy. The business plan should be summarized by both the steering committee and the project team to highlight those logistics-related areas of the plan that can be IT-enabled. Three aspects of the business strategy must be surfaced for successful, strategy-aligned IT planning:

• Critical success factors, or "things that must go right" in order to achieve stated goals and objectives

FIGURE 7–6   Information Technology Planning

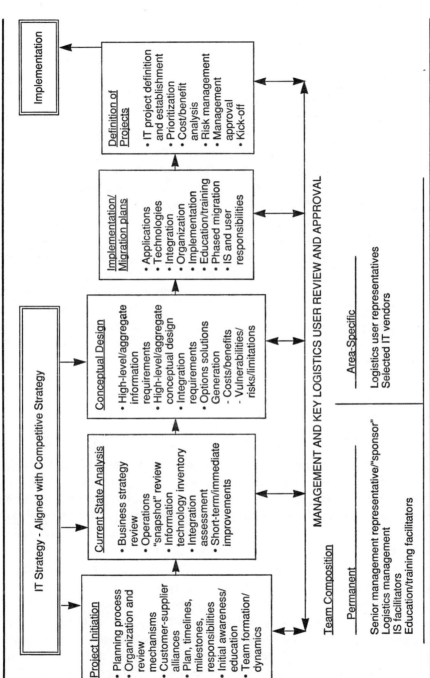

IT Strategy - Aligned with Competitive Strategy

Implementation

Project Initiation
• Planning process
• Organization and review mechanisms
• Customer-supplier alliances
• Plan, timelines, milestones, responsibilities
• Initial awareness/ education
• Team formation/ dynamics

Current State Analysis
• Business strategy review
• Operations "snapshot" review
• Information technology inventory
• Integration assessment
• Short-term/immediate improvements

Conceptual Design
• High-level/aggregate information requirements
• High-level/aggregate conceptual design
• Integration requirements
• Options solutions Generation
  - Costs/benefits
  - Vulnerabilities/ risks/limitations

Implementation/ Migration plans
• Applications
• Technologies
• Integration
• Organization
• Implementation
• Education/training
• Phased migration
• IS and user responsibilities

Definition of Projects
• IT project definition and establishment
• Prioritization
• Cost/benefit analysis
• Risk management
• Management approval
• Kick-off

MANAGEMENT AND KEY LOGISTICS USER REVIEW AND APPROVAL

Team Composition

Permanent

Senior management representative/"sponsor"
Logistics management
IS facilitators
Education/training facilitators

Area-Specific

Logistics user representatives
Selected IT vendors

• Obstacles, or "things that need to be removed" from the current operating state in order to achieve the business plan

• Business implications, in terms of competitiveness, cost, time, and quality, if the obstacles are not removed or if the goals are not met (This is important to provide an impetus for change and a basis for IT cost-benefit/risk analysis for prioritizing projects in the IT plan.)

Review business operations. This involves making an objective and rigorous analysis of the processes, methods, and performance of the logistics chain vis-à-vis cost, time, and response to customer service requirements. Suppliers must be interviewed, as must line management representing all organizations (and levels within each organization), to further define the critical success factors, obstacles and implications surfaced earlier. Obtaining the "voice of the customer" during this analysis is essential to ensure that a future state system will provide the customer with appropriate, cost-effective levels of service. A key part of this "snapshot" analysis is the rigorous collection and analysis of data to effectively characterize the operations. (Methods have been discussed further in Chapter 8.)

Conduct an information technology inventory. This inventory focuses on surveying and documenting current IT in place to support the business. The existing architecture must be mapped to illustrate the integration issues of the system, followed by a performance evaluation and cost effectiveness analysis of the current system. It is important at this point that the steering committee and project team carefully monitor the cost of the process. If not managed properly, or if performed at too high a level of detail, this task can get out of hand, costing a great deal in terms of time and money, and frustrating progress in the IT planning process. The best solution, of course, is to have well-documented systems already in place. If this is unavailable, or if documentation is marginal, the process should be closely managed to obtain the most accurate picture of the system with the least amount of expenditure.

Identify short term/immediate improvements. This important step is often ignored in many companies—the identification of "quick hit", fast payback projects which can be implemented immediately. A well-assembled team (experienced and knowledgeable in operations, systems, and technology) can quickly surface several high savings opportunity/low cost improvement initiatives during the preceding phases. The project team should optimally bring these initiatives to the steering committee for approval and delegation to functional implementation teams. These, in turn, should be empowered to install solutions under the auspices of the project team.

These initiatives are necessary for two reasons. They demonstrate to senior management, to system caretakers, and, especially, to users along the supply chain that progress is being made, and that the IT planning team is really a proactive task force. They also generate improvements to the "bottom line," thus demonstrating that the initial planning project is self-funding. These short term improvements are necessary to maintain enthusiasm and commitment. In too many companies, lack of perceived progress has resulted in management and user frustration and skepticism, ensuring the failure of the IT planning process.

Conceptual Design

Develop high-level/aggregate information requirements. By reviewing the current state, and matching it to the requirements of line management, the team will be able to develop a set of high-level information requirements. Processing requirements should be summarized and the volume of transactions should be quantified roughly by function. Any issues dealing with the current system environment should also be noted and quantified as to their impact on future state designs. The next step involves the identification of key benefits in terms of time, cost, and response of the new system—the "delta" between the current and planned environments.

Develop high-level conceptual design. This activity results in the development of a system overview. A hardware configuration "strawman" (preliminary case to be discussed as a starting point) should be developed to get the concepts on paper, followed by the formulation of a data usage model to illustrate the data path for system use. Typically, a management review is required at the end of this task to gain management and user consensus on the new high-level design.

The conceptual design must include interfaces and integration requirements; risks and risk management; major features; decision parameters and decision-support points; key success factors necessary for the information system to be used effectively; and major outputs. A danger here is the tendency (particularly when IS personnel drive the process) to attempt to drive the conceptual design to excruciating levels of detail. This usually results in reviewers and managers neglecting the all-important review (wearying of the volume to be read) or dismissing the conceptual design as another "IS effort". Care must be taken to maintain the conceptual design at a "business" level of detail.

Develop solutions options. Based on issues raised during the management review and the parameters identified in the aggregate requirements and conceptual design, solutions options should be identified. These options should respond to the following issues:

- Total costs of implementation (education, training, modification, systems development, personnel, time, hardware, software, peripherals, and communication technologies)
- Benefits (tangible, intangible, quantifiable or non-quantifiable, economic, tactical and strategic)
- Software and hardware limitations and performance negatives
- Risks and vulnerabilities

Implementation/Migration Plans

Develop application plans. This basically involves taking the "strawman" system architecture and adding specifics to create the architecture of the applications to be used. Descriptions of potential applications must be generated and must describe the application, its operating parameters, modifications required (if any), and integration with other applications. The implementation of the application set must be prioritized and phased to balance the implementation cost and reduce system implementation risks.

Develop technology plans. The hardware requirements must be planned to ensure that the appropriate hardware is specified for the chosen application. The configuration must be solidified to support the system in terms of performance and implementation schedule. An approach to, and a discussion of, technology assessment is outlined later in this chapter.

Develop organization plans. Staffing requirements, information system organization, and user organization need to be identified and designed to fit the needs of the application and technology implementation plans; future system operation; and system maintenance. The management of staff resources and procedures must be finalized at this stage.

Definition of Projects

Establish projects. Summaries, schedules, and cost estimates of each project must be developed to incorporate the application, technology, and organizational plans. The projects must then be phased in relationship to each other, to determine the best schedule (considering cost and technology implementation dependency issues). For discrete (rather than integrative) IT projects, prioritization can be done on a cost impact versus strategic urgency versus improvement potential versus value to customer basis. (The prioritization process is outlined in more detail in Chapter 8—Assessing Logistics Performance.)

Part of the project definition and planning process involves a risk analysis of the impacts of the proposed technologies and systems on customer service, competitiveness, recovery plans (should a portion or schedules expand), response, payback, and user acceptance. Should some of these risks appear significant (that is, highly important to success and seem likely to occur), risk management and contingency plans must be developed.

Obtain management review and approval. The project team needs to raise the project plan to the senior management level to gain approval and the go-ahead for implementation. In practice, these sessions can be intense, and it is imperative that the project team be prepared to respond to issues ranging from the technologies to be utilized to the bottom line costs and benefits associated with the implementation plan.

Key Factors for Success

Several factors must be in place for the planning process and the resulting implementation to be successful. There are two aspects to these key success factors:

1. *Planning process success factors.* As discussed earlier in this chapter, commitment of the entire value chain is essential. Top management of the manufacturer must be completely convinced of the merits of the entire effort. They must also communicate their commitment, in word and action, to all stakeholders of the value chain. System users must be actively involved throughout the planning process, and must be actively involved in the design effort to ensure ultimate success—a term used by one major company for this involvement is "submersed." Project team members should be committed full-time to the effort. Very often, whole segments of a planning effort can be weakened or fail due to lack of team participation. Management must dictate the necessity, and instill the importance, of full-time participation.

Core members of the project team must represent (at a minimum) all major organizational entities within the enterprise. Representative experts should also be included from external stakeholders (i.e., suppliers, customers, transportation companies). Finally, the project team *must* be cross-functional, and empowered to "break down" departmental barriers.

The results of such departmental barriers are negative and, in an effort as important as IT planning, can be detrimental to the company's competitiveness and success. Classic symptoms of departmental barriers include information hoarding, multiple databases with duplicate data, non-integrateable and incompatible applications, and an IS department which undertakes every IT application as an in-house development effort.

2. *Implementation success factors.* These include those factors central to successful implementation. It is far better to have a poor system which is well implemented than a great system which is poorly implemented. These success factors begin with successful integration of projects, people, and technology. If projects are developed in a vacuum, the system will lose its cost and impact efficiencies. Suppliers need to be invited to share in the implementation effort. They are more likely to incorporate parallel systems, extend existing systems, or invest in new technologies if they see benefits to be gained from links to the company's engineering, planning, and procurement systems.

Working capital is required to begin the investment process. Building new IT systems can be very expensive, and re-engineering existing systems, while less expensive, is still costly. However, good planning will reduce the likelihood of unexpected overruns. The impact of external fiscal pressures on implementation can also be reduced by careful monitoring of plans and their quick alteration if needed. It is essential, however, that the plans be well developed and robust to permit such changes in direction or emphasis.

Technology Assessment

An important part of the IT planning process, as well as of the ongoing management of processes and technology, is technology assessment (Figure 7–7 provides an approach to Technology Assessment). Using the framework established in the planning process, the company must maintain its focus on satisfying the goals and objectives of the business—not on the mere acquisition of "interesting" technology. This end is achieved by focusing on the critical success factors for the logistics chain (identified earlier) as the departure to choosing the most effective solution. The real danger at this point is wasting precious capital on technology without a purpose. Once the critical success factors have been reviewed for technology requirements, a five-step process should be initiated:

1. *Analyze the activities of the value chain.* This involves the

FIGURE 7-7 Technology Assessment

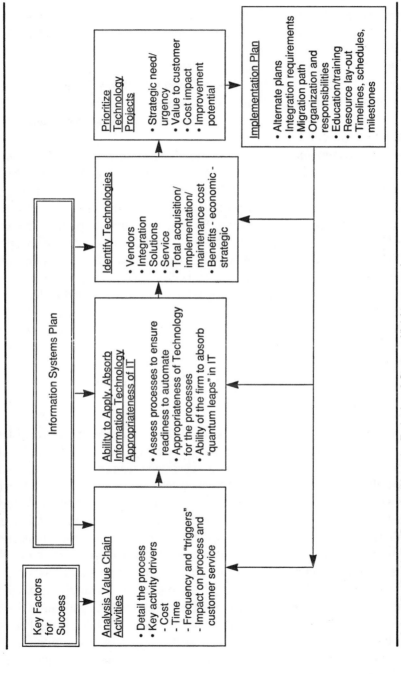

process of identifying technology applications to specific activities and should be performed only after the drivers of each activity have been identified. Drivers are those elements of an activity that influence its effectiveness. Some drivers include: cost of performing the activity (direct, material, indirect/support); time required to perform the activity, and its response to initiating "triggers"; occurrences of the activity, its frequency, and the "triggers" that initiate it; critical path impact; and impact on customer service.

2. *Determine the ability to apply and absorb information technology and its appropriateness for the process.* Each activity must be analyzed to determine if the application of technology is appropriate. The activity may be improved procedurally without the need for expensive technology; this avenue of simplification must first be applied. The result of this activity will generate "no cost—low cost" improvement opportunities whose payback can help finance technology for more demanding activities. Additionally, many organizations and/or functions may not be organizationally or culturally ready for some sophisticated technologies. It then becomes all the more important to focus on the process rather than blindly applying technology as a solution. "Simplify, standardize, optimize, integrate, and automate" should be the guideline for managing the process-technology interaction.

3. *Identify technologies.* This is the point where the team moves from an analysis to a solution orientation. The analysis should lead to the objective choice of technology alternatives. Too often, the process and individual projects can be compromised by team members who are biased toward a particular solution (either the classic case of a solution looking for a problem, or vested interests precluding team members from being objective), thereby adversely affecting the company as a whole. A major pharmaceutical company, looking for an IT system for its manufacturing and quality control, found itself proceeding very slowly because of the IS department's reluctance to consider anything besides the applications from a certain vendor. The IS department was uncomfortable with other technologies and platforms (it would have to acquire new skills), and the vendor provided much of the justification, support, and technical advice that it lacked (but did not wish to admit). Finally, the senior finance executive broke the logjam by announcing that all vendors would be considered on an equal footing. Too narrow an approach can either end in disaster, cause the architects to miss subtle opportunities, or increase the cost of modification.

Technology suppliers and their products should be evaluated on how well they can meet business requirements in total. These requirements should include product effectiveness, cost effectiveness, system design assistance, reliability, ability to deliver, ability to solve problems, maintainability, and long-term support. Some of the key technologies that must be considered in logistics are listed in Table 7–1.

4. *Prioritize technology.* Chapter 8—Assessing Logistics Performance—discusses an approach to justifying technology as well as the issues and methods involved in prioritizing projects. Essentially, they involve criteria of strategic need or urgency, cost impact, improvement potential, and value to the customer. These criteria must be quantified (at the very least, in relative terms) objectively if cost-effective and competitiveness-based technology is to be acquired or developed.

5. *Develop implementation plan.* The plan for implementation is the result of a very rigorous analysis. Many companies enhance their level of success by using computer-aided software engineering (CASE) tools. These tools assist the system architects (project team) in the planning process. The technologies identified earlier are placed into the plan, illustrating primary and alternative approaches. The plan should prioritize the implementation of technology to incorporate an approach for the enterprise to achieve the greatest benefit from resources expended.

Pitfalls

There are several pitfalls which can lead to failure of the IT planning and implementation process. Chief among these is the lack of commitment of the executive management team to the process. Needless to say, lack of a coherent, documented, and articulated competitive strategy nullifies the effort. Other pitfalls that must be avoided include:

- *IT perceived as a tool.* IT should be treated as an integral part of the business plan, not just a tool for support of its execution. The proper perspective can result in an IT plan that provides an integrated system of process flow, people, information, and capital. Viewing information technology merely as a tool could result in technology without a purpose or the "technology for technology's sake" syndrome. With this perspective, user groups often acquire technology in a piecemeal fashion to satisfy immediate automation requirements.
- *Localizing the IT strategy and planning effort.* The process must be

TABLE 7–1
Some Key Logistics Technologies—Technology Assessment

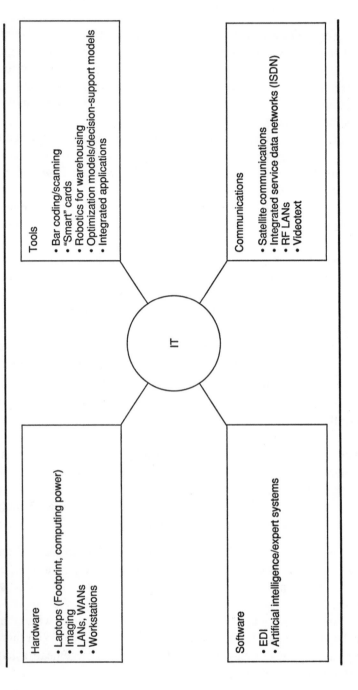

Hardware
- Laptops (Footprint, computing power)
- Imaging
- LANs, WANs
- Workstations

Software
- EDI
- Artificial intelligence/expert systems

IT

Tools
- Bar coding/scanning
- "Smart" cards
- Robotics for warehousing
- Optimization models/decision-support models
- Integrated applications

Communications
- Satellite communications
- Integrated service data networks (ISDN)
- RF LANs
- Videotext

enterprise-wide. It cannot be functional in scope, or encompass just part of the organization. A significant danger to the process and the competitiveness of the company is the assigning of planning and implementation responsibilities to a single department. (A natural reaction by executive management is to assign responsibility to the IS or finance department.) Their lack (in many companies) of logistics and manufacturing operations, customer and supplier requirements, and the basic business processes endanger the effort and place the company at risk. IS departments are often conceptually tied into a single platform and vendor and, in many firms, they have a track record of acquiring technology for technology's sake. Furthermore, they have a vested interest in maintaining IT development and selection in-house, while centralizing information under their control. These can be dangerous behaviors in today's global and competitive market.

• *Planning without implementation.* The IT plan cannot be "shelfware"—it must be implemented. Executive management is responsible for implementation. If the plan is not being followed because it is cumbersome, unrealistic, or out-of-date, change the plan. If the reason is lack of acceptance from logistics personnel, the plan must be recommunicated. However, if the plan is not effective due to employees unwilling to adopt new business practices and change, the people must be changed.

• *Internal conformance.* This is a major risk to visioning an IT-enabled future state of logistics. As stated earlier, IT must be an integral part of the logistics process approach, not a means to automate existing practices. This implies change. Change can be a very traumatic experience in any enterprise. If every stakeholder has not "bought into" the need to change, the system will loose effectiveness; everyone in the logistics supply chain must become a manager of change. Success will be measured by how well the enterprise will adapt. Change cannot be forced, at least in the short term, but must be proactively managed.

INTEGRATED LOGISTICS SYSTEMS

Integrated logistics systems must span, in a seamless manner, the activities of the entire logistics supply chain. IT strategy alignment with competitive strategy, managing the logistics strategic planning process, and integration of IT with the major business processes can develop the requirements for integration and information sharing. IT integration and information sharing along the supplier-customer chain are crucial for quick response, reduced time to market, quick delivery, and excellent quality.

A conceptual diagram of one company's plan for an integrated logistics system is show in Figure 7–8. It possesses some important characteristics:

Shared database and networks provide the supply chain with common, easily accessible information. (The type, use, and storage of data, and stores will become competitive features of the enterprise, particularly as the value of information as an asset grows in importance.)

EDI, electronic data interchange, is the tool to disseminate information to the appropriate stakeholder in the right form and at the appropriate time. EDI can take several forms, most of which deal with protocols for the exchange of data to similar and dissimilar computer systems and networks. This technology links elements of the dispersed supply chain, and enables the alliances and partnerships necessary for success.

Multi-plant/multi-DC facilities are vital. An integrated logistics system must encompass all the facilities in the supply chain network—it must be system-wide to be effective.

Applications and tools are also important. An integrated logistics system is not monolithic in nature—it must support the many major business processes in the supply chain. (Figure 7–8 illustrates the variety of applications and decision making tools necessary for an effective integrated logistics system.)

Management reporting is necessary for monitoring and management. Effective, flexible, real-time management reporting (in both summary and detailed formats) must be designed into the system, for both periodic and ad-hoc information requirements.

Customers' and suppliers' information systems/databases are all linked. EDI enables the information linking of all the stakeholders in the supply chain. Equally important is the flexibility to use and provide different data formats, and use different computing philosophies to link with customers and suppliers.

FIGURE 7-8
Components of an Integrated Logistics System

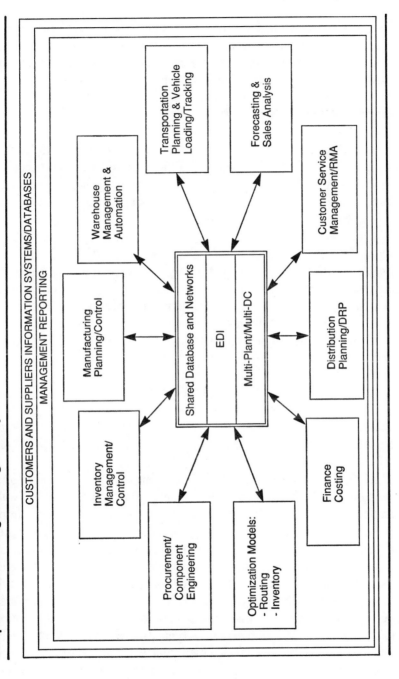

245

Figure 7–9 outlines the logistics information system developed by one multinational computer company. It can be seen that integration with the various product divisions is of critical importance in light of short product life cycles and the dynamic nature of the product technology.

Examples of Applications

The following pages provide some examples and outlines of various applications components of an integrated logistics system. The discussion focuses on four important applications within an integrated system—distribution requirements planning (DRP), financial/cost systems, procurement systems, and field service systems.

DRP and the Relationship of DRP Systems and MRP II

A major component of an integrated logistics system is distribution requirements planning (DRP). This is a requirements generation information system that applies material requirements planning (MRP), time-phased logic, to the distribution function. Consistent with the MRP logic, DRP anticipates and aggregates distribution needs by individual distribution center. Moving backward in the supply chain, the logic then allocates specific distribution needs to a specified plant or group of plants. The plants, in turn, use these needs as time-phased requirements for input to the master production schedule. Figure 7–10 outlines the DRP planning process and key underlying logic elements, while Figure 7–11 illustrates the relationship of DRP and MRP II systems to the planning flow. Figure 7–12 outlines some key features of a DRP system.

MRP II (manufacturing resource planning) systems have very often been sold (and perceived) as "silver bullets" to cure inadequacies in the manufacturing process. DRP should not carry the same perception simply because the distribution process can present the same challenge. The project team must ensure that the distribution and manufacturing processes are capable of producing *and* delivering product to customer satisfaction *before* applying DRP. DRP is a planning tool encompassing a philosophy of doing business that recognizes all forms of inventory as interrelated. It allows management to transfer forecast responsibility to the regions and/or regional distribution centers—typically, the most knowledgeable about local demands. As a management tool, DRP also coordinates globalized system-wide planning and flow of material to meet customer service requirements. The most important aspect of DRP, however, is its

FIGURE 7-9
Logistics Information Systems

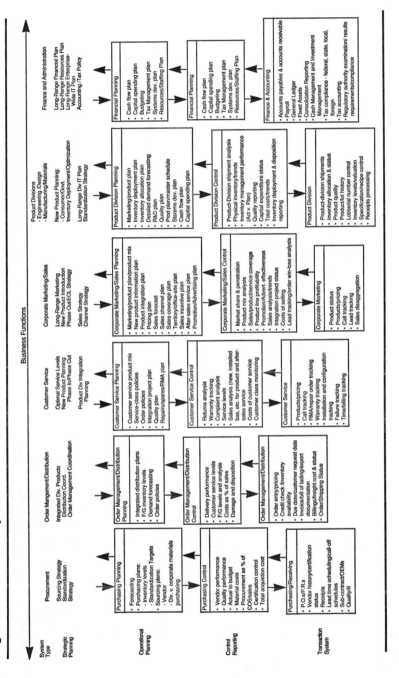

247

FIGURE 7–10   The DRP Planning Process

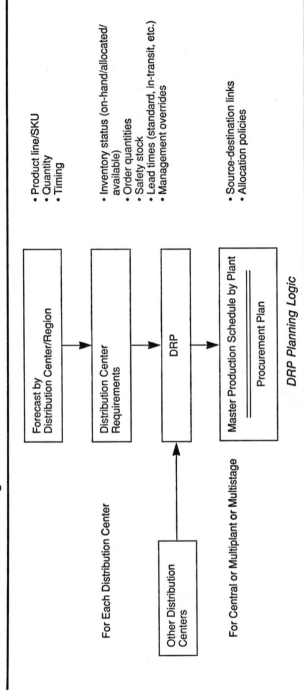

For Each Distribution Center

Forecast by Distribution Center/Region
- Product line/SKU
- Quantity
- Timing

Distribution Center Requirements

DRP
- Inventory status (on-hand/allocated/available)
- Order quantities
- Safety stock
- Lead times (standard, in-transit, etc.)
- Management overrides

For Central or Multiplant or Multistage

Other Distribution Centers

Master Production Schedule by Plant

Procurement Plan
- Source-destination links
- Allocation policies

DRP Planning Logic

- For each distribution center, calculates when the on-hand and in-transit inventory will be consumed, based on market/forecast requirements (net of allocated)
- Uses order quantities and safety stocks to calculate planned shipments to each distribution center
- Uses lead times to calculate shipping dates for planned shipments
- Recommends shipments for each source and destination by latest ship date
- Includes planned shipments and projected on-hand, and continues this process to the end of the planning horizon
- Uses source-destination links and allocation policies by product for application of logic
- Can suggest alternative shipment routes based on specified rules and parameters

248

FIGURE 7–11
Relationship of MRP II and DRP Systems to the Planning Flow

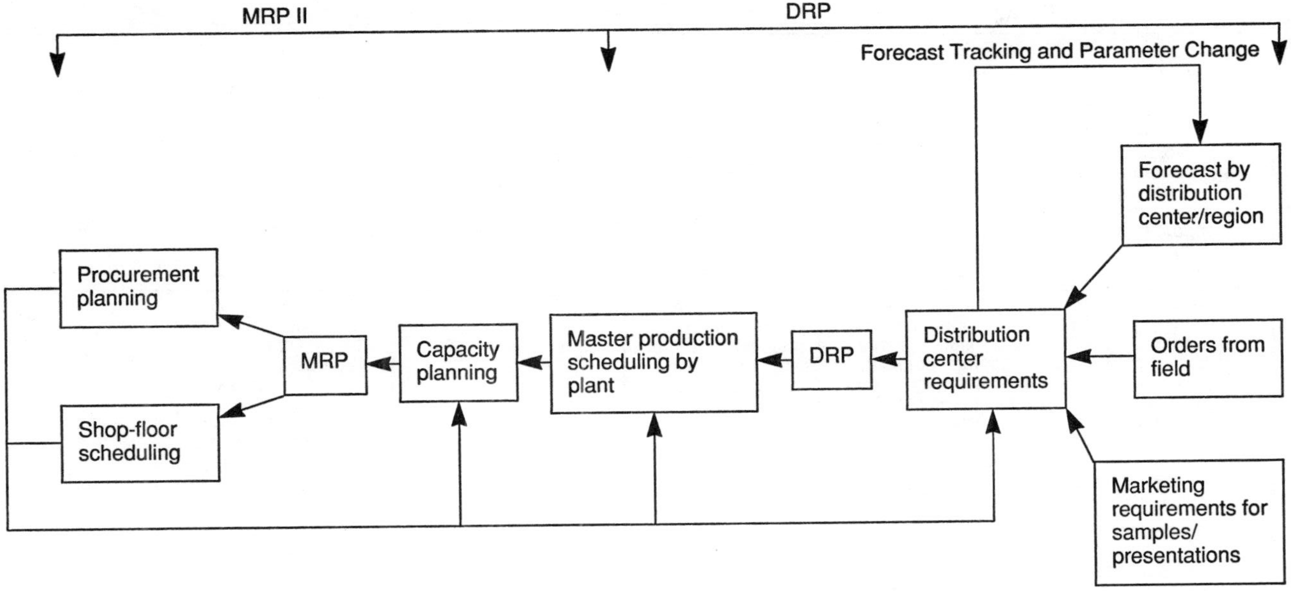

FIGURE 7–12   Key Features of a DRP System (Excluding Manufacturing and Procurement)

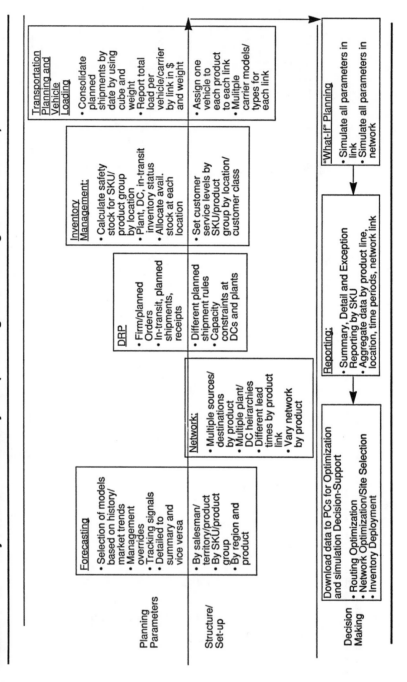

potential to improve the planning of *all* distribution resources, when applied properly.

Successful implementation of DRP requires close attention to three aspects of the system.

- *Parameters* must be set and then analyzed and updated regularly. Parameters should include:
  - Safety stocks by product and DC
  - DC and warehouse capacity standards by product
  - Stocking locations by product
  - Source-destination links by product
  - Order quantities and ship quantities by product
- *Planning* policies need to be created and implemented to ensure the following:
  - Localized responsibility to forecast by DC or region
  - Centralized planning and aggregation
  - A planning horizon at least greater than the cumulative lead time
  - Review and updating of the DRP parameters
  - Enterprise and regional customer service policies
  - Product allocation
  - Effective network flows by product
- *Operational aspects* of the system should include visibility of:
  - DC and warehouse stock status by product
  - Source-destination ship schedules
  - In-transit inventory
  - Shipments and receipts
  - Expected delivery and receipt dates

Generally speaking, the most important operational issues are accuracy, accuracy of data, system parameters, and the updating process.

For successful planning with DRP, the logistics organization must interface with, and jointly set policies and forecasts with, the other organizational stakeholders.

Financial Systems

A core portion of an integrated logistics system, and central to the success of a logistics strategy is the financial and costing system which will collect cost data and provide management with effective decision making information. The steering committee and project team must take special care to ensure, during the planning process, that an integrated mechanism for capturing cost is built into the system. The key to effective logistics strategy and management is accurate and timely cost and profitability information. Changes made to the supply chain (material cost and content, transportation mode and link, volume, inventory, etc.) must be reflected in the cost data being collected. An activity-based costing system that provides *true* profitability and cost by product is essential in the dynamic environment in which many companies operate today. It must provide information and costs for key cost drivers identified, and must include direct costs, as well as all indirect and support costs associated with delivery from the supplier to the customer. This includes total costs of customer service by customer class, product profitability, sales return, and volume costs/savings. Above all, the system must be flexible, providing a strategic and operational management tool in addition to playing the traditional role of accounting reporting.

Among the critical information that the financial system must provide to management are the following:

- Logistics costs in the areas of product contribution, regional sales/ management/support, and customer delivery
- Accurate and timely reporting of costs associated with current service levels and in providing increased customer service levels
- The incremental costs associated with trade-off decisions, such as those required to establish optimum service levels and transportation consolidation
- Periodically recalculated inventory carrying costs to reflect changes in the overhead pool
- Transporation costs by mode, class, and lane (often through reporting third-party freight cost and billing services)—if possible, cross-referenced by product, region, and customer
- All indirect and operating costs associated with the distribution centers
- Production costs by product and product group on a plant-by-plant basis
- All administrative and order processing costs
- Ability to incorporate, or download to, a spreadsheet-type analytical package in order to assess various cost trade-offs for strategy formulation and line management

Procurement Systems

The virtual supply chain concept requires that the company address issues of supplier partnerships or alliances before defining the requirements of the procurement information system. The inclusion of suppliers in the planning process will facilitate defining a procurement system, its database requirements, and connectivity standards, as the supplier becomes an integral part of the information stream. Management of the supply chain for competitive customer service *demands* timely communication of data, parameters, schedules, issues, and trends. The urgency of rapid responses and quick decisions requires a more instantaneous means of communication. Discussion and partnership with suppliers, OEMs, and other third-party partners will enable the company to redesign its processes and to provide the guidance needed for the system architect to plan for future state systems requirements.

Important features of a "world class" procurement system include:

- Access of all supply chain entities to a single, integrated, logical master data base
- Capability to edit and update in an on-line mode
- Institutionalization of the on-line query process versus hard copy reporting
- Hardware considerations and their effect on suppliers and partners (The ability must be present to access supplier inventory position on-line, and to transmit electronically purchase order and specification data.)
- Capability to track information to multiple, often remote, areas (i.e. transport, warehouse, etc.)
- A supplier rating system that measures performance in terms of impact on cost, response, quality, and cycle time
- A supply chain performance management system to provide a mechanism to manage the effectiveness of individual partnership from both perspectives
- Quality delegation programs to reduce and, ultimately, to eliminate incoming inspection steps and create a dock-to-line/WIP environment
- Capability for financial and inventory analysis to maintain equitable pricing using simulation
- Positive material tracking using bar code technology

• Make or buy analysis capability with focus on supplier involvement

As mentioned earlier, open, quick, and accurate communication is essential if the supplier-customer relationship is to give the company a competitive advantage. The most effective way to achieve this communication with the supplier is by building an electronic data interchange (EDI) network between the supplier and customer. EDI must be used as a tool to augment the speed at which data can be exchanged. Even with the implementation of EDI, however, both customer and supplier must continue to dialogue on a regular basis through personal visits. Information technology cannot substitute for personal relationships in maintaining effective partnerships.

Communication with suppliers requires that good internal systems be in place to support the supply chain. Procurement systems should be integrated with, and have visibility of, other subsystems. These include:

• *Research and development engineering design*, to capture new product and product cost data in advance of the procurement cycle
• *Financial*, to capture the standard and actual costs associated with the product (for instance, to be used in the make/buy decision)
• *Inventory*, to track on-hand, planned, and shipped quantities and their locations/status
• *Material planning*, to capture quantity and timing requirements of new and reorder issues and receive electronic requisitions for purchase
• *BOM*, to gather past numbers and their associated engineering specifications
• *Engineering/quality*, to provide to all supply chain entities the quality data of procured material (specification conformance; test results; reliability in the field; delivery performance and response; packaging quality/use; etc.) and the corrective recovery actions required

Field Service Systems

Recent, highly visible surveys of several computer companies have demonstrated the strategic importance of field service. In order to support a high, competitive level of service, it is essential that the manufacturer have a field service applications system that is integrated, on a worldwide

FIGURE 7–13
Field Service Information System Components

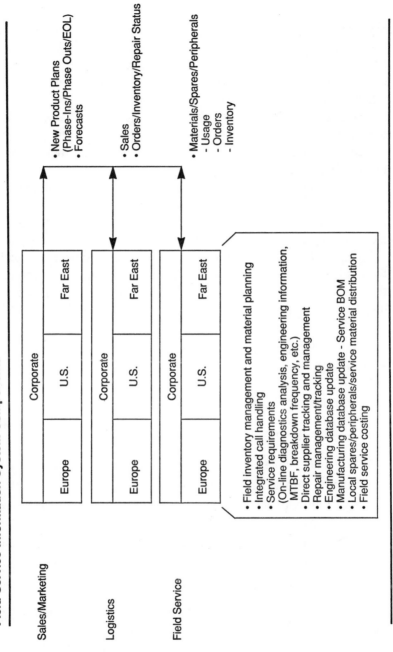

basis, with logistics, sales/marketing, engineering, and manufacturing. (Figure 7–13 outlines the major components of a field service system.) Of particular importance in such a system is the ability to manage service requirements (on-line diagnostic analysis, MTBF [mean time between failures], breakdown frequency, prediction of service calls, replacement before actual breakdown, integration with engineering for technical feedback and enhancements, and integration with manufacturing for repair status). Also important are costing and field inventory management and planning (including OEMs, spares, peripherals, etc.).

Often ignored (relatively speaking) in favor of manufacturing and materials systems, the field service information system must be viewed today as the key factor in influencing repeat sales, since after-sales service is an important component of the buying decision. Defining and developing such a system requires the inclusion and active participation of the engineering, marketing, and manufacturing functional personnel on the project team, and the presence of a senior line operations executive on the steering committee.

Off-the-Shelf Software versus Contractor-Developed versus In-House Developed

Sooner or later in the planning process, the steering committee and project team have to deal with choosing the most effective means for building the system. Several factors are involved in this decision:

Size and complexity of the supply chain and its requirements

Current, in-place information systems

Availability of software applications packages and hardware migration paths

Confidence in vendor and/or in-house capability

Capital and timing

Resources in terms of people and time

There are significant advantages to acquiring (and later modifying or enhancing) off-the-shelf applications packages:

• If vendors have already developed a great deal of the functionality, it does not make a great deal of sense for the in-house IS department to reinvent the wheel.

- Good packages are flexible and can easily be tailored to user requirements.
- Third-party applications are almost always lower cost.
- More rapid implementation ensures quicker results.
- Unlike many (if not most) in-house developed systems, third-party applications software is well documented.
- Third-party software is usually well supported with maintenance and future enhancements.

Similarly, there are some significant disadvantages to developing software in-house:

- It is costly in terms of money and time to build and maintain.
- In-house IS systems analysts often lack the functional expertise in which software vendors invest.
- High turnover in IS departments contributes to frequent time and cost overruns.
- Documentation during development and future enhancements is often poor.
- Rigid coding does not allow flexibility.

A large components manufacturer built a system through a combination of acquisition and in-house development. A year later, the worldwide materials planning department grew so frustrated at the lack of IS response to requests, lack of system flexibility, and lack of user documentation of the in-house developed planning system, that it developed its own spreadsheet-based capacity and time-phased planning system. There was no consultation with the IS department in making this move. This led to a planning system that could not be integrated with the WIP tracking system—consequently, all updates had to be done manually. A year after that, at the request of the vice president of materials, the firm began the process of evaluating third-party materials tracking and application packages to replace its entire set of planning systems.

Another large manufacturer, assuming its needs to be unique (and finding itself under considerable pressure from a large IS department), decided to develop a major demand management system in-house. Two years later, the system is still under development; the users are frustrated; a host of small PC-based systems have proliferated; and the company is still without an integrated system.

The trend toward focusing on core competencies has highlighted one important fact—systems development is not a core competency for most manufacturers. Proprietary and unique systems can still be built with a considerable degree of confidentiality, and there are several large third-party firms with the methodologies, tools, and experience (functional and IT-based) to do so.

GLOBAL IT APPLICATION TRENDS

We have discussed, in an earlier chapter, the trends in globalization of markets and the management of global companies. Michael Porter identified some of these trends as increased geographical dispersion of the configuration/network and the coordination of like activities along the value chain (*Competition in Global Industries* [Boston: Harvard Business School Rep. 1986]). These trends are forcing manufacturers to acquire and develop new or greatly expanded applications to provide the information and decision support to manage in this new competitive environment—in other words, to move toward the virtual supply chain. Figure 7–14 illustrates some of these application trends superimposed over Porter's framework. Briefly, they include:

- *Global supply-demand planning systems* (with global access)
- *Electronic information exchange (including EDI)* to include other stakeholders in the firm—customers, suppliers, transportation companies, freight forwarders, distributors, and value-added resellers—as the firm moves toward a greater degree of outsourcing
- *Worldwide engineering-production databases* to enable geographically dispersed engineering and manufacturing units to work simultaneously toward developing new products; designing them for manufacturability, serviceability, testability, packaging, and customer usage; and bringing them to market rapidly
- *Global resource balancing*, incorporating optimization modeling to manage assets (capital and inventory) along the supply chain (discussed later in this chapter)
- *Worldwide inventory and order status (including lot status) and visibility*
- *Key indicator performance measurement and reporting* on a worldwide basis

FIGURE 7–14
Global IT Application Trends

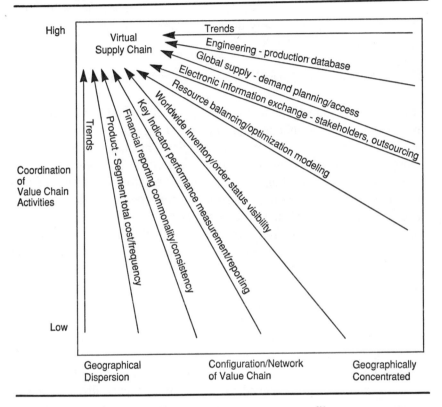

- *Financial reporting commonality/consistency* for management and investors
- *Consistent, accurate systems to analyze product-segment costs* for decision making

Attempting the successful management of a global company on a sustained basis in today's highly competitive environment without the functionality and integration accorded by these applications is well-nigh impossible. While several companies are attempting to develop these applications in-house (a number are experiencing problems with time, cost, functionality, and user frustration—one large components company is in its second major reincarnation of the in-house development of a worldwide forecasting and planning system), others are using a combination of in-house and off-the-shelf packaged software. Lessons from successful companies show that the latter approach is more successful, generally because, for third party developers, this is their core competency and most are very good at it.

Global Network IT Operations Supporting the Supply Chain

In response to globalization, to competitive trends, and to the resultant management, usage, unique acquisition requirements, and systems maintenance pressures imposed by these applications, many companies are reorganizing their IS functions and responsibilities. They are responding to the challenge by viewing the issues involved from a strategic IT perspective—they are moving away from the concept of user data access to that of user self-sufficiency. The key strategic issue facing companies is that of centralization versus decentralization. IT today does not require the traditional IS functional roles of managing a "black box" and providing users a semi-autonomous service capability. The lack of a business and competitive perspective among IS personnel, the problem of priority-setting in responding to user requests, and a "silo" mentality have long hindered the ability of companies to integrate IT with their processes. Additionally, trends toward outsourcing (at the least, in non-critical areas) have encouraged local supply chain users to move some traditional IS functions (local integration, maintenance, management of upgrades etc.) to external firms and vendors. The traditional centralized IS department which reports to finance is being changed. Figure 7–15 illustrates the types of IS roles and responsibilities that are emerging in several multinational companies. The new responsibilities represent a balanced autonomy within the organization. Briefly, they are divided into two areas.

   1. *Key functions and functional responsibilities.* Increasingly, corporate IS is being called upon to play a facilitation and planning role. The essence of this role is integration. Global enterprises are realizing that the best IT applications acquisition decisions, applications usage, and maintenance are done at the local supply chain level. Hence, centralization is ensuring that the enterprise can be fully information integrated, as well as maintaining the core systems necessary to manage the enterprise from corporate IS. Included are basic functions such as core systems maintenance but, more important, also the value-added role of facilitation in

FIGURE 7–15 Global Network Information Technology Operations

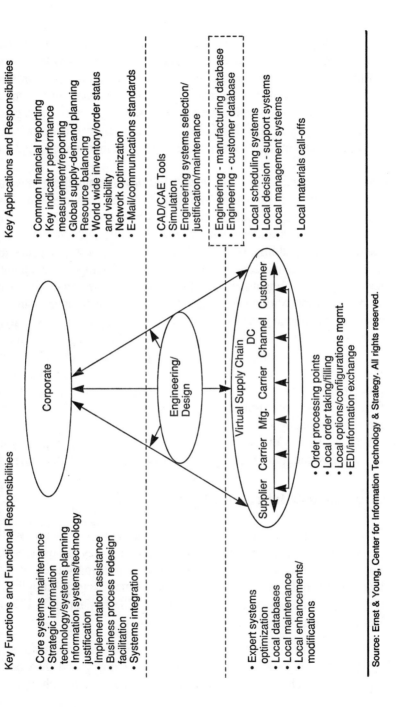

Key Functions and Functional Responsibilities

- Core systems maintenance
- Strategic information technology/systems planning
- Information systems/technology justification
- Implementation assistance
- Business process redesign facilitation
- Systems integration

- Expert systems optimization
- Local databases
- Local maintenance
- Local enhancements/ modifications

Key Applications and Responsibilities

- Common financial reporting
- Key indicator performance measurement/reporting
- Global supply-demand planning
- Resource balancing
- World wide inventory/order status and visibility
- Network optimization
- E-Mail/communications standards

- CAD/CAE Tools
- Simulation
- Engineering systems selection/ justification/maintenance

- Engineering - manufacturing database
- Engineering - customer database

- Local scheduling systems
- Local decision - support systems
- Local management systems

- Local materials call-offs

Corporate

Engineering/ Design

Virtual Supply Chain

DC
Supplier Carrier Mfg. Carrier Channel Customer

- Order processing points
- Local order taking/filling
- Local options/configurations mgmt.
- EDI/information exchange

strategic IT planning and justification; business process redesign; and systems integration. An equally important aspect of this role is standards setting for the enterprise in terms of communications standards, protocols, and integration requirements. On the other hand, several functions, long the purview of a centralized IS group, have been disaggregated and pushed to the local facilities/SBU level in the supply chain, including the acquisition of key applications, their usage, enhancement, and maintenance.

2. *Key applications and responsibilities.* Among the trends inherent in globalization are increased coordination of key activities and geographical dispersion of the logistics network. These pose unique challenges in applications selection, acquisition, development, and maintenance. Companies are responding by centralizing core applications necessary for managing the global enterprise, and decentralizing those applications necessary for management at a local supply chain level. For instance, such core applications can include global supply-demand planning and resource balancing; worldwide inventory/order status and visibility; common financial and key indicator measurement and reporting; and standards setting. Key applications at the supply chain level include scheduling, decision-support, order configuration and fulfillment management, procurement, and expert systems applications. The engineering design function has unique applications (CAD/CAE, simulation, etc.), and these are usually managed within the group—regardless of the location/co-location decision. Centralization–decentralization here is typically not the issue—it is integration with production, suppliers, and customers.

Electronic Data Interchange (EDI)

EDI is the integrative technology for the virtual supply chain. While it is massively used in situations involving large volumes of business transactions and data tracking requirements, it is increasingly used by firms to link their supply chains and build the virtual factory (suppliers, customers, intra-company transactions, etc.). The key intent in EDI implementation is to:

> *Reduce time* in communications with suppliers and customers, and within geographically dispersed manufacturing and distribution locations (schedules, plans, material and engineering change release, etc.)

Increase accuracy of communications regarding orders; inventory status and visibility; engineering and supplier product and process designs; and customer requirements

Streamline transaction-based operations (order entry, accounts receivable, and accounts payable)

Reduce redundancy of data flowing from one entity to the other along the supply chain

Increase response in order fulfillment, supply management (delivery, design, location), and schedule changes within the network

Reduce pipeline inventory levels

Improve sales productivity

Improve customer service levels

Figure 7–16 illustrates some of the information companies are transmitting along the virtual supply chain through the use of EDI. The adoption of EDI is, by no means, mechanistic. It involves several major IT and organizational issues, including the following.

Information sharing. Information is power in an organization, and certainly is power outside the organization along the supply chain—it can threaten organizational relationships. One major supplier of a large company hedged on its EDI commitment for a long time—it did not want to reveal its true schedules and stock status to its customer. EDI must be a mutually agreed upon strategy, with firm definitions of data to be transmitted, periodicity, and content. Where the data is subject to manipulation, it is sometimes necessary to link databases. The benefits of EDI, therefore, must be articulated and made clear to all parties. One major computer manufacturer has written connectivity requirements into its purchase agreements for suppliers, and explains the mutual benefits to all affected parties

Standards. Standards must be set carefully after reviewing the operating environment and the industries involved. EDI standards are often industry-dependent, and clear agreements must be defined regarding standards, data elements, and transaction sets. Similarly, multinational firms will probably have to implement more than one standard.

Applications and communications. It is important to review current applications and communications networks within the company for integration, standardization of data within the company, and the systems' abilities to support EDI. EDI is a means for functional and, therefore,

FIGURE 7–16   EDI/Data Linkages for the Virtual Supply Chain

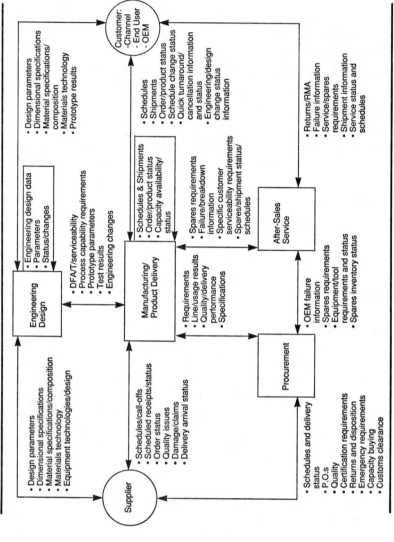

Source: Ernst & Young, Center for Information Technology & Strategy. All rights reserved.

information integration. Given this, many companies are centralizing their evaluation and standards setting on an enterprise-wide basis. The company must proceed carefully before investing in conversion or translation applications. These must be flexible and capable of supporting multiple EDI standards; have control and report capabilities; have interfaces with existing hardware, software, and databases; and provide for security.

Some of the specific issues to be resolved include communications (time zones, communications protocols, hardware types), data standards (user data versus standards, cross-industry standards, and maintenance of standards), and the EDI environment (implementation with trading partners, applications interfaces, and translation issues involving the host, network, front-end, etc.). The major issues, though, revolve around organizational implementation, and are similar to those encountered in any implementation of integrative technology. Companies must, however, guard against acquiring technology for technology's sake—not all implementations of EDI have proven effective. The case of the electronics supplier who installed EDI terminals and networks in a major customer's engineering department has been discussed earlier. On the other hand, the case of the large manufacturers who use EDI applications to link design engineering in several countries constitutes a success story. One of these firms has linked its engineering design databases and departments to those of its major customer. This ensures a partnership and provides strategic benefits to both the supplier (ensuring that its components will be designed into new products) and the customer (providing a mechanism for simultaneous engineering involving the supplier, and reducing time to market for new products). Several large components manufacturers have linked their supply databases (inventory status, allocation, availability) to those of their distributors (stock status, demand, orders) in order to ensure end customer satisfaction through service, availability, and low pipeline inventory levels. On the other hand, a major multinational, following a thorough cost-benefit analysis of its remote-site communications needs (involving California, Taiwan, Japan, Europe, Illinois, and New Jersey), defined its EDI strategy for the following 12 months in one word—"fax".

IMPLEMENTATION

Figure 7–17 illustrates the criteria necessary for the successful implementation of a major IT system.

FIGURE 7-17   Logistics Information Systems Implementation Criteria for Success

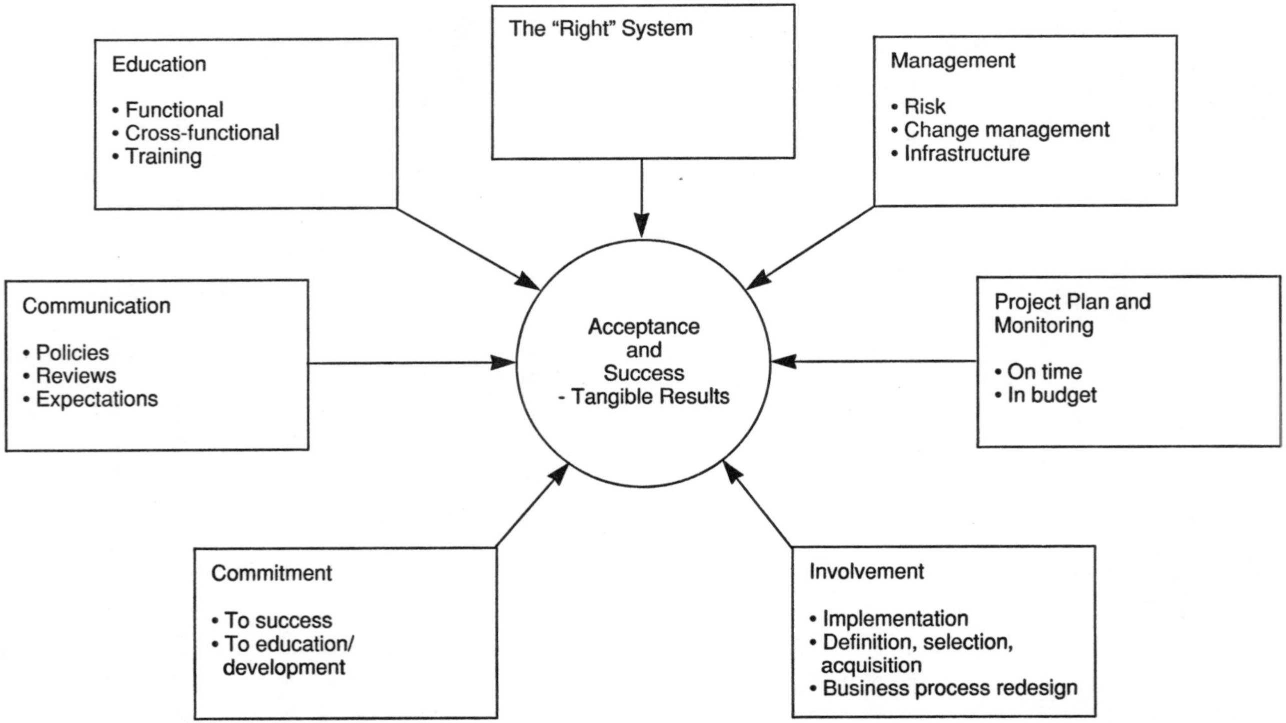

Successful implementation may be defined as a combination of organizational acceptance (no technology should ever be perceived as the IS department's system, or another IS attempt at righting previous errors), and "success"—the tangible results—(reduced inventory, increased customer service levels, tighter alliances with stakeholders, improved decision-making, etc.) obtained from the implementation of the system. These success criteria include:

• *The "right" system.* Selection, acquisition, and development/enhancement of an IT with the necessary features for the processes involved; ease of use; migration path; flexibility and integration capabilities; and technical and functional support. It is one of the great myths in IT selection that "users know what they want". Typically, users know their requirements for automating and extending their current processes. It is imperative that IT definition be the result of a business vision and incorporate an examination of the processes involved (business process redesign).

• *Education.* The old adage still holds true, "If you think education is expensive, try ignorance." Lack of education is the primary cause of IT implementation failure. Education is expensive—it involves the cost (and opportunity costs) of people's time, cost of training and trainers, and also the cost of training materials and facilities. Education must encompass functional education and IT system use training, as well as cross-discipline education. This involves addressing the questions: "What decisions do I make that would impact on other functions?", "What is the type and level of this impact?", "What are the decisions made by others that would impact me?", and, finally, "What do my internal suppliers and customers require of me?".

• *Communication.* The communication of policies and results of reviews is essential for successful system implementation. However, communication must be coupled with *management commitment* to the requirements of success, including education, resource allocation, and a realistic expectation of results. IT involves change, and communication and commitment must be backed up by *management willingness to foster change* and to set in place the necessary infrastructure to accommodate and manage change. Additionally, change is risky—a moving away from the status quo—and the commitment to undertake reasoned risks must be an integral part of IT implementation.

• *Involvement of all concerned.* Traditional implementation wisdom defines this aspect as "user involvement". It is much more than that—it requires the active involvement and participation of higher-level management, IS, users, support/indirect personnel, and other functional groups along the supply chain.

• *Implementation organization.* The infrastructure and decision-making roles necessary to successfully implement a major IS must include: senior management to set direction and be the arbiter of strategic viability and resource allocation; an overview management structure for the implementation process; and cross-functional representation and involvement to ensure organizational and supply chain management success. Figure 7–18 depicts one such organization structure for the implementation of a major logistics information system in a large manufacturing firm.

• *A detailed project plan* (with timelines, milestones, deliverables, roles, and responsibilities) and a budget to measure and monitor time and cost are the final requirements for successful IT implementation.

Some suggestions for successful implementation include

1. *Start with the easiest.* An integral part of implementation success is organizational acceptance. The organization must be convinced the effort will be successful, and obtaining early success is an excellent way to achieve this. Another aspect of this strategy is to *implement in "pieces"* to obtain better project control and the necessary early benefits and paybacks.

2. *Plan and execute for a quick implementation.* The traditional 18 to 24-month timelines associated with implementation were part of the conventional wisdom in a period of relatively low IT sophistication. Furthermore, industry and competitive dynamics change so rapidly that IT should not become a bottleneck or constraining factor.

3. *Try initially for an 80 percent solution.* A comprehensive, 100 percent solution is likely to take an inordinately long time, probably causing management and users (and suppliers and customers along the supply chain) to lose interest. The incremental balance of benefits will accrue in due course.

In the final analysis, successful implementation of a major IS depends upon achieving multifunctional integration and planning. It requires a transition from traditional approaches of segmented planning, functional objectives, and the specialized/generalist skill sets of logistics managers and practices to the new integrated logistics imperatives imposed by the market. (Figure 7–19 illustrates these differences.)

FIGURE 7–18   An Implementation Organization

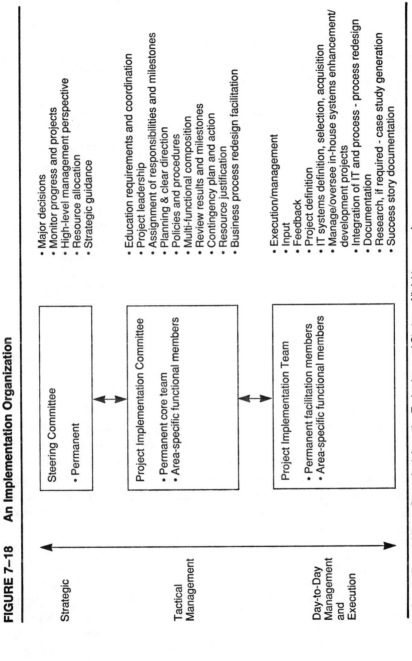

FIGURE 7–19
Achieving Multifunctional Integration and Planning in Logistics New v.
Traditional Practices and Philosophies

Planning Requirements	Traditional	New Imperatives
Planning	Segmented	The Logistics supply chain
Objectives	Functional	Systemic
Performance Measures	Localized	Enterprise-wide
Management Development	Specialized/ generalists	Multifunctional/ internal-external supplier/customer-oriented
Results	Optimize parts; suboptimize entire system—enterprise	Optimize the system for effective competitive performance

JUSTIFICATION

IT project justification is a vital element of a company's implementation
and resource allocation process. Traditional cost-based methods (for instance, internal rate of return, net present value, discounted payback period, etc.) are no longer sufficient or even appropriate in many cases of
strategic IT projects. Chapter 8—Accessing Logistics Performances—
discusses an approach to justification. The justification techniques employed should range from economic to strategic analysis, depending on
the scope, organizational impact, level of IT, and its integrative capabilities. Most important, the strategic nature of the IT project must be
considered—it is virtually impossible to quantify, in dollar value, many
strategic IT projects that are key to competitiveness.

Figure 7–20 provides the justification matrix utilized by one company for project prioritization. The prioritization parameters are based on
strategic urgency/benefit (the strategic impacts of the project) and on improvement potential, with a focus on time, response, cost, and quality.
While the strategic aspect was essentially qualitative (rated on a fixed
scale by executives following a discussion of industry and competitive
trends and the firm's performance), the improvement potential was quantified using benchmarking. The selected projects included some for busi-

FIGURE 7–20   Information Technology Project Prioritization

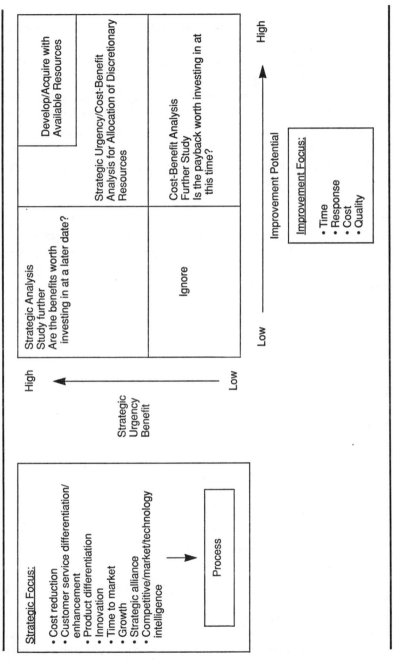

ness process redesign, as well as certain applications and connectivity development projects.

For such projects, much of the justification rests on confidence in the business process redesign and on strategic analysis processes. If the company is an industry follower in terms of technology, justification is fairly simple and can be based on documented case study benefits from the leaders (in this case, the company is striving to catch up and has probably lost some market advantage through excess conservatism). For leaders, however, justification is more difficult and its success rests on the rigor of the IT strategy and planning processes.

In any event, too many companies place artificial and arbitrary hurdle rates on the justification process (often a weighted average cost of capital plus some risk premium). These often pose serious problems. One large pharmaceutical company set an internal rate of return hurdle of 20 percent, and retained it for five years while its business, products, and competitive thrusts changed. Finally this resulted in a major strategic IS, necessary to manage quality (a mission-critical function in this industry), being rejected because the IS department could not come up with sufficient dollar benefits to justify the cost on an economic basis.

A cost-benefit analysis must consider all relevant costs—indirect, support, maintenance, training, and direct. Benefits must include cost savings and cost avoidance; ongoing operational and one-time (balance sheet) savings; and revenue enhancement benefits. One large company quantified the following revenue enhancement benefits for a logistics system:

Product availability

Improved service for after-sales support

Increased sales from ramp-up/delivery to distributors (another aspect of product availability)

Faster response to orders for configured products (including OEM material)

Cost recovery from warranty tracking of returned OEM products

Finally, justification must account for the risk inherent in IT projects. Large IT projects are inherently risky in terms of time (system development and integration), quality (functioning as intended), implementation, and cost (overruns). These must be identified and planned for. An excellent justification process can be a proprietary advantage.

CHAPTER 8

ASSESSING LOGISTICS PERFORMANCE

The periodic assessment of logistics performance is a very important aspect of planning for and managing the logistics function. It is an integral part of the process of logistics strategy development and management. Assessment encompasses comprehensive data identification and collection, and a number of methods of analysis and evaluation. Essentially, a logistics assessment serves three functions:

1. *It identifies key data necessary* to effectively manage costs, customer service, response, quality, and time within the logistics function. It also determines whether the data required can be easily collected in the company; actually exists; is available in a form conducive to summary management reporting, manipulation, and extraction for analysis; is easily available for all authorized users on a global basis; and has security mechanisms to prevent access by unauthorized parties (some data is competitively sensitive). Equally important is the data base built up through regular logistics assessments (the auditing function). This data base can be used in an ongoing manner for performance evaluation and trend analysis.

2. *It details and understands the current environment* as an initial step to developing logistics strategies. As discussed in Chapter 2, key steps in the planning process involve understanding ourselves, the customer, and the competition. The process of logistics assessment can provide this understanding.

3. *It audits the logistics function* to ensure that it meets the needs of the marketplace (defined here as that unique combination of product, customer, and competitor), as well as operates in a cost-effective, flexible, and responsive fashion. Equally important, it determines whether the

logistics function is changing and adapting to changing corporate strategies, product developments, customer preferences, and competitor efforts.

The assessment should be conducted periodically—many companies do this annually—and the key indicators identified during the process monitored frequently.

LOGISTICS ASSESSMENT—ISSUES TO BE ADDRESSED

The logistics assessment should address the following six questions:

1. Are current logistics strategic objectives consistent with current corporate, marketing, and manufacturing strategies?

2. What is the company's current customer service level performance? Does the company meet customers' *requirements* and *preferences* in the following areas?

- *Order management*
  - Order fill rates
  - Order completeness
  - Order turnaround time and lead time (as measured by customer ask date, not sales-committed due date)
- *Delivery*
  - Delivery performance
  - Delivery lot sizes
  - Delivery frequencies
  - Delivery locations
  - Emergency requirements response
  - Damage rates
  - Claims processing
- *Field service/support*
  - Field service response
  - Repair turnaround
  - Spares delivery
  - Technical support
  - Documentation completeness
- *Information*
  - Information availability (planning, shipping, inventory availability)

- ○ Part numbering to conform to customer requirements
- ○ Inventory availability (prevent stockouts)
- ○ EDI for speed and customer convenience
- ○ Inventory proximity
- *Packaging*
  - ○ Packaging convenience (unitization, dock-to-stock, point-of-use packaging)
  - ○ Bar coding to customer requirements
- *Buying patterns/preferences*
  - ○ Customers' priorities that determine or influence buying decisions (drawn from the components listed above)
  - ○ Performance and service levels needed to ensure that we are the sole suppliers (to form a real or virtual supply chain alliance)
  - ○ Customer reaction when faced with a stockout of the company's products—do they buy another company's product, or defer purchase until our product is available (return, backorder)?

3. What is the true total cost and how is the company doing vis-à-vis the industry and competition by product line, major customer category, and geographical segment? These costs include:

- *Warehouse operations costs allocated by storage space and number of orders processed*
  - ○ Direct and indirect personnel
  - ○ Utilities (power, telephone, etc.)
  - ○ Maintenance
  - ○ Facilities (lease, rent, etc.)
  - ○ Taxes
  - ○ Value-added operations (packaging, labeling, assembly, etc.)
  - ○ Costs of technology—investment, return (automation, AS/RS, AGVs, etc.)
- *Transportation costs (inbound and outbound) by line, weight, volume, and modes (air, LTL/TL, etc.)*
  - ○ Supplier to plants/warehouses
  - ○ Warehouses to plants
  - ○ Inter-plant
  - ○ Plant to distribution centers
  - ○ Inter-distribution center

- ○ Plant, distribution center to customers
- ○ Supplier to customers (OEMs, spares)
- *Manufacturing costs per unit allocated by key cost drivers*
  - ○ Facilities
  - ○ Maintenance
  - ○ Direct and indirect personnel
  - ○ Equipment and automation
  - ○ Production space
  - ○ Engineering change notices
  - ○ Scrap
  - ○ Rework and rejects

4. Is the company using its resources and capacity effectively in the following areas?

- *Shipping, supply, and inter-plant*
  - ○ Overnight/second-day air
  - ○ Truckload/less-than-truckload
  - ○ Air freight
  - ○ Rail
  - ○ Sea
  - ○ Multi-mode
  - ○ Routing trucks
- *Manufacturing plants and distribution centers*
  - ○ Throughput
  - ○ Space utilization (cubic feet for warehouses)
  - ○ Capacity utilization

5. Is the company managing its material flow effectively through the supply chain in these areas?

- *Inventory levels*
  - ○ Raw material
  - ○ OEMs
  - ○ Components, peripherals, sub-assemblies
  - ○ Work-in-process and semi-finished
  - ○ Finished product
  - ○ Packaging material
  - ○ In-transit material
- *Forecast accuracy*
- *Planning schedule accuracy*

- *Cycle times* (Typically, lead times are obtained as averages.)
  - Vendor lead times for critical path items (purchase order placement to receipt)
  - Total manufacturing lead time (forecast issue to finished goods)
  - Outbound distribution lead time
  - Inbound and outbound transportation times

6. Are the information systems and technologies meeting the needs of the users, the business, and customers in the following?

- Information required
- Ease of access
- Ease of data manipulation and analysis
- Integration across the supply chain
- Response time
- MIS response to user requests

Obviously, not all the components outlined above are applicable to all companies or to all industries. However, most of them are, and should be considered, or at the very least, used as a checklist during logistics assessment.

Data Collection

Data collection and the determination of the availability of such data is an important first step. Today, data is power in an organization—a key impediment to the achievement of the information-integrated company. Many companies, however, collect an enormous amount of data, much of which is in an unusable form or is never used by line management. In many companies, such data is perceived as the responsibility of the MIS function, leading to several unfortunate consequences:

- MIS hoards data and assumes the role of central conduit through which all requests for data access are funneled. This has a considerable damping effect on the enthusiasm of line management to access certain types of data on an ad-hoc basis (that which is not required on a daily or weekly basis).
- Response time for accessing data and obtaining new reports can be painfully slow.
- The propensity for central MIS functions to acquire certain platforms (because they are used to it, or have been trained in it, or have come to

rely on vendor support for technical assistance) has led to huge, unwieldy data base management systems, rather than quick-access, easy-to-manipulate relational databases. Systems have evolved into cumbersome beasts in many corporations, leading to great difficulty in users accessing some data.

• IT strategy is not aligned with competitive strategies.

• The lack of centralized strategic IT planning or standards-setting (many users and line personnel oppose the concept because of past experiences with corporate MIS) has resulted in many corporations possessing incompatible systems, through which it is difficult to pass data. This situation is one that companies—global, large and small—must address in coming years.

Many of the data required for a logistics assessment are typically resident within the company, so existing reports can be used (if necessary, new reports can be written). It usually, however, is an eyeopener for management to discover that a great deal of the important data is private—maintained in individuals' log books and personal computers—rather than in the company's computer system. Some of the data will have to be compiled in usable form from several different reports and sources. If the data are deemed important enough, new requirements must be developed for the information system(s).

The sources of data within the company include:

Periodic internal/external customer surveys

Finance/accounting

Functional areas

IS—corporate, divisional, and plant–level

Manual data maintained in logs

Personal computer files maintained/generated at the operational level (plant, distribution center)

Managers' estimates and knowledge

Third-party freight billing agencies

Sometimes, specific data are not available. In such an event, one can use proxy data (but make the assumptions clear) to provide an indication of trends and order-of-magnitude effects.

It is apparent that, if a company has not conducted a logistics assessment prior to this, the task of data collection can be sometimes painful and disruptive to the organization. Our experience has shown that the process proceeds best if the senior logistics executive steers the task force and appoints a high-level manager to direct it.

Logistics Assessment: Analysis and Identification

Figure 8–1 outlines the steps and suggested methods of data collection used in logistics assessment. The first five steps involve analysis and identification.

Step 1: Consistency of Logistics Strategic Objectives
This is a fairly rapid step and may take two paths.

If the company has written corporate, manufacturing, marketing, and logistics strategies, the first path is to identify the critical success factors associated with the corporate, marketing, and manufacturing strategies, and then to check against the logistics objectives to assess consistency.

If the company has no written strategies, then they must be identified through a series of facilitated executive sessions with senior management to arrive at the critical success factors. There are several frameworks within which to accomplish this. One such framework and approach, used successfully on numerous occasions, is provided in Figure 8–2.

Should the logistics strategy and objectives be inconsistent with the corporate, manufacturing, and marketing objectives, the company should embark on a logistics strategy planning process as described in this book. Among the keys for successful implementation are: institutionalizing the process, changing strategies periodically to reflect internal and external changes, and monitoring results.

Step 2: Determine Customer Requirements and Preferences and Obtain Targets for Performance
Customer requirements are best obtained from the customers themselves and those nearest the customers—line management. Instruments to obtain this information include:

- *Written, facilitated, and telephone customer surveys*
- *Interviews with customer management*
- *Structured interviews with internal:*
  - Line management

FIGURE 8–1   Logistics Assessment

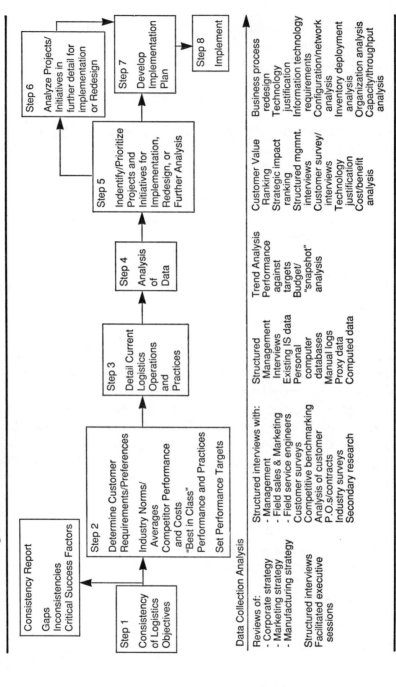

FIGURE 8–2
Facilitated Executive Sessions

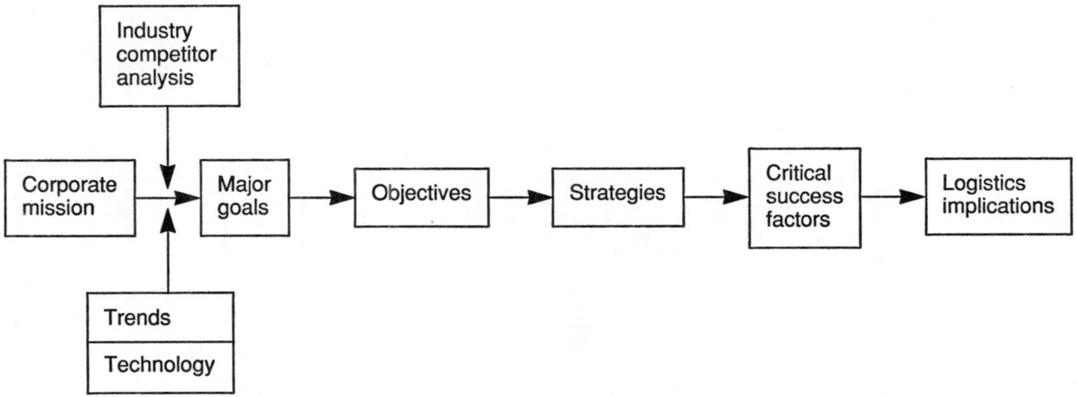

- ○ Field service engineers
- ○ Field sales force
- ○ Marketing
- ○ Channel representatives
- *Analysis of purchase orders and contracts to ascertain typical customer delivery preferences*

If possible (and it is not always so), management must check and confirm internal perceptions and analysis results with the customers themselves. An example of a customer survey is shown in Figure 8–3. Typically, customers are usually eager to discuss their needs with suppliers serious about filling them.

While the instruments listed above are excellent for determining customer requirements, the firm must go further to obtain information on competitors and on the industry. Secondary research (trade journals, etc.) provides some information, but a far better approach is to use a structured benchmarking method. (Some of the major issues and techniques of benchmarking have been discussed in Chapter 5.) An example of such an analysis for a major foods company is shown in Figures 8–4—8–8. It involves a definition of on-time delivery by major customers. (The company itself was confused about what it and its customers meant by the term, yet it was used as a key indicator of performance.) It further involves comparisons of the company versus its major competitors in terms of: percentage of orders complete per year; lead times until order delivery; on-time delivery performance per year; and customer perceptions of best customer service.

As can be seen, the company in question is not doing too well versus its major competitors. Proceeding with the assessment process from this point, several major opportunities surfaced for the company to improve its business processes, cost management efforts, inventory management and deployment, and information technologies. The information obtained through step two provided the company with targets that can be used to measure performance, and against which to set objectives. Figure 8–9 provides an example of the output of this exercise.

Step 3: Detail Current Logistics Operations and Practices
Earlier in this chapter, the specific operational and cost data that must be collected were outlined. This provides a baseline from which we can improve or redesign our operations. Additionally, this baseline model

FIGURE 8–3   Example of Customer Service Levels Survey

CUSTOMER SERVICE LEVELS SURVEY

COMPANY A

Company Data

Respondent/Interviewee/Title: _____

Company: _____

Division: _____

Revenues: _____

Major Products:

Produced: _____
Sold: _____
Distributed: _____

1. Products purchased from Company A?

_____
_____

2. Percentage of products purchased from Company A vs. other Suppliers?

Supplier	**Line 1**	**Line 2**	**Line 3**	**Line 4**
a. _____Company A_____	____%	____%	____%	____%
b._____	____%	____%	____%	____%
c._____	____%	____%	____%	____%
d._____	____%	____%	____%	____%

3. Describe the overall quality of Company A's product vs. that of its competitors.

	Poor Excellent	Comments
a. Receipt Quality	1 2 3 4 5	_____
b. Functional/Spec Qualty	1 2 3 4 5	_____
c. Packaging Quality	1 2 3 4 5	_____
d. Others (Specify): _____	1 2 3 4 5	_____

FIGURE 8–3 (*continued*)

CUSTOMER SERVICE LEVELS SURVEY
COMPANY A

4. What lead time do you get from your customer for an order?

	Low	Avg	High
Line 1			
Line 2			
Line 3			
Line 4			

5. How often do your major suppliers deliver product to you?

	Supplier	**Order Frequency (Days, Shifts, Hours)**
a.	Company A	
b.		
c.		

6. What are your most used and preferred methods for placing an order or calling off for delivery with your major suppliers?

	Supplier	**Method generally Used**	**Preferred Method**
a.	Company A		
b.			
c.			

1. Mail order
2. Call distribution center/warehouse
3. Call sales office/sales rep
4. Call distributor
5. Personally hand to sales rep
6. Use a pre-set call-off schedule
7. EDI
8. Fax
9. Call supplier's plant
10. Other (specify)

FIGURE 8–3

CUSTOMER SERVICE LEVELS SURVEY
COMPANY A

7. How do you respond when a supplier fails to meet service expectations (quality, delivery performance, response, cost, quantity, off-contract delivery, etc.)?

		% of time
a.	Call salesman	_____
b.	Refuse current order	_____
c.	Halt future orders/call-offs	_____
d.	Reduce future orders/call-offs	_____
e.	Look for alternative source	_____
f.	Other (specify)	_____

8. When you decide to buy a product from Company A, and it is not immediately available, do you:

a.	Backorder	_____
b.	Go to an alternative supplier	_____
c.	Buy a substitute	_____
d.	Defer purchase until the product is in stock	_____
e.	Other (specify)	_____

9. Please specify the service levels you require (necessary to do business) and those that define your expectations of excellence that your suppliers need to meet along the following dimensions.

Additionally, what service levels are currently being provided by Company A and the major competitors?

Dimensions of Customer Service	Required Levels	Expectations of Excellence	Company A	Competitors 1	2
a. Order cycle time (Placement to delivery)	_____	_____	_____	_____	_____
b. Order accuracy	_____	_____	_____	_____	_____
c. On-time delivery	_____	_____	_____	_____	_____
d. Order fill rates/ availability	_____	_____	_____	_____	_____
e. Delivery lot sizes	_____	_____	_____	_____	_____
f. Delivery frequency	_____	_____	_____	_____	_____

FIGURE 8–3 (*continued*)

CUSTOMER SERVICE LEVELS SURVEY

COMPANY A

Dimensions of Customer Service	Required Levels	Expectations of Excellence	Company A	Competitors 1	2
g. Claims processing					
h. Field service response					
i. Spares availability					
j. Packaging convenience					
(% pkged lots usable on line)					
(% pkged lots ready for stock)					
k. Order completeness					
Other (specify)					
l.					
m.					

10. Which supplier provides the best overall service?_____

    Why do you think so?_____

11. How long have you been a customer of Company A? _____

12. What are your impressions of it as an excellent supplier? _____
_____
_____
_____

FIGURE 8–3 (*concluded*)

CUSTOMER SERVICE LEVELS SURVEY
COMPANY A

13. Do you believe that its performance has improved over the past year? ___

14. Rank the following 15 attributes of a supplier in terms of importance that contribute toward your buying decision for each product line.

Attribute	Product Line 1	Product Line 2	Product Line 3	Product Line 4	Generally
a. Price	___	___	___	___	___
b. Delivery performance	___	___	___	___	___
c. Order turnaround	___	___	___	___	___
d. Product quality	___	___	___	___	___
e. Product reliability	___	___	___	___	___
f. Order fill rates/ availability	___	___	___	___	___
g. Order completeness	___	___	___	___	___
h. Order accuracy	___	___	___	___	___
i. Response to emergency requirements	___	___	___	___	___
j. Inventory proximity	___	___	___	___	___
k. Field service support	___	___	___	___	___
l. Information on order status and availability	___	___	___	___	___
m. Packaging convenience	___	___	___	___	___
n. Frequent delivery	___	___	___	___	___

FIGURE 8–4
Definition of On-time Delivery Major Consumer Products Firm

Definition of On-time Delivery	Retailers (22)	Wholesalers (32)
Within one day	20%	28%
On a given day	60%	52%
A.M. or P.M. definition	12%	6%
Within 1 hour of specified time	6%	8%
Within half-hour or less	2%	6%

FIGURE 8–5
Order Completeness Large Electronics Firm

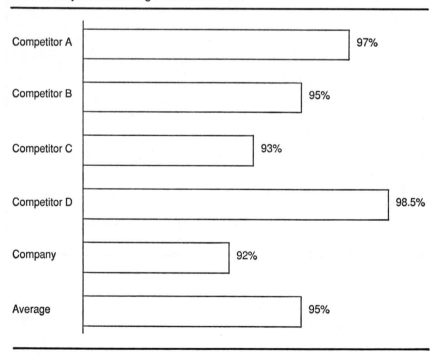

FIGURE 8–6
Order Turnaround Time Large Electronics Firm

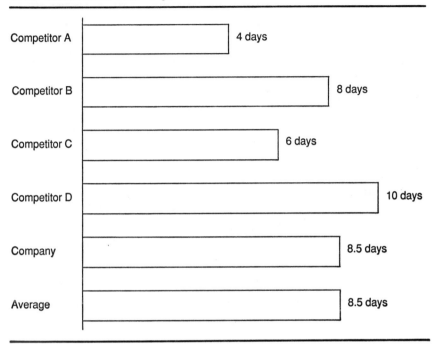

provides the basis for developing logistics strategies and analyzing major structural changes.

It is important that each piece of data be confirmed and its source documented. This ensures the integrity and accuracy of the data, as well as determines future requirements for information systems. Confirmation must be obtained through a combination of hard copy data and line management interviews.

Step 4: Analysis of Logistics Data

There are several types of analysis that can be conducted, depending on the key performance indicators developed as part of the logistics objectives. The key indicators are derived from the critical success factors ("What must go right in order to achieve this?"). This analysis need not be taken to the process level of detail. Its purposes are to isolate problems, danger areas, and performance shortfalls; identify projects and areas to improve or redesign; identify costs and benefits (for prioritization

FIGURE 8–7
Delivery Performance Large Electronics Firm

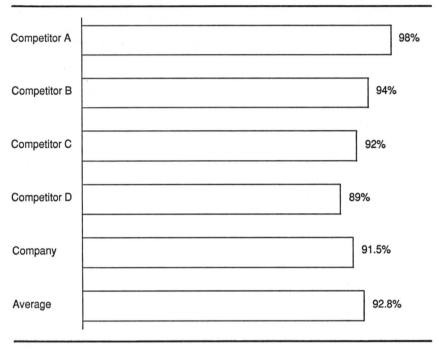

Competitor A	98%
Competitor B	94%
Competitor C	92%
Competitor D	89%
Company	91.5%
Average	92.8%

FIGURE 8–8
Overall Customer Service Level Performance Defined by Customer Survey

Company	Ranking by %
Competitor A	40%
Competitor B	25%
Competitor C	15%
Competitor D	6%
Company	14%

FIGURE 8–9
Example—Customer Requirements/Preferences vs. Performance

Customer Account/Segment	Requirements/ Preferences	Performance	Comments
Company A Colorado Plant	Delivery performance −2 to +1 days on-time Frequency: every 2 weeks avg.	60% on time 23% early 17% late	17% Late: 12% store on hand shipped late 5% stockouts 23% Early: Early shipments due to release/pick errors
California Plant 2	Delivery performance −2 to 0 hours on-time Frequency: twice a day	94% on time 6% late	6% Late: 2% by 0–4 hours 4% by 8–24 hours Late receipts from plant
California Plant 2	Claims processing 1 week	Avg: 2.5 weeks 0.5–3.5 weeks	82% greater than 1 week 24% incorrect info from customer
California Plant 3	Order accuracy Permissible: −0 to +2 quantity 10% line items	Avg. quantity +1% Line item accuracy 99%	Line item accuracy mainly due to incorrect customer P.O.

and justification) of such projects and initiatives; assess current and potential vulnerability to changing customer demands and competitor performance; and establish the baseline for logistics strategy development.

The different types of analysis are as follows.

Trend analysis. Trend analysis charts historical performance, both in relative and absolute terms. It provides a good indication of the operating efficiencies of the business, and surfaces issues regarding cost control and containment. To be meaningful, trend analysis must be done by logistics component (by distribution center, outbound transportation, etc.). Trend analysis includes:

- Cost component trends relative to sales and volumes
- Absolute cost and volume/throughput trends
- Volume trends relative to sales
- Inventory turns and levels
- Customer service level trends relative to sales and volumes

Performance against targets. This type of analysis provides a true picture of company performance in terms of cost, customer service levels, asset management, and material management through the supply chain. Company performance is measured against customer requirements and buying patterns, competitor performance, "best in class," and industry norms.

"Budget/snapshot" analysis. The term "budget and snapshot" analysis indicates the analysis type and result. It includes measuring actual performance against budgeted, planned, and "ideal" measures. As with all analysis techniques, in order to be meaningful it must be conducted by logistics component. Analysis types include:

- "Ideal" inventory levels and safety stocks (based on demand patterns and lead times) compared to actuals
- Budgeted costs versus actuals as a function of sales and volumes
- Budgeted/planned volumes versus actuals
- Planned versus actual customer service levels

Internal information technology. This assesses all the important aspects of IT support, within the company and from the users' perspective. It includes the capabilities of the information systems (features, functions, data maintained required by logistics, other functions, customers, suppliers, and management reporting), and takes into account its ease of access, usage, and user-friendliness. It also includes the response of the MIS department to user requests for enhancements, modifications, new package acquisition, new system development, and support. Expanding upon the targets identified in step two, Figure 8–9 shows summary results from such an analysis.

Step 5: Identify and Prioritize Projects and Initiatives for Implementation, Redesign, or Further Analysis

The analysis outlined above typically leads to several projects and initiatives which address, and seek to close, gaps in performance and information technology. These projects can include the following areas.

Information technology projects. These could range from applications development and modification to new technology introduction, to integration requirements between two systems. For instance, one company's projects included: modifications to the forecasting systems to incorporate certain types of analytical capabilities; evaluation and justification of a DRP system; EDI links with a major dealer account; and information integration between the production shop floor management VAX in Singapore and corporate supply-demand planning in California.

Processes to be improved or redesigned. Processes identified could span the entire supply chain. One company identified claims processing, order turnaround in a particular distribution center, the supply-demand planning process (from receipt of projections from the field as a forecasting input, to release of manufacturing and ship schedules), and the credit approval process for customers.

Specific areas where costs need to be reduced or contained. Cost reduction or containment areas are generally identified vis-à-vis industry norms, increasing trends, or competitors' cost structures. For instance, the company mentioned above recognized that transportation costs as a percentage of sales and volumes had increased over the past year. Additionally, safety stock levels relative to sales volumes increased for a certain product line over the past six months, even though the product was quite mature and there had been no production ramp-up for marketing and sales purposes.

Automation investment projects. Projects such as these must be very closely evaluated and justified. One company invested a great deal of money in automated storage and retrieval systems (ASRS) and automated guided vehicles (AGV). The initial justification was based on some heroic assumptions about potential benefits (Included were direct and indirect labor based on throughput, and a reduction in order turnaround time based on little more than the vendor's pitch.). Two years later, utilization is less than 50 percent, and total order response times to the customer have decreased only marginally. Total costs (which include a large complement of maintenance personnel, programmers, and support engineers) have risen—to be added, of course, to the cost of capital invested in the project. The company's shift in strategy and geographical changes in market (a major customer consolidated its manufacturing facilities on the West Coast) have resulted in a white elephant. Additionally, the real issues in order turnaround time lay not with warehouse turnaround time, but with the product mix stocked at the location.

Whereas technology justification is not within the scope of this book, some points are worth mentioning.

- *Consider all costs—direct, indirect, support, maintenance, administrative, and working capital.*
- *Consider all investments—equipment, up-front training, peripherals, add-ons, and software.*
- *Consider all benefits:*
  - *Quantitative—cost savings, cost avoidance, and revenue enhancement.*
  - *Qualitative/intangibles—employee satisfaction, customer satisfaction, strategic and integrative benefits.*
- *Consider timing—costs, investment, cost savings and avoidance, revenue enhancement, and discount rates.*
- *Identify and evaluate risks—business, market, technological, operational, and implementation (see Chapter 2)—and their impacts on the proposed project.*
- *Use the appropriate justification techniques—from economic and financial to value analysis, strategic impact, and customer satisfaction—based on the purpose of the project (replacement, major change, integration).*
- *Examine carefully assumptions used in the analysis.*

An assumption that inventory levels will automatically decrease because of technology is a poor assumption, as is that which projects increased sales merely because of improved order turnaround. There are a host of other dimensions of customer service which may be much more important to the customers' buying decisions. Figure 8–10 shows one such approach to technology and project justification.

FIGURE 8–10
An Approach to Justification

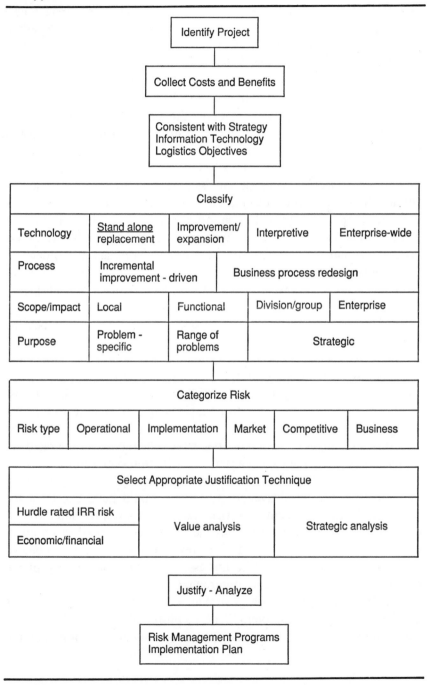

Methods to determine inventory levels and safety stocks. If the current methods and programs of setting stocking levels and safety stocks are not working—some indications are increased backorders, longer lead times to fill customer orders, too much inventory at the wrong location, or increased overall inventory levels relative to sales—then they must be modified or changed. Chapter 6 discusses this particular issue.

Areas, processes, major problems, performance shortfalls, and potential vulnerabilities to analyze prior to decision making. These are current or potential problem areas that pose threats to the business.

One company identified its current distribution channel as a potential vulnerability. Low-priced imports were posing a threat and the company's shelf space and dealer loyalty were decreasing. After analysis of its strategy, it decided to tackle this issue on two fronts. It expanded its product line to provide a complete range of products for end users (thereby attempting to provide a one-stop shop for its dealers). Further, it invested in an IS linking dealer inventories to the company's own ordering process and system. The company placed terminals in the dealers' outlets at no charge to the dealers, and managed their inventory for them. Benefits to the dealers were so great (in terms of reduced overall inventory levels, fewer stockouts, and decreased purchasing and ordering costs), the company effectively succeeded in closing out its competition from this channel.

Another company identified the order entry process as a potential vulnerability. It re-engineered its IS to automate approval cycles, credit checks, and order configuration management, thereby succeeding in drastically reducing response time while increasing convenience to the customer.

A third company identified a potential vulnerability in the rated capacity of one of its plants and a major distribution center in the Atlantic region. A new product was due to be released shortly, and the production ramp-up to meet initial availability targets would have exceeded the plant's manufacturing, and the distribution center's storage and throughput, capacities—adversely affecting the success of the product introduction. The company analyzed the situation and, as a result, negotiated outsourcing contracts to handle the assembly and warehousing of the product on the East Coast during introduction.

Yet another high technology firm identified its forecasting process as a current and potential problem. With its proliferation of products (electronic components), the forecasting process—already a major problem—

would be hard-pressed to provide the company's operating units any sort of meaningful information. After detailed analysis, the process was redesigned and integrated with a new IS.

Changes in organization and coordination. One electronics firm found that the production planning and delivery processes posed a significant problem. Trends revealed that plan and schedule accuracy was declining, and that 60 percent of the monthly output for most of its plants took place within the last week. After further analysis of the process and the organization, the company decided to place the entire supply-demand planning process under a single vice president. (Previously, it had been in pieces, under manufacturing planning's two different product-based functions, procurement and distribution.)

Logistics Assessment: Prioritizing Projects

There are several different dimensions along which one can prioritize projects. The only one that should not be adopted is management instinct, or "gut feeling." Valid dimensions include cost impact on the business and improvement potential of the project.

These two are typically quantified in:

- *Value to the customer.*

    Value to the customer can be determined by a combination of quantified data and customer perception—dollar impacts and customer survey data along a Likert-type scale (1 to 5 or 1 to 7).

- *Strategic impact.*

    Strategic impact is typically determined by a combination of management interviews and surveys, as well as a review of the business strategy.

Obviously, initiatives and projects that have some combination of high cost impacts, high improvement potentials, high value to the customer, and high strategic impact on the business should be implemented or further analyzed for implementation feasibility. Figures 8–11—8–12 show prioritization grids developed for one company to prioritize projects along several of these dimensions.

The following three steps in the logistics assessment process are involved with prioritization and implementation.

FIGURE 8–11
Prioritization Grid High Improvement Potential/High Cost/Service Level Impact
Prioritization

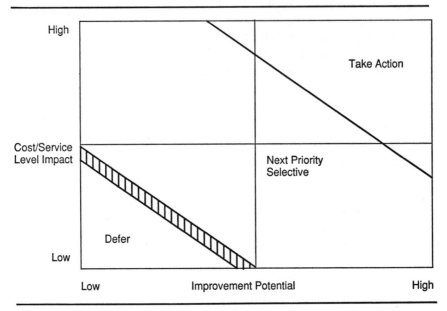

Step 6: Analyze projects and initiatives in further detail for implementation or redesign

This step involves those projects, technologies, and processes identified as candidates for further analysis prior to implementation. In some cases, analysis is a necessary prerequisite to implementation. For instance, the redesign of business processes involves comprehensive process and enabling technology assessment. Step six can involve several different types of analysis and technique, depending on the nature of the project or initiative (most of which would require separate chapters or books to examine thoroughly). Some of these are:

• Business process redesign (a fairly complex undertaking that encompasses several analytical techniques and seeks to integrate IT with the process)
• Technology justification
• Information technology requirements
• Configuration/network analysis

FIGURE 8–12
Prioritization

Partial Prioritization List

PMES:	Procurement module enhancements
EDIX:	EDI links between company and supplier X
SOPT:	Start-up optimization package
WHSQ:	Training in SPC tools for warehouse
OPSC:	Production scheduling for options
CONM:	Configuration manager
CSSO:	Customer satisfaction survey – OEMs
DC2C:	Conveyor system for shipping in DC2

1 Take action

2 Next priority

3 Defer till allocations for 1 and 2 complete

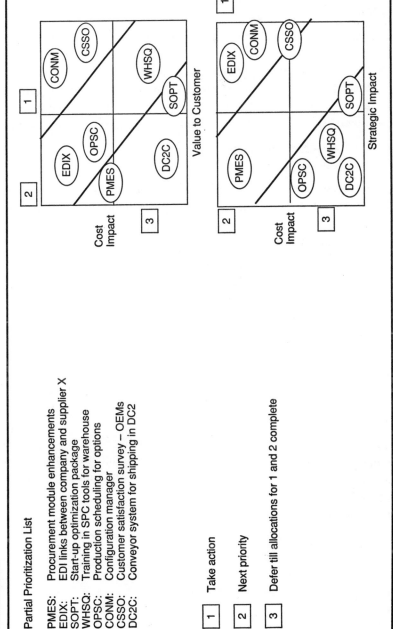

- Inventory deployment analysis
- Organization analysis
- Plant/warehouse capacity and throughput analysis;

Step 7: Develop an Implementation Plan
Characteristics of an implementation plan have been discussed in Chapter 2. Some bear repeating here. An implementation plan that increases the likelihood of success (nothing is guaranteed) must include:

- Timelines/schedules
- Responsibilities
- Resources—investment capital, working capital, personnel, outsourcing, etc.—and their time-phased allocation to the effort
- Milestones and progress status points
- Monitoring mechanisms for progress
- Key indicators and the monitoring system to evaluate the success of the effort

Step 8: Implement
The logistics assessment is an important management tool and should be incorporated in the annual planning process. It is an integral part of logistics strategy development and ongoing management, and provides the crucial picture that identifies the company's vulnerabilities in the marketplace; its performance shortfalls on customer-critical issues; and the gaps in major processes, IT, and cost management efforts. Many successful companies in a variety of industries conduct such an assessment on a periodic basis, and have based construction of data bases on the results, to ensure easy monitoring, convenient analysis, and rapid response to market changes.

REFERENCES AND BIBLIOGRAPHY

This section acknowledges those authors whose work is referenced in this text and whose concepts and intellectual capital are embodied in this book. It forms the basis for a reference library for those managers who wish to probe deeper into logistics management. This section can help such managers successfully develop and implement logistics strategies.

Abernathy, William J., et. al. "Industrial Renaissance." New York: Basic Books Inc., 1983.

Anderson, David L., and Robert Calabro. "Logistics Productivity through Strategic Alliances." *Council of Logistics Management Annual Meeting Proceedings.* Volume I, 1987, pp. 61–74.

Anderson, David L., et. al. "Integrated Operations: Redefining the Corporation." *Council of Logistics Management Annual Conference Proceedings.* Volume I, 1989, pp. 229–252.

Arthur, Jerry G., et. al. "Baxter/Trammell Crow Company: Value Managed Relationship." *Council of Logistics Management Annual Conference Proceedings.* Volume II, 1990, pp. 31–66.

Aucamp, Donald C. "The Evaluation of Safety Stock." *Production and Inventory Management.* Second quarter, 1986, pp. 127–132.

Balam, Brian. "European Partnerships." *Council of Logistics Management Annual Conference Proceedings.* Volume II, 1990, pp. 267–274.

Beer, Michael, et. al. "Why Change Management Programs Don't Produce Change." *Harvard Business Review.* November–December 1990, pp. 158–166.

Bender, Paul S., et. al. "Practical Modeling for Resource Management." *Harvard Business Review.* March–April 1981, Volume 59, No. 2, pp. 163–173.

Bhote, Keki R. "Next Operation as Customer (NOAC): How to Improve Quality, Cost and Cycle Time in Service Operations." *AMA Memberships Publications Division*, 1991.

Bishop, Daryl. "Outsourcing Transportation and Traffic Management Services."

Council of Logistics Management Annual Conference Proceedings. Volume II, 1989, pp. 207–211.

Bishop, Thomas, and Seven H. Wunning. "Third Party Logistics: A Competitive Advantage." *Council of Logistics Management Annual Conference Proceedings.* Volume II, 1988, pp. 1–13.

Blackburn, Joseph D. *Time-Based Competition.* Homewood, Ill.: Richard D. Irwin, Inc., 1991.

Blanding, Warren. "Customer Service Logistics." *Council of Logistics Management Annual Meeting Proceedings.* Volume I, 1986, pp. 361–375.

Bowersox, Donald J., et. al. "Logistics Strategy and Structure: Strategic Linkage." *Council of Logistics Management Annual Conference Proceedings.* Volume I, 1990, pp. 53–64.

Bowersox, Donald J., et. al. "Integrated Logistics: A Competitive Weapon. A Study of Organization and Strategy Practices." *Council of Logistics Management Annual Meeting Proceedings.* Volume I, 1987, pp. 1–14.

Buckner, Dennis, et. al. "Third-Party Logistics: Key to Survival." *Council of Logistics Management Annual Conference Proceedings.* Volume II, 1989, pp. 341–351.

Busher, John R., and Gene R. Tyndall. "Logistics Excellence." *Management Accounting.* August 1987, pp. 32–39.

Byrne, Stephen. "European Partnerships." *Council of Logistics Management Annual Conference Proceedings.* Volume II, 1990, pp. 285–301.

Camp, Robert C. *Benchmarking.* Milwaukee, Wis.: ASQC Quality Press, 1989.

Chambers, John C., et. al. "How to Choose the Right Forecasting Technique." *Harvard Business Review.* July–August 1971, pp. 45–74.

Champa, Domenic J., and Gary T. Long. "The Supply Chain Perspective: The Customer Service Mix." *Council of Logistics Management Annual Conference Proceedings.* Volume II, 1989, pp. 149–155.

Christopher, Martin. "Assessing the Costs of Logistics Service." *Council of Logistics Management Annual Meeting Proceedings.* Volume I, 1987, pp. 195–204.

Christopher, Martin. "Customer Service Strategies for International Markets." *Council of Logistics Management Annual Conference Proceedings.* Volume I, 1989, pp. 325–335.

Class, David J., and Craig K. Thompson. "Managing the Logistics Infrastructure." *Council of Logistics Management Annual Conference Proceedings.* Volume II, 1990, pp. 31–44.

Clayton, Brian R., et. al. "International Transactions . . . An Integrated Systems Approach." *Council of Logistics Management Annual Conference Proceedings.* Volume I, 1988, pp. 133–160.

Close, Steve M., et. al. "Knowledge-Based Systems: Achieving the Potential in Logistics." *Council of Logistics Management Annual Conference Proceedings.* Volume II, 1988, pp. 85–111.

Cooper, Martha C., et. al. "Logistics as an Element of Marketing Strategy both Inside and Outside the Firm." *Council of Logistics Management Annual Conference Proceedings.* Volume I, 1988, pp. 53–71.

"Corporate Profitability and Logistics: Innovative Guidelines for Executives." Prepared by Ernst & Whinney for the Council of Logistics Management and The National Association of Accountants. *The Council of Logistics Management,* 1987.

Coyle, John J., and Joseph C. Andraski. "Managing Channel Relationships." *Council of Logistics Management Annual Conference Proceedings.* Volume I, 1990, pp. 244–258.

"Customer Service: A Management Perspective." Prepared by the Ohio State University for the Council of Logistics Management. *The Council of Logistics Management,* 1988.

Davenport, Thomas H. "The Impact of IT on Future Business Processes." *Executive Report: CASE, No. 1,* Winter 1991.

Davis, Stanley M. *Future Perfect.* Reading, Mass.: Addison-Wesley Publishing Company, Inc., 1987.

Emmelhainz, Margaret A. "UCS/EDI: The Impact." *Council of Logistics Management Annual Meeting Proceedings.* Volume I, 1987, pp. 301–307.

Fischel, Dennis, and Ronald S. Potter. "Opportunities in Third Party Logistics." *Council of Logistics Management Annual Conference Proceedings.* Volume I, 1990, pp. 259–276.

Fox, Mary Lou. "Closing the Loop with DRP II." *P&IM Review with APICS News.* May 1987, pp. 39–41.

Fox, Mary Lou. "Integrating Forecasting and Operations Planning in Promotion Driven Companies." *Council of Logistics Management Annual Conference Proceedings.* Volume II, 1988, pp. 67–79.

Garvin, David A. "What Does 'Product Quality' Really Mean?" *Sloan Management Review.* Fall 1984, pp. 25–43.

Gopal, Christopher. "Developing Logistics Strategies for Competitive Advantage." *American Production & Inventory Control Society.* 31st International Conference Proceedings, 1988, pp. 370–372.

Gopal, Christopher. "Manufacturing Logistics Systems for Competitive Global Manufacturing." *Information Strategy: The Executive's Journal.* Fall 1986.

Gopal, Christopher. "Technology Justification: Obtaining Resources for CIM Acquisition and Implementation." *Pharmaceutical Technology.* April 1989.

Gunn, Thomas G. "Integrated Manufacturing's Growing Pains." *Electronic Engineering Manager, Electronics Engineering Times.* February 1986, pp. 1–8.

Gunn, Thomas G. "Manufacturing for Competitive Advantage: Becoming a World Class Manufacturer." Cambridge, Mass.: Ballinger Publishing Company, 1987.

Harrington, Thomas C., et. al. "A Methodology for Measuring Vendor Performance." *Journal of Business Logistics.* Volume 12, No. 1, 1991, pp. 83–104.

Harris, Diana B. "Logistics Partnerships: Opportunities and Risks." *Council of Logistics Management Annual Conference Proceedings.* Volume I, 1990, pp. 213–224.

Hart, Christopher W.L., James L. Heskett, and W. Earl Sasser, Jr. "The Profitable Art of Service Recovery." *Harvard Business Review.* July–August 1990, pp. 148–156.

Hayes, Robert H., and Steven C. Wheelwright. *Restoring Our Competitive Edge: Competing Through Manufacturing.* New York: John Wiley & Sons, 1984.

Hayes, Robert, Steven Wheelwright, and Kim Clark. *Dynamic Manufacturing.* New York: The Free Press, 1988.

Helferich, Omar K., et. al. "Application of Artificial Intelligence—Expert System to Logistics." *Council of Logistics Management Annual Meeting Proceedings.* Volume I, 1986, pp. 45–86.

Henderson, John C., and N. Venkatraman. "Understanding Strategic Alignment." *Business Quarterly.* Volume 55, No. 3, Winter 1991, pp. 8–14.

Herron, David P. "Managing Physical Distribution for Profit." *Harvard Business Review.* May–June 1979, pp. 121–132.

Heskett, James L. "Leadership through Integration: The Special Challenge of Logistics Management." *Council of Logistics Management Annual Conference Proceedings.* Volume I, 1988, pp. 15–21.

Hiromoto, Toshiro. "Another Hidden Edge—Japanese Management Accounting." *Harvard Business Review.* July–August 1988, pp. 22–26.

Hoffman, Lowell M. "The First Strategy in Integrated Logistics: Management Development." *Council of Logistics Management Annual Conference Proceedings.* Volume II, 1989, pp. 385–393.

Holcomb, Mary C., et. al. "Managing Logistics with a Quality Focus." *Council of Logistics Management Annual Conference Proceedings.* Volume I, 1990, pp. 161–170.

Hull, Darel R., and Edward J. Tracy. "AT&T Benchmarking: Fundamental Priority." *Council of Logistics Management Annual Conference Proceedings.* Volume I, 1990, pp. 187–211.

Ishikawa, Kaoru. "What Is Total Quality Control." Translated by David Lu, *Central Japan Quality Control Association*, 1979.

Johnston, Russell, and Paul R. Lawrence. "Beyond Vertical Integration—The Rise of Value-Added Partnership." *Harvard Business Review*. July–August 1988, pp. 94–101.

Kallock, Roger W., and David G. Robinson. "Reengineering Business Logistics." *Council of Logistics Management Annual Conference Proceedings*. Volume I, 1990, pp. 171–186.

Kallock, Roger W. "The Challenge of Managing Logistics in a Global Environment." *Council of Logistics Management Annual Conference Proceedings*. Volume I, 1988, pp. 83–93.

Kratkiewicz, Gary L., and Bruce C. Arntzen. "Forecasting and Reporting Materials Flows in a Large Manufacturing Firm." *Council of Logistics Management Annual Conference Proceedings*. Volume II, 1989, pp. 325–340.

Lambert, Douglas M., and Jay U. Sterling. "Developing a Strategic Logistics Plan." *National Council of Purchasing and Distribution Managers Proceedings*. October 1986, pp. 312–322.

Lambert, Douglas M., and Jay U. Sterling. "Developing a Strategic Logistics Plan." *Council of Logistics Management Annual Meeting Proceedings*. Volume I, 1986, pp. 313–322.

"Leading Edge Logistics: Competitive Positioning for the 1990s." Prepared by Michigan State University for the Council of Logistics Management. *The Council of Logistics Management*, 1989.

Livingston, David B., and Gregory Lane. "Integrating Customer Service into the Firm's Strategy: The Times They are a Changing." *Council of Logistics Management Annual Meeting Proceedings*. Volume I, 1987, pp. 15–31.

Livingston, David B. "Logistics as a Competitive Weapon: The Total Cost Approach." *Council of Logistics Management Annual Conference Proceedings*. Volume II, 1988, pp. 15–45.

Lounsbury, Charles B. "Profit Through Transportation Partnerships." *Council of Logistics Management Annual Meeting Proceedings*. Volume I, 1987, pp. 105–116.

Macklin, Colin L. "Third Party Logistics in Europe." *Council of Logistics Management Annual Conference Proceedings*. Volume I, 1988, pp. 95–121.

Markides, Constantinos C., and Norman Berg. "Manufacturing Offshore Is Bad Business." *Harvard Business Review*. September–October 1988, pp. 113–120.

Mason, Richard O., and Ian I. Mitroff. "Challenging Strategic Planning Assumptions." New York: John Wiley & Sons, Inc., 1981.

Masters, James M. "Analysis of the Life-of-Type Buy Decision." *Journal of Business Logistics.* Volume 8, No. 2, 1987, pp. 40–56.

Miller, Martin. "Strategic Planning: Visions for the 90s." *Council of Logistics Management Annual Conference Proceedings.* Volume II, 1990, pp. 241–245.

Miller, Martin. "Strategic Planning: Where the Rocks Are." *Council of Logistics Management Annual Conference Proceedings.* Volume II, 1990, pp. 247–250.

Muller, E.J. "Pipeline to Profits." *Distribution.* September 1990, pp. 32–40.

Mundy, Ray A., et. al. "Innovations in Carrier Sourcing: Transportation Partnership." *Council of Logistics Management Annual Conference Proceedings.* Volume II, 1989, pp. 109–113.

Murray, Robert E., and Samuel D. Calaby. "Outsourcing, Networking and the Hollow Corporation." *Council of Logistics Management Annual Conference Proceedings.* Volume I, 1988, pp. 171–235.

Neuschel, Robert P. "The New Logistics Challenge—Excellence in Management." *Journal of Business Logistics.* Volume 8, No. 2, 1987, pp. 29–39.

Novack, Robert A., and Stephen W. Simco. "The Industrial Procurement Process: A Supply Chain Perspective." *Journal of Business Logistics.* Volume 12, No. 1, 1991, pp. 145–167.

Novack, Robert A. "Logistics Control: An Approach to Quality." *Journal of Business Logistics.* Volume 10, No. 2, 1989, pp. 24–43.

Novich, Neil S. "Developing Superior Service as a Competitive Tool." *Council of Logistics Management Annual Conference Proceedings.* Volume II, 1990, pp. 257–266.

O'Malley, William J. "Japanese Logistics Systems: 'No Time for Tea.'" *Council of Logistics Management Annual Conference Proceedings.* Volume II, 1990, pp. 275–283.

Ohmae, Kenichi. *The Mind of the Strategist.* New York: McGraw-Hill Publishing Co., 1982.

Ploos van Amstel, M.J. "Managing the Pipeline Effectively." *Journal of Business Logistics.* Volume 11, No. 1, 1990, pp. 1–25.

Porter, Michael E. *Competition in Global Industries.* Boston: Harvard Business School Press, 1986.

Porter, Michael E. *Competitive Strategy: Techniques for Analyzing Industries and Competitors.* New York: Free Press, 1980.

Powers, Richard F. "Optimization Models for Logistics Decisions." *Journal of Business Logistics.* Volume 10, No. 1, 1989, pp. 106–121.

Pyburn, Philip J. "Redefining the Role of Information Technology." *Business Quarterly.* Volume 55, No. 3, Winter 1991, pp. 25–30.

Rao, Kant, et. al. "Corporate Framework for Developing and Analyzing Logistics Strategies." *Council of Logistics Management Annual Conference Proceedings.* Volume I, 1988, pp. 243–262.

Rauch, Thomas J., and James Rust. "The PC Model: A Strategic Planning Tool." *Council of Logistics Management Annual Meeting Proceedings.* Volume I, 1987, pp. 159–181.

Robeson, James F., ed. *The Distribution Handbook.* New York: The Free Press, 1985.

Robeson, James F. "Logistics 1995." *Council of Logistics Management Annual Meeting Proceedings.* Volume I, 1987, pp. 381–388.

Schmenner, Roger W. *Making Business Location Decisions.* Englewood Cliffs, N.J.: Prentice-Hall, Inc., 1982.

Schmenner, Roger W. "The Merit of Making Things Fast." *Sloan Management Review.* Fall 1988, pp. 11–17.

Schneider, Lewis M. "New Era in Transportation Strategy." *Harvard Business Review.* March–April 1985, pp. 118–126.

Schonberger, Richard J. *World Class Manufacturing.* New York: Free Press, 1986.

Scott Morton, Michael S., ed. *The Corporation of the 1990s: Information Technology and Organizational Transformation.* New York: Oxford University Press, Inc., 1991.

Sease, Gary J. "Innovative Use of Information Management Models in Distribution." *Council of Logistics Management Annual Meeting Proceedings.* Volume I, 1987, pp. 149–166.

Sharman, Graham. "The Rediscovery of Logistics." *Harvard Business Review.* September–October 1984, pp. 71–79.

Sheehan, Willam G. "Contract Warehousing: The Evolution of an Industry." *Journal of Business Logistics.* Volume 10, No. 1, 1989, pp. 31–49.

Stalk, George, Jr., and Thomas M. Hout. *Competing Against Time.* New York: The Free Press, 1990.

Stenger, Alan J., and Joseph L. Cavinato. "Adapting MRP to the Outbound Side—Distribution Requirements Planning." *Production and Inventory Management.* Fourth quarter, 1986, pp. 1–13.

Sterling, Jay U., and Douglas M. Lambert. "A Summary of the Accounting Techniques Used to Measure the Profitability of Marketing Segment." *Council of Logistics Management Annual Meeting Proceedings.* Volume I, 1987, pp. 205–229.

Stern, Louis W., and Frederick D. Sturdivant. "Customer-Driven Distribution Systems." *Harvard Business Review.* July–August 1987, pp. 34–41.

Stock, James R., and Douglas M. Lambert. *Strategic Logistics Management,* 2nd ed. Homewood, Ill.: Richard D. Irwin, Inc., 1987.

Sullivan, Lawrence P. "The Seven Stages in Company-Wide Quality Control." *Quality Progress.* May 1986, pp. 77–83.

Taylor, Charles A., et. al. "Developing and Managing Distribution Partnerships." *Council of Logistics Management Annual Meeting Proceedings.* Volume I, 1987, pp. 93–104.

Tucker, Francis, Seymour M. Zivan, and Robert C. Camp. "How to Measure Yourself against the Best." *Harvard Business Review.* January–February 1987, pp. 8–10.

Tyndall, Gene R., and Seymour M. Zivan. "Corporate Profitability and Logistics: An Update on Logistics Excellence." *Council of Logistics Management Annual Conference Proceedings.* Volume I, 1989, pp. 283–306.

Tyndall, Gene R., et. al. "Corporate Profitability and Logistics." *Council of Logistics Management Annual Meeting Proceedings.* Volume I, 1986, pp. 295–311.

Tyndall, Gene R. "Logistics and Profitability: Are the Two in Conflict?" *Journal of Cost Management for the Manufacturing Industry.* Volume 1, No. 2, Summer 1987.

Van der Hoop, J.H. "Geographic Perspectives of International Logistics: Europe." *Council of Logistics Management Annual Meeting Proceedings.* Volume I, 1987, pp. 245–254.

Watson, James F., and Herb Johnson. "The Value of Strategic Logistics Partnership." *Council of Logistics Management Annual Conference Proceedings.* Volume II, 1988, pp. 277–290.

Weidenbaum, Murray. "Filling in the Hollowed-Out Corporation: The Competitive Status of U.S. Manufacturing." *Council of Logistics Management Annual Conference Proceedings.* Volume I, 1989, pp. 1–13.

Wheelwright, Steven C., and Robert H. Hayes. "Competing through Manufacturing." *Harvard Business Review.* January–February 1985, pp. 99–109.

Zemke, Douglas E., and Douglas M. Lambert. "Utilizing Information Technology to Manage Inventory." *Council of Logistics Management Annual Meeting Proceedings.* Volume I, 1987, pp. 119–139.

Zinn, Walter, and Donald J. Bowersox. "Planning Physical Distribution with the Principle of Postponement." *Journal of Business Logistics.* Volume 9, No. 2, 1988, pp. 117–136.

INDEX

OTHER BUSINESS ONE IRWIN TITLES OF INTEREST TO YOU

Common Sense Manufacturing
Becoming a Top Value Competitor
James A. Gardner
The Business One Irwin/APICS Series in Production Management

Using Gardner's straightforward, easy-to-apply planning suggestions, manufacturers can generate order quantities that are exactly equal to the net requirements for the period in which they are scheduled. He shows you how to reduce floor space through better plant layout, gradually eliminate work-in-process inventory, and eliminate the "end of the month crunch" in production.
ISBN: 1-055623-527-5 $34.95

Computer Integrated Manufacturing
Guidelines and Applications from Industrial Leaders
Steven A. Melnyk and Ram Narasimhan
The Business One Irwin/APICS Series in Production Management

Computer Integrated Manufacturing (CIM) can greatly improve speed and precision in manufacturing operations. But because confusion surrounds the theory and practice, few manufacturing executives have readily adopted this powerful strategy. *Computer Integrated Manufacturing* takes a management/strategic perpective and offers case studies to illustrate the implications of the CIM approach to manufacturing.
ISBN: 1-55623-538-0 $45.00

Forecasting Systems for Operations Management
Stephen A. DeLurgio and Carl D. Bhame
The Business One Irwin/APICS Series in Production Management

Understand and implement practical, theoretically sound, and comprehensive forecasting systems. *Forecasting Systems for Operations Management* will assist you in moving products, materials, and timely information through your organization. It's the most comprehensive treatment of forecasting methods available for automated forecasting systems.
ISBN: 1-55623-040-0 $44.95